Local Politics and Development
in the Middle East

Also of Interest

The Problems of Arab Economic Development and Integration, edited by Adda Guecioueur

Industrial Progress in Small Oil-Exporting Countries: The Prospect for Kuwait, edited by Maurice Girgis

Migration, Mechanization, and the Agricultural Labor Market in Egypt, edited by Alan Richards and Philip L. Martin

Arab Aid to Sub-Saharan Africa, Pamela M. Mertz and Robert A. Mertz

*Political Behavior in the Arab States, edited by Tawfic E. Farah

*Religion and Politics in the Middle East, edited by Michael Curtis

*Rich and Poor States in the Middle East: Egypt and the New Arab Order, edited by Malcolm Kerr and El Sayed Yassin

The New Arab Social Order: A Study of the Social Impact of Oil Wealth, Saad Eddin Ibrahim

*A Concise History of the Middle East, Second Edition, Revised and Updated, Arthur Goldschmidt, Jr.

Women and Revolution in Iran, edited by Guity Nashat

Imlil: A Moroccan Mountain Community in Change, James A. Miller

PROFILES OF THE CONTEMPORARY MIDDLE EAST:

South Yemen: A Marxist Republic in Arabia, Robert W. Stookey

*Syria: Modern State in an Ancient Land, John F. Devlin

*Jordan: Crossroads of Middle Eastern Events, Peter Gubser

*The Republic of Lebanon: Nation in Jeopardy, David C. Gordon

*Available in hardcover and paperback.

Westview Special Studies
on the Middle East

Local Politics and Development in the Middle East
Edited by Louis J. Cantori and Iliya Harik

Although development at the local level is a primary goal of most assistance schemes, most development agencies and banks know little of politics at the local level in developing countries. As a result, assistance programs generally lack relevance to indigenous populations and are--at the community level--viewed as being controlled from the "outside."

The authors of this book concentrate on how local politics influence development in the Middle East, with the intent of encouraging more appropriate--and thus more effective--assistance programs. They discuss general policy issues and the nature of center-periphery relations in Middle East countries and delve into specific problems encountered in Egypt, Jordan, Lebanon, Syria, Iraq, Turkey, Tunisia, and North Yemen, showing how information about local political schemes can aid administrators of development programs in providing assistance that is acceptable--and accepted--at the local level. The case studies provide a broad base for planning, encompassing capitalist, state capitalist, and socialist systems in both rural and urban settings.

Louis J. Cantori is chairman of the Department of Political Science at the University of Maryland, Baltimore County. *Iliya Harik* is professor of political science and director of the Center for Middle Eastern Studies, Indiana University.

Local Politics and Development in the Middle East

Edited by Louis J. Cantori
and Iliya Harik

Westview Press / Boulder and London

Westview Special Studies on the Middle East

Published in 1984 in the United States of America by Westview Press, Inc., 5500 Central Avenue, Boulder, Colorado, 80301; Frederick A. Praeger, President and Publisher

Library of Congress Catalog Card Number: 84-50188
ISBN: 0-86531-169-2

Composition for this book was provided by the editors
Printed and bound in the United States of America

10 9 8 7 6 5 4 3 2 1

To the members of the Committee for the

Comparative Study of New Nations,

University of Chicago, who stimulated

our thinking on things local

Contents

x

Preface

The papers in this volume are the product of a conference organized jointly by Indiana University and the University of Maryland, Baltimore County, and held at Donaldson Brown Conference Center, Port Deposit, Maryland. It appears slightly more than a decade after a similar conference was held at Indiana University to discuss the nature of change in rural areas of the Middle East and North Africa, the proceedings of which have since appeared in a volume edited by Richard Antoun and Iliya Harik.* The present volume is not intended as an effort to bring us up to date on developments that have occurred since the first conference was held, but to open a new chapter.

At the time the first Indiana conference was held, we were in great need of understanding the nature of rural society and the changes which it was undergoing. We were then involved in a diagnostic effort: What are the characteristics of the rural community and why was it changing? New literature has appeared since and enriched our library with a wealth of material on local societies in general and rural communities in particular.

The new undertaking had for an objective the examination of the impact of change-oriented policies. At the time the first conference was held policy studies with a local focus were still in their infancy as far as the Middle East area was concerned. The Port Deposit Conference sought to draw more attention to the importance of policy studies in the development process and to encourage research in that line.

For three days, scholars from various parts of the world met in one assembly to discuss their research and findings on local development strategies and assessing policy impact. Papers included a vast array of topics including research agendas and some

---

*Richard Antoun and Iliya F. Harik, eds. Rural Politics and Social Change in the Middle East (Bloomington: Indiana University Press, 1972).

blue prints for development strategies. However, it was decided by the editors that only the case studies should be included in this volume in order to preserve unity of treatment and coherence in the volume as a whole. Moreover, including all the papers would have made the volume much too large for our purposes. The price we paid for excluding valuable contributions made at the conference, we hope to compensate for by maintaining the coherence of the volume as a unit.

Many people have contributed at various stages to making the conference and subsequently the volume possible. They include institutions and individuals. As organizers of the conference and editors of the volume, we would like to thank Indiana University and the University of Maryland, Baltimore County,for their support. Also the Agency for International Development deserves extension of special thanks for providing our two universities with a conference grant. None of the above mentioned institutions, however, are responsible for what is in this volume. Individual authors bear the exclusive responsibility for what has appeared in their contributions.

Many individuals participated in the conference and contributed significantly to making it a success. We wish to acknowledge therefore appreciation to Milton Esman, Cornell University; Ernest Grigg, Save the Children Federation; James Dalton, Near East Bureau of AID; Khalid Ikram, The World Bank; Amal Rassam, Queens College; Robert Fernea, University of Texas at Austin; Dale Eikelman, New York University; Sayid Yasin of the Ahram Center for Political and Strategic Studies, Cairo; John Waterbury, Princeton University; Michael Hudson, Georgetown University; Robert Webb, Acting Vice Chancellor and presently Chairman, Department of History, University of Maryland, Baltimore County; Joseph Wheeler, Assistant Administrator, Near East Bureau, AID; Fredj Stambouli, University of Tunis; and Linda Schatkowski-Schilcher, Institut fur Europaische Geschichte, Mainz, W. Germany. The editors wish to thank Nicholas Hopkins, American University in Cairo, for his able assistance in editing some of the contributions.

Finally, thanks are due the University of Maryland, Baltimore County, for a grant to cover the costs of the preparation of the typescript. Jane Gethmann ably typed the final copy for which we are also indebted to Helen Pasquale.

L.J.C.
I. H.

1
Introduction

Louis J. Cantori and Iliya Harik

Scholarly attention to the study of local societies in the Middle East reflects three kinds of emphases. The first reflects the cultural and social concerns of anthropologists as expressed in ethnographic studies. This approach considers the local community as the unit of analysis by itself. A second scholarly concern views development of local societies in terms of center inspired service delivery or in terms of efforts to establish a dynamic developmental structure at the local level. A third emphasis is of a political nature and concerns the impact of national politics on local communities. Whether expressed in terms of political system, elites or class, the tendency in the third approach has been to focus more upon the macro national level rather than the micro local level. It is accurate to say that anthropological and developmental concerns account for the overwhelming majority of scholarly studies of local communities.

There are, however, four ways in which the political understanding of local communities is important. The first has to do with the policy aspect of development. How, where and by whom, and for whom development policy is formulated are important questions. A second factor has to do with the tendency in the Middle East, and perhaps the Third World generally, to institute policies of decentralization. By so doing, they give additional significance for the study of local communities. A third factor has to do with what Kesselman and Rosenthal have called a "national culture of localism," i.e., the manner in which local political relationships and values are projected on to the national level.(1) Whether observed in the kinship/consulative bedouin political style of Saudi Arabia or in the images of family and village in President Sadat's speeches, the tendency of national leaders to express or act in accordance with local values is in evidence. Related to the foregoing is a fourth political importance, namely the relationship of local societies to political stability. Political stability seems affected by local politics in at least two possible ways. The first has to do with political revolt itself (e.g. revolution, demonstrations, etc.). The Iranian revolution of 1979 appears to have been a relatively rare case of a rural based rebellion.

1

Otherwise, political revolt appears more normally as an urban and not a rural phenomenon. Political stability is threatened less dramatically but in the long run just as seriously by the weakening of the legitimacy of the government. At a minimum such an eventuality can lead to economic non-performance in the often crucial agricultural sector which in turn might contribute to overall political deterioration and revolt.

The studies in this volume reflect the diversity of the research interests of their authors to say nothing of the ethnic, religious, cultural and geographical diversity of the Middle East. There are two perspectives, however, which are common to all the studies: the relationship between central political power and the local community and the nature of local political processes themselves. Hopkins focuses upon technology and the international economic order as background factors to his consideration of center-periphery relationship. Thus, the introduction of new techniques of agriculture in the nineteenth century was accompanied by the integration of the agricultural economies of the Middle East into the world capitalist system. In the period of the 1950's and 1960's, new social frameworks for development emerged (e.g., the revolutions and coups in Egypt, Iraq and Syria). In the third phase of the 1970's and '80's new technology such as dam construction, and mechanization ushered in a new phase of agribusiness under capitalist or state-capitalist auspices. Hopkins then goes on to enumerate what he feels are the characteristic patterns of center-periphery relations. Empirically Hopkins sketches the international economic system within which the succeeding studies in the volume are located. Theoretically, he presents an alternative conception of the locus of political power implicit to most of the studies. Hopkins offers the point of view of dependency theory that locates significant, if not total power, in the international capitalist system. Most of the other studies, however, tend to view such power as an aspect of the national center or the sub-national governmental institutions.

The studies of Egypt by Harik and Khadr deal with a country with a large history of continuous and highly centralized political authority. To a significant extent, that authority system was based upon a closely linked and politically effective combination of a landowning class and a modern professional middle class. When the British unilaterally granted Egypt a qualified national independence in 1922, this class of people gained greater power. The revolutionary regime of Gamal Abd al-Nasser eliminated this class and replaced it at the local level by new institutions of central governmental authority. Anwar al-Sadat's presidency, which started in 1970, inaugurated a policy of administrative and political decentralization in which local authorities were intended to exercise extensive responsibility for managing local affairs.

Khadr's study of the fishing society in Aswan shows clearly that during the Nasser period central political authority was in fact exerted in such a way as to reinforce a pre-existing local elite in its dominant position. It also documents whether as a result of alternative strategies to obviate this elite during the Nasser period or later in the Sadat period (only hinted at inasmuch as field research was carried out in 1975-76), the local elite may have changed its membership but it still governed local affairs.

Harik's study timewise deals with the period of President Sadat's policy of decentralization and the changes which were made in the Nasser implemented local institutions. It offers an outline of the different development strategies of Nasser and Sadat and makes an assessment of their failures and achievements at the local level. Unlike the Aswan fishing community studied by Khadr, elites in upper and lower Egypt examined by Harik changed character under Nasser and Sadat, and political administrative structures became diversified. In terms of the impact of the center upon the periphery, it would appear that development is perhaps leading as a policy and a process towards reinforcing local elite dominance and possibly towards a greater degree of local political autonomy.

While this may be true of rural Egypt, Cantori and Benedict's study of a local Egyptian urban quarter differs significantly from those of Khadr and Harik both in terms of geographical location and in terms of focus. It complements a rural Egyptian representation by being concerned with urban Egypt. Its concern is primarily with perceptions of leadership roles rather than elite structure or center-periphery relations. Urban neighborhoods are purely residential in character and consist of individuals playing a diversity of occupational roles. If there is a single enterprise, as in the case of the madbah (slaughterhouse) in the Cantori and Benedict study, its relationship to the political center is legal and organizational but not one of government service delivery and/or supporting programs. Thus the urban neighborhood which is geographically closer to the political center is significantly more free from central control. An important factor contributing to the solidarity of the madbah neighborhood is the Sa'idi or southern Egyptian regional point of origin of its inhabitants. The strength of kinship factors among the people from that area of Egypt is well known by other Egyptians and contributes to a live and let live attitude towards the quarter.

Both Khadr's and Harik's studies identify the phenomenon of economically little diversified communities in their relationship to an assertive political center. The Tunisian community studied by Larson, on the other hand, is socially and economically mixed by reason of service, agricultural and mining occupations. She notes that policies from the center were hampered by their authoritarian nature and inadequacy for local conditions. She also stresses managerial deficiencies as impediments to successful implementation.

Center-periphery relations in Syria, on the other hand, appear different in nature due to institutional importance of the Ba'th Party as an instrument of mobilization. As Hinnebusch points out, however, the Ba'th Party is not a monolithic structure with strong authority at the center. Instead, for reasons having to do with its past history, its center has been fragmented and its local organization emanated less from the center than from particularly local conditions. Not only are its local branches dominated by local political elements but such ancillary organizations as the Youth Union and the Peasant Union are also locally dominated. Less like the case of Egypt and Tunisia, development seems to proceed within locally adapted governmental structures rather than around them or in spite of them. Egypt and Tunisia are political systems with a long tradition of centralized political rule. Syria is a new state in comparison, having been created after World War I, and therefore is less nationally integrated and stable than the other two countries.

Another new state, Jordan, has accomplished a similar degree of integration and extension of centralized political authority in a very different manner. Gubser presents a case study of the way in which effective political leadership from the center had first coopted nomadic domination of sedentary/urban populations, and then, by making them politically/socially mobile, was able to supplant their authority at the local level. The key to the success of this process has been the strong character of the king.

All of the preceding case-studies discussed so far, with the exception of Jordan, have been of socialist or socialist-oriented political systems, where the political role of the center has been an assertive one. Jordan is not different in this respect even when a market economy approach is the basis of analysis. The political center in Jordan asserted itself locally in order to establish political control.

Although a republic, Turkey resembles Jordan in that the political center asserts strong political control over local communities and lacks a socialist orientation. Kiray's study documents the impact upon the local community of the expansion of the modern market economy and the contraction of the traditional economy, as the communities livelihood shifts from near subsistence grain agriculture to fruit and vegetable truck farming and to industry. The study also indicates how a portion, at least, of the traditional local elite is able to capitalize upon this process and enrich themselves. Consistent with the general pattern of the preceding studies, development results in a greater degree of integration into the national political system but this is accompanied by the reinforcement of a local elite and the maintenance or even increase in local autonomy.

The question of local elites, the local autonomy of communities and a weaker role of the political center appears in an exaggerated form in the cases of Yemen and Lebanon. As Tutweiler points out in the case of Yemen, it is the local community that takes the initiative in development, both because it historically enjoyed autonomy and because of the political instability of the center in the years following the proclamation of a republic in 1962. Not only does Tutwiler's study document this process with respect to such projects as road building, but also how local elites have used traditional resources such as zakat (religious charitable contributions) for modern purposes. Tutwiler also shows how a traditional local elite is eventually replaced by a younger more modern one. As development proceeds, the periphery comes into a more dependent relationship to the center but there remains a sense in which the periphery appears to be sacrificing its local autonomy more on its own terms rather than those of the central government.

Joseph deals with a local urban community of Armenian refugees who settled in Beirut in the twenties and thirties and have since become naturalized Lebanese citizens. She points out that the Armenian community in Borg Hammond possesses both a highly disciplined political party and a variety of cultural organizations including ones with linkages to the world Armenian community. This effective organization is important to maintaining the Armenian community within the neighborhood, and in gaining benefits from the political center. In fact, however, the Armenians possess so much communal self-sufficiency that the political center figures little in their political or developmental progress. This ability to prosper on the basis of their own resources and through access to international agencies reflects the potential for autonomous community growth in a democratic system even while it also reflects the as yet unresolved question in contemporary Lebanon, of the proper balance of central political authority, and degree of local political autonomy.

In conclusion, two sets of concerns have been addressed in this volume. There are first the empirical generalizations relating parts of the system to each other. Second, there is the emphasis in policy and its impact on the process of local political and economic development.

The first of the empirical generalizations begins with a consideration of the nature of the political system within which the local community is located. It is obvious from the examples of Egypt and Yemen that the political center varies considerably in its effectiveness. Even when the center is effective the range of its impact upon the periphery will vary with its economic orientation toward development. This is reflected in the cases of the state socialist regimes such as Egypt, Syria and Tunisia on the one hand and the more free enterprise-oriented Turkish and Jordanian systems, on the other hand. In most of these regimes, rural communities are more likely to be targeted by central government. The largest sector of the labor force is in rural areas and government revenue is derived to a larger extent from the agricultural sector. The economic betterment of rural lower income populations, on the other hand, is most often a secondary objective. Urban populations, in contrast, are the focus of government bounties and services for considerations of their potential political threat in view of their physical location at the political center.

The second concern focuses on policy and underlines the importance of decentralization, local participation, effective management and human resources for the success of development strategies. It is possible to speculate on the preceding aspects of policy that while development may mean an increasing impact of the center upon the periphery, local autonomy may also be preserved or even increased in the process.

It should be clear from what already has been said and from a reading of the specific contributions that political development is the focus of this volume. Each one of the papers reflects a policy concern relevant to broader developmental perspectives, and may also hopefully serve the concerns of development students of other developing areas.

FOOTNOTES

1.   Mark Kesselman and Donald Rosenthal, Local Power and Comparative Politics (Beverly Hills, California: Sage Professional Papers in Comparative Politics, 1974).

2
Development and Center Building in the Middle East

Nicholas S. Hopkins

INTRODUCTION

This paper deals with the relationship between development and the creation of a strong central government in the Middle East. It explores the idea that those who sponsor development programs are interested not only in the potential economic benefits, but also in the political consequences. The outcome is thus to create a different kind of society, or perhaps to reinforce imaginatively an existing one, in which their own role and position will be enhanced. If development programs are designed at one level to improve the economic situation of one or another category in the population, that is never done without political calculation as well. Thus for instance, programs designed to raise the income level of the poorest segment of the population can be construed as strengthening the political position of the dominant sponsoring elite both directly in that such an improvement in the standard of living removes some of the pressure for a larger share in the pie from such populations, and also indirectly in that it absorbs such populations into the socio-economic structure organized and run by the elite and thus it gives the non-elite an interest in the continuity of this economic structure.

In other words, if we were to ask the questions, "Does development develop?", "What does development develop?", or "Whom does development develop?", the answers might be, for instance, that the real benefits of rural development are felt in the capital, while the relative difference between urban and rural, between rich and poor, may even increase. "Development" might be seen as developing above all a socioeconomic structure centered around the extraction of the surplus from the rural areas to the benefit of the wealthier urban areas, and aiding in the creation of new classes part of whose project it is to organize the integration of the country as a whole into the world capitalist system. Thus while the manifest function of "development" carried out under government auspices might be to raise the income of the poor, or improve agricultural productivity or raise health standards, the latent function might rather be to reinforce the weight of the

7

central government, the political center and its associated class, within the total social formation: To the extent, on the other hand, that local community development is the outcome of forces within the local communities it is the structures of these communities which find themselves reinforced.

The purpose of this paper is to examine the relationship between economic development and the balance of power between central government and local rural communities in the Middle East.[1] The format of this paper will be first, to present some general ideas about local and rural development in the Middle East and some concepts for grasping this process, second, to review a number of cases and situations, and finally, to draw all the information together into a concluding analysis.

The three waves of rural development

The transformation of Middle Eastern society in the last century has been tremendous. Here we are concerned with the social, economic and political changes that can be seen to result from some combination of a number of factors: 1) the introduction of new forms of technology, such as improved irrigation techniques, motor pumps, tractors and combine harvesters, improved transport by rail and road, improved record keeping, and stronger institutions of bank credit; 2) the emergence of stronger political centers, partly under colonial impact as in the Maghreb, Egypt and the fertile crescent, and partly as a response to factors of internal evolution; and 3) the changing mode of relationship between the various Middle Eastern societies and the powerful "external center," the capitalist structure whose center is geographically in Western Europe and (more recently as far as the Middle East is concerned) in North America or even Japan.

The historical pattern of transformation can be broken down into three phases, with different dates depending on the area or country in question. The first wave began in the 19th century in Egypt, and somewhat later in the other parts of the Middle East. Phase I involved the introduction of new techniques of agriculture which renewed the technological basis of rural life. In the Nile Valley the major shift from annual basin irrigation to perennial canal irrigation protected the fields from the floods of August and September. This permitted the cultivation of cotton as a major cash crop and allowed the introduction of multiple cropping so that farmers were occupied throughout the year and had less time for other pursuits. In the Maghreb and the plains of the upper Tigris and Euphrates, the principal shift was towards the mechanization of the extensive cultivation of cereals (Warriner 1962, Yalman 1971), though there were also other areas that were transformed through marsh drainage (Benedict 1974) or through the introduction of the intensive cultivation of grapevines or fruits (Chaulet 1971, Peters 1972). The gradual spread of this new "package" of technology led to the integration of formerly isolated rural communities into the world capitalist system. On the whole, this process resulted in the material improvement of the countryside but it also implied a high degree of social differentiation between the few who profited fully and the many who did not. The legal structure came increasingly to protect the advantages of the few through the introduction of private property in land on a large scale, and through the creation of a market in land. In Egypt, the Maghreb and upper Mesopotamia there was a trend towards large landowners (most of whom were Europeans in the Maghreb) running estates on the one hand, and landless workers, a rural proletariat, on the other. Even in areas less directly affected, there was usually a change in the nature of the dominant group -- from agas to merchants in the southwestern Turkish town of Ula (Benedict 1974), or from learned men to professionals in the southern Lebanese village studied by Peters (1972).

The second wave began with the Egyptian revolution of 1952. Phase II consisted in the elaboration of new social frameworks for action which would retain the technical advantages of the first wave but would attempt to neutralize the built-in tendency towards social differentiation that they entailed (Nash and Hopkins 1976). In other words, revolutionary governments starting with the Egyptian in 1952 tried to keep technology constant while cancelling out the negative or disruptive social impact of that technology. These new social frameworks were built around land reform and rural cooperatives. A policy of land reform and cooperative formation represented a political decision taken by a national elite which was no longer rooted in the traditional agrarian system, and so was free to establish a government around a new class alliance (Zghal 1969). The extent to which it reflected rural aspirations is another matter altogether. In the Arab world this effort to offer a more equitable social system for the rural areas and thus to reduce the social tension resulting from the unbridled introduction of new technology for private gain is characteristic of Egypt, Syria, Iraq and Tunisia. In each case the real impetus for this change came not from the rural workers and peasants but from the "administrative elite" anxious to reorganize the vital structures of the country. The case of Algeria began differently, in the direct social action of the rural workers after 1962 when they occupied the "biens vacants" (Chaulet 1971), but the projects of the mobilizing elite shortly became the dominant force (Clegg 1971). In Iran, land reform was decreed from above in 1962 by the Shah, in his "White Revolution," which was designed at least partly to break the power of large landowners and prepare the way for modern estate agriculture (H. Richards 1975).

At present one can distinguish a third wave of agrarian transformation in the Middle East. Phase III is primarily based on the new patterns of agricultural technology that have emerged in the second half of the 20th century: dam-building, "Green Revolution," computers, and on a pattern of economic incentives that draw people into the realm of market forces. In the Middle East the clearest examples of this new stimulus to technological transformation are a) the construction of major dams such as the

Aswan dam in Egypt and the Euphrates dam in Syria as well as smaller projects from Morocco (Benhlal 1977) to Iran (H. Richards 1975); b) the development and extension of major irrigation and land reclamation schemes such as the Gezira and its annexes in the Sudan; c) the various manifestations of the Green Revolution such as the introduction of improved varieties of barley and wheat ("Mexican Wheat") in Algeria, Tunisia, Lebanon and Syria; and d) the expansion of agribusiness enterprises into Iranian agriculture. In Egypt, where modern technology had been restricted to irrigation and transport, there is now tremendous interest on the part of the government in mechanizing work in the fields through the use of tractors and other machines. In the present context of the open door policy, such a mechanization goes directly against the intent of the agrarian reform of 1952 which was to create a smallholder agriculture, for the plots of the majority of Egyptian farmers are far too small to make mechanization a paying proposition: either the machines will impose a restructuring of the "access-to-lane" patterns, or they will be rejected.

Agriculture in the Middle East is increasingly into a world market, so that countries such as Egypt, Lebanon and Tunisia are modifying their production to suit the demands of the European market while Saudi Arabia and Kuwait are looking to the agricultural development of the Sudan through such projects as the Jonglei canal and drainage scheme to provide them with the goods they need to support their expanding populations of oil and industrial workers and bureaucrats. These pressures are also felt at the local level, where the response is various: one Egyptian village has recently built over 20 sheds where chickens are raised for a local market; farmers in a Tunisian town produce fruit and vegetables for the Tunis wholesale market; Turkish farmers seek ways to expand and profit from their tangerine crop -- and through the Middle East many rural areas live increasingly from the money sent home by those who are working abroad (Maghreb, Yemen, Turkey, Egypt, the Levant).

The three waves of agrarian transformation have had considerable impact on patterns of rural local politics. In the first place, the balance of forces within local communities has been altered. The effect of the first and sometimes the third wave has been to allocate to a few people the basis for wealth and power (landownership and access to machinery, bank credit, etc.). The Egyptian agrarian reform or the Iranian White Revolution reinforced the status of the middle peasantry while neglecting completely the mass of the poor and landless peasantry. In some cases the agrarian transformation has strengthened or exacerbated existing patterns of stratification, or called a class system into overt existence.

In the second place, the agrarian transformation has altered the nature of the political and economic relationship between the local agrarian community on the one hand and the city and the state on the other. The various national governments have acquired a stronger desire and capability to intervene in local politics through the creation of new institutions in the countryside which are responsive to national policies. A key set of institutions are the commercial marketing networks that tie the rural economy more firmly to a national, even an international system. Yet these pressures from the central government must be filtered and understood through the local social structure, and, moreover, they do not obliterate the political dynamics of the rural community itself. The struggle for local leadership, rivalries between old families, the competition for control of local economic resources, or the continued symbolic importance of traditional distinctions phrased in religious terms -- this is the stuff of local politics. Projects formulated at the national level will be reinterpreted at the local level, and fed into pre-existing patterns of rivalry.

The change in the economic relations between state and local community is also reflected in the cultural attitude of the administrative elite who frequently decide that they must make the rural people conform to urban and national ways of life. The Egyptian anthropologist Hamed Ammar has written

"The national group in its endeavour to transform the folk communities into conscious citizens of the society and to incorporate them fully into the nation's structure, exercises its authority through social and economic institutions, and through complex systems of legislation and administration ... In their exposure to the new forces of acculturation, communities may assimilate or select, according to their pre-existing value system, they may also develop resistances and hostility or show manifestations of apathy or indifference. The nation-state however, pursues its acculturation activities by further pressure and expansion through its officials and institutions. Mechanisms of conflict and adjustment on both sides continue to develop ... A great challenge for Arab social thinkers and workers lies at present in the problems involved in the integration of the folk culture -- mainly in the rural areas -- with the national culture (Ammar 1960:29-30).

Similar attitudes of disdain towards the rural and the peasant are expressed throughout the Middle East. Warriner reports that "For Baghdad opinion in 1964, the peasants were still non-persons ... an attitude reflecting an age-old hostility between tribes and townspeople ... On the side of the peasants, this hostility was reciprocated. Visits to villages were accompanied by an armed military escort" (Warriner 1969:101). In Algeria, the government sees itself as "giving" appropriate modern institutions to the peasantry (Zghal 1977:310, quoting the Algerian National Charter) whose response was supposed to be one of gratitude.

Yet rural people are much more than just the passive

recipients of technology and government action. They react creatively to their situation. They have their own projects, just as the national governments have theirs. Part of the task of a successful government is to make these local and national projects coincide. Yet as Ammar points out, the relationship between national and local politics is dynamic. Rural people attempt to defend their integrity of action from government interference and try to manipulate the government themselves. A cooperative initially founded by a mobilizing bureaucracy can be taken in hand by its members and turned into an authentic local institution expressing the social base of local politics. In local communities throughout the Middle East, ambitious individuals take advantage of the cleavages and new opportunities presented by national politics to forward their own schemes and achieve their ends. In this way, the processes of local politics feed into and help form the processes of national and international politics. Yet from one end of the Middle East to the other, the form of popular participation in politics is shaped by the degree of agrarian transformation. The new technology reinforces the power of governments and the urban elite class who mostly run them. Yet the longterm efficiency and even survival of the evolving agrarian structure is dependent upon the creative participation of the rural people in organizing and operating it. This is the continuing dilemma posed by the transformation of the agrarian structures of the Middle East.

Patterns of relations

Development is dialectically related to the growth of a stronger central government. "Center-building" implies the structural differentiation of the "center" of a society -- its government, but also the "political class" of people who dominate the government -- and its consequent reinforcement as a weight in society in relation to other sectors. Such other sectors include here local communities and rural people. One form that this differentiation takes is the clearer emergence of class relations. This is not surprising if we think that development generally involves the appearance of capitalist relations of production, and that these in turn imply the existence of two or more classes. These classes have their roots in local events and local relationships, for the capitalist relations of the production are in the first instance between individuals in local settings. Their full significance only appears when the local manifestations of class are tied into a system corresponding to the state and culminating in the class or alliance of classes that controls the state.

This suggests that one of the most significant things that can happen to a local community as development occurs and the "center" is strengthened is that its relations to that center begin to take the form of class relations, instead of, as in the past, patron-client relations or other vertical links (Grandguillaume 1976; Hopkins 1977a). In such a relationship, the greatest class differentiation should occur at the center (Stambouli 1977).

Whatever degree of differentiation or inequality that might exist within the local community, it may stand as one class or perhaps two in relation to the center, and it will appear towards the bottom of the class system linked to the state. For this reason, the resistance of a community to the initiatives of the center may not appear directly as a class relationship, but rather as the efforts of a community to retain integrity. Moreover, the expression of an ideology that stresses small town and local community values may serve to disguise the class nature of the relationship. To the extent that a consciousness of class does not develop, then local communities will remain rivals for the attention of the state's representatives.

In the pre-modern days, relations between local communities and the states that then existed may indeed have had something of this quality. These communities were fairly autonomous, and settled many of their affairs themselves (Hopkins 1977b). Their relationship with the central authority was likely to be brief and brutal, frequently taking the form of a military tax-collecting expedition. If they were dissatisfied with the central authority, they might try either to withdraw from its sphere of authority, or to revolt against it in the hopes of breaking away if not of changing it. If satisfied, local communities would attempt to manipulate the central authority, perhaps through promising support in exchange for some favor. Manipulation could then be seen as "opting in," to use the terms of Vinogradov and Waterbury (1971), while withdrawal is "opting out," revolt simply adds the ingredient of force to the equation.

It is of course still possible analytically to speak of relations between some local community and the enveloping society and state, to treat them, as Bailey (1969) does, as the two sides of an equation. One could then show that each on occasion tries to influence the other. Thus one could say that the "center," or its dominant class alliance, might try to impose a certain kind of political life on villagers by obliging them to participate in a single-party structure or a cooperative scheme. The Middle East, like the rest of the world, is full of examples of this kind. A regime decides it must destroy or thrust aside some aspect of local community life in order to advance its development plans, or another conceives the need to mobilize all the people behind it. In Bailey's terms, the encapsulating society ("structure B") tries to make people in the encapsulated communities ("structure A") play by rules determined at the center and so absorb them fully into the national game. This emphasis on the freedom of manoeuvre of the local communities is correct, for one should never underestimate the ability of people to create elbow room for themselves. Yet in a fundamental sense it misses the point that the system deployed around a center is more than the sum of its parts.

Looking from the top down -- from the viewpoint of the encapsulating society -- two terms seem to describe the kind of relationship that exists between the "center" that is a-building and the local communities that willy-nilly are a part of that process. From the political point of view there is dominance: the center tries to bend everyone else to its will, or perhaps tries to mobilize them. This is the model that planners entertain when they hope or think that all critical decisions are to be made by a national elite at the "center" on the grounds that others are "too backward" and "do not understand." At best, this "top-down" model is based on enlightened paternalism, but the myth of the backward peasantry which requires guidance if it is to progress also disguises class attitudes and relations.

From the economic point of view, we can speak of exploitation. The new technology can facilitate the incorporation of all the productive activity into a single system directed by the national planners (in the case of state socialism) or through market forces controlled by central banks (in the case of a more liberal economy). What these systems have in common is that they are designed to extract the maximum of surplus from the rural areas in order to feed the urban population and to finance urban projects, from industrialization to a high standard of living for the urban elite. To the extent that the agrarian changes described in the previous section has led to the appearance of capitalist relations of production, and so to a class structure, then the patterns of exploitation can be channeled along those lines rather than the older lines of individual patron-client relations.

It remains true, however, that the class alliances that dominate the center cannot totally alienate the remainder of the population. For one thing, there may be two or more coalitions competing for popular support in order to establish their right to take charge of the "center." Or perhaps the entire country needs to galvanize itself in response to an outside threat. This need for support creates its reflection, the existence of manipulation of the "center." Certain particular processes and events can thus be analyzed simply as an interaction, but we would be missing the point if we halted the analysis there without considering the class framework within which all this occurs. Thus one tactic for the "center" would be to co-opt the local projects (Fallers 1974) of the country, and argue, through a process of translation, that they are but versions of the single national project. Such translation may be necessary if there is to be mutual support, or mutual manipulation.

As the Middle East develops and a stronger central state organization appears, classes associated with the capitalist relations of production make their appearance. In an analytical sense, one can see the state apparatus controlled by one or more of these classes. Since a class system characterizes the national (societal) level, the emergence of classes presages a new form of integration of local communities into the larger system, orchestrated around a "center."

An examination of cases

A. Egypt

Since Egypt was the first to enter Phases I and II, it is a good place to start. Our picture of rural/local life in Egypt is woefully inadequate, despite a number of suggestive studies. In Egypt, research has tended to concentrate at the national level, and there are a number of studies of the effects of technology, land reform and cooperatives that encompass the whole country (Warriner 1962; Saab 1967; Mayfield 1971; Abdel-Fadil 1975; and Radwan 1977).

In 1957 Jacques Berque published a study of the large Minufiyya village of Sirs al-Layyan which summed up the impact on this village of the technological changes of what I have called Phase I. This village was switched from flood irrigation to canals as a result of the construction of the Delta barrages between 1875 and 1900. The result was to stabilize land holdings and to make a different kind of agriculture possible. One of the chief features of this new agriculture was a market orientation, and in general people became oriented towards the acquisition of money. Education was used as a pathway to jobs in the city, and towards the new social category of intellectual. National level politics penetrated the village in the form of a rivalry between the Wafd and Watani parties. Although Phase I led to a certain number of social and cultural changes, the basic continuity of the village pattern was not disrupted at this time. In other parts of the Delta, marked by estate agriculture from the 19th century, social relations became polarized around a class of large landowners on the one hand, and the landless workers and permanent estate workers (tamaliyya) on the other (A. Richards 1977, 1978, 1979).

Harik's study of the village of "Shubra el-Gedida" in Behaira is the most complete study of Phase II (Harik 1974). This village is located in an area that was on the frontier of the land that was cultivable before the technological changes of the 19th century (Lozach 1935). As was frequently the case in these areas, the social form that resulted was estate agriculture: before 1952 one-third of the village land was owned by the royal family, and two-thirds by eight other families. As a consequence, the impact of the new forms of social organized proposed by the Egyptian government in Phase II was particularly strong in "Shubra," more so than in villages or areas such as Minufiyya where smallholding agriculture continued despite the technological innovations. Harik makes clear the struggle for power in the village between those whose power base lay in the new structures such as the land reform cooperative or the party structure, and those whose power base lay in the continuity of the village stratification and differentiation system. The land reform process led to the creation of cooperatives that provided a structure for the peasants who were to work the land expropriated from the large landowners; the cooperative structure also functioned as a political device to

mobilize opposition against the remaining large landowners.
Further political structures in the village were the village
council and party branch. All of these structures were "given" to
the village in the sense that they were invented by planners at the
national level and deliberately spread to all of rural Egypt in
order to provide a structure that would allow for the cooptation of
people into a single nationally-dominated political-economic
system.

The contrast between the picture given by Berque of pre-1952
Sirs and by Harik of "Shubra" 15 years after the 1952 revolution is
instructive. The political relation between village and center in
Sirs seems to have been that of "support" in that two parties,
representing different groups of the national elite, were competing
for the support of the villagers in order to "win" at the national
level (cf. al-Sayyid-Marsot 1977). In "Shubra" the national
government's policy clearly falls into the category of "dominance,"
to which the villagers are beginning to learn to respond in terms
of "manipulation." Harik stresses the gap between the political
process at the national level and at the local level. Economically
it is hard to judge the amount of "exploitation" between the two
Delta villages fifteen years apart. In "Shubra" the pattern of
exploitation through private landholding had itself been undergoing
a rapid evolution before the revolution, since 17% of the tillers
of the soil paid rent in money in 1939 compared to 75% in 1952. As
a result of land reform and the efforts to establish bureaucratic
dominance over the countryside, the engine of exploitation may have
shifted from private hands to the government, with its myriad of
regulations including the power to impose a cash crop (cotton) and
the price for it.

The studies by Berque and Harik represent Phase I and Phase II
in Egypt. What about Phase III? Egypt currently seems on the
verge of entering into a new phase of high technological inputs.
The technological revolution of the first wave affected crop mix,
transport and irrigation technology. As irrigation became highly
mechanized and centralized, local shaykhs lost control of
irrigation to the central government (Lozach and Hug 1930:194), and
it seemed that the new perennial agriculture would allow surplus
population to find work -- "at least as long as the standard of
living of the rural people remains so low" (Lozach and Hug
1930:201). Since the actual work in the fields was not affected to
a great extent, the initial effect of more intensive agriculture
was to increase the need for labor. It also increased social
tension, so that Besancon (1957:190) refers to:

> "... the urgency of a structural reform in order to
> avoid serious explosions among the poor peasants (in June
> 1951, there had been a peasant riot on the estate of
> Badraoui Pasha)."

Ayrout (1952:45-46, 55-57) also gives many examples from the 1930's
and 1940's of tension between landlords and peasants.

At present in rural Egypt mechanization is limited to some extent geographically and to a great extent in terms of the task. Thus while tillage and threshing are largely mechanized (because they use the tractor), planting and harvesting are not. Water lifting is completely mechanized in some areas -- in the village of Musha, near Assiut, the first pump dates back to 1908, locals say, and all water lifting is now done mechanically -- and not at all in others. In the Delta and parts of the Sa'id the saqia (water wheel) is still common, though there is a tendency to replace it by a mobile pump. Currently there is a strong push towards farm mechanization, and the subject is one of considerable debate among Egyptians and the foreign aid community. Both the World Bank and USAID are committed to mechanization projects, though significantly neither one involves supplying large numbers of new machines and both stress the social context and impact of mechanized farming. On the other hand, Egyptian government authorities appear to prefer the introduction of large tractors and similar machines, rather than the intermediate or appropriate technology associated with the idea that "small is beautiful."

Mechanization of this kind will have tremendous impact on rural and local social structures (A. Richards 1980). On the whole it is possible to make the equation that the larger the input of mechanization the greater the reinforcement of some kind of centralized power, so the introduction of machines of this kind will strengthen central institutions, whether governmental or private enterprise in type. Furthermore, the introduction of large machines implies some kind of land consolidation, and thus a modification of the basic land tenure structure which since the Agrarian Reform of 1952 has been oriented towards the creation of a small-holding pattern (Abdel-Fadil 1975:23). One of the authors of the 1952 reform wrote: "A peasant who owns the land he cultivates (self-supporting) is considered a sound basis for a democratic society" (Marei 1957:243). Whatever the truth of this expression of faith, since land consolidation is a reversal of policy it would have a profound impact on all the local political structures that have been tied to the existence of small and medium farmers. The land consolidation necessary for effective mechanization would seem to imply that some people will be "consolidated in" while many more are "consolidated out." This is the current trend in the debate on the proper use of the new lands (Springborg 1979). The result will be perhaps some kind of agribusiness oriented toward use of the most modern technology and capital- rather than labor-intensive, as happened in the Khuzistan area of Iran under the Shah (H. Richards 1975).

Before this process goes too far, some debate on its implications is called for, so that the third wave does not end up creating the same social tensions that the first wave did. The spread of mechanization and what is sometimes called the "Green Revolution,"[2] coming after a period during which cooperatives, land reform and political mobilization created a different mood in

the countryside, may foment a new round of social tension. This is
what has happened in India and other countries where the Green
Revolution is more advanced:

> "... The 'green revolution' has created contradic-
> tions inherent in capitalist development, the most
> important being a sharp increase in inequalities of
> income distribution. Thus the 'green revolution' seems
> to be forcing a choice on the policy-makers of the
> developing countries: whether to have an egalitarian land
> reform or to accept the consequences of the 'green
> revolution' in terms of increasing unrest among the rural
> proletariat (Chaudhri 1974:169-170).

Areas of Egypt such as the land reclamation zones exemplify
the combination of first wave technology with second wave social
reorganization patterns. One such area is Ibis, outside
Alexandria, studied by Tadros (1975, 1976). Farmers were moved
into this area from overcrowded sections of the Delta and
established in villages built for them by the government. Some of
these farmers were given ownership rights to land while others were
tenants on government-owned land, but all had to belong to a
cooperative which regulated many aspects of agriculture such as
crop rotation and water use. Tedros found that this structure,
which was "given" to the farmers by the government, had not taken
root, in part because of bad conception on the part of the planners
(villages too far from services, and inadequate provision for
animals), and in part because the program itself was poorly
implemented (inadequate staff for the cooperative, inadequate
supply of seeds and fertilizers, difficulties in organizing timing
and pricing when the corp had to be marketed). The farmers were
able to organize themselves for self-help projects when they
involved building mosques or cemeteries, but not when they involved
government projects.

The Nubians who were resettled in Upper Egypt after their
homelands were flooded by the High Dam give another idea of the
adaptation of people to this kind of milieu (Fernea and Kennedy
1966; Fahim 1975). The most complete study is of the village of
"Kanuba" near Daraw which was settled by Nubians displaced by the
raising of the old dam in 1933 (Fahim 1973; Kennedy 1977). The
origin of the village was different from Ibis, although the form
was similar. Here, however, the dominant form of relationship
between the community and the national government seems to have
been manipulation. Fahim escribes the Nubians as being very
skilled at playing on the values and attitudes of the government
people:

> "Since relocation to date, the relocatees have
> developed a tendency to function as a pressure group on
> the local settlement administration through sharp and
> wide complaint-techniques with the nation's top
> officials. Nubians justify such an attitude towards the

government on the ground that development, as a Nubian
local leader once put it, is a 'Nubian right rather than
a government favor'" (Fahim 1975:27).

They argue that since they had to give up their homes and land for
the national interest, then the nation/government owes them
"development." Like the people of Ibis, the Nubians are willing to
organize themselves to build new mosques, guesthouses or even
schools, but prefer to try to extract other resources from the
government. One successful practitioner of these arts told Kennedy
how he would organize "harakat" in order to get, say, a dispensary
for the village (1977). But the same process of social movement in
the village also gave rise to religious disputes that ultimately
resulted in a more urban form of Islam in "Kanuba" (Fahim 1973,
Kennedy 1977). The Nubians are willing to participate in
development in ways that they define, even though the government
has done nothing to encourage notions of participation (Fahim
1975:31).

The overall picture from the literature on Egypt is that of a
constant pressure on rural economic and political life from the
central government which first organized the technological changes,
then after 1952 sponsored the changes in social organization, and
is now once again encouraging technological transformation together
with such institutional changes as the shift from cooperatives to
village credit banks. The ability of people in local communities
to respond to these government initiatives is less well documented.
Harik's picture of local politics in "Shubra" is convincing
evidence that the village is not the "empty box" it is sometimes
held to be -- an empty box waiting for someone to put something in
it. The accounts of the Nubians give us an additional idea of the
kind of manipulation that people can oppose to the tactics of
dominance or exploitation. But our ignorance of the social
structure of the agricultural lands of Egypt along the Nile is
enormous, and so our ability to evaluate the consequences of a
development policy currently based around high technological inputs
is correspondingly low.

B. Syria and Iraq

Our knowledge of social processes in these two feuding
enemies is also not very high. Phase I has been fairly well
described for the open plains between Aleppo and Mosul where the
introduction of tractors led to the cultivation of large areas of
land that had not been accessible under earlier forms of technology
(Warriner 1962:84-93); and the impact of controlled irrigation in
southern Iraq has been analyzed by Fernea (1969, 1970). Both
countries tried agrarian reform, cooperatives, and other Phase II
social innovations during the 1960's and 1970's. The degree of
real success in Iraq at present is something of a mystery, although
the early stages are generally considered not to have been very
successful (Warriner 1969:77-108; Fernea 1969; Guerreau and
Guerreau 1978:221-235). Rassam (1974, 1977) has analyzed the

changing relationship between patrons and clients in the north around Mosul, and suggests that there is now more flexibility in choosing intermediaries since both traditional urban landlords and patrons and government officials are available. Guerreau and Guerreau sum up the dilemma from the point of view of the government:

> "... the dilemma of the cooperatives is as follows: either one organizes the fellahs according to their tribal origins, and thus one contributes to the reinforcement of the very structures one wants to destroy, or one does not take these origins into account and so runs into very violent disputes which are capable of blocking the running of the cooperatives entirely" (Guerreau and Guerreau 1978:234).

Two recent accounts of Syria differ in their interpretation. Khader (1975) gives an account of the evolution of land reform, he sees the problem of the emergence of the "kulaks" as privileged intermediaries and recommends instead that the cooperative system be generalized. The account given by Ismail (1975) of a poor farming village in the Alawite country gives a sensitive version of the gradual process whereby a local community reaches out to the central government, principally through its educated youth. The youth have been largely responsible for the introduction of party branches, revolutionary youth and women's organizations, and the cooperatives. The cooperative is basically a service cooperative that has lessened dependence on merchants but has done little to modernize agriculture. The earlier relationship of Ismail's village to the government is shown by the fact that it was the center of a revolt against the French colonial administration from 1918 to 1922; now there is a slow interpenetration of village and national life, a growing together of national and local projects. In Syria more than in Iraq the regime has attempted to devise social forms for its rural population, and to diffuse them; as Hinnebusch (1977) points out, the regime never also forgets the implications of these policies for the kind of support it can expect to receive from the rural population.

The theme that recurs in the writing on Iraq and Syria is that the increasing power and penetration of the state is causing the old intermediary elites to give way to new ones. Thus Fernea (1970) traced the replacement of the tribal shaykh by the technocratic engineer in the management of the local irrigation system, and pointed to the essential foreignness of all such officials.

> "The government employees who administer, teach and police southern Iraq are often outsiders with respect to both the people of the market and the tribesmen ... Only recently have villages begun to be administered by country-bred employees. Many Baghdadis, sent out from their city offices to work in the provinces, regard

themselves as exiles in a savage land ... Until recently, when a uniform code of justice replaced a special tribal code in rural areas, administrators with city backgrounds were obliged to rely heavily upon tribal leaders for the interpretation of local custom and the unraveling of historic relationships between tribal groups, a fact which many muwadhafin resented (1971:187)."

Warriner (1962) emphasized that the lack of adequate intermediaries between rural communities and urban government is one of the problems that faced Iraq both before and after the revolution: Ismail shows how the mukhtar and the religious shaikh-s in his village are losing their function to party and government officials, who are often rural themselves. Hinnebusch sees the education of many youth from lower social classes, especially rural, as one of the factors enabling the social transformation of Syria in the 1960's and 1970's. Khader argues that the cooperative structures have simply replaced the older structures of patronage and come to provide a support for the regime in place as their prime function (1975:77-79). The role of the intermediaries is to facilitate manipulation in exchange for support.

C. Turkey

Unlike the countries we have discussed so far, Turkey has never undergone a land reform. Although Turkish agriculture has been tied into the European market since the 18th century, the real impact of modern technology (Phase I) was delayed until after the second world war. Yalman's analysis (1971) of the introduction of tractors into the extensive grain agriculture of the Diyarbekir area (adjacent to the area of Syria and Iraq where similar developments occurred) shows that they only appeared there in force after 1950. His account shows that mechanization reduced formerly essentially independent farming villages (mostly Kurdish) to the status of wage laborers on the new mechanized farms of the landlords (mostly Turkish). Or the peasants simply migrated to the cities. Similar accounts have been given by Kiray (1974) and others. The rosy picture of prosperity due to mechanization in the Antalya area given by Karpat (1960) can be taken either as a contradiction or as a sign that the process is different in ecologically and socially distinct areas.

Western Turkey has produced a number of village and small town studies. Mansur's (1972) study of the coastal town of Bodrum shows that until the 1960's the community held itself aloof from national and international affairs although it was to some extent tied into a regional market for its fish and tangerines. By the early 1970's, more involvement in the external market has caused prices to rise locally to urban levels, and the poor appeared to be worse off. In Ula (Benedict 1974), near Bodrum, modernization of agriculture and improvement in transportation after 1930 are two of the factors that have led to the replacement of a dominant stratum of agas by a rising group of merchants. Contrary to the case of

Diyarbekir, the draining of the marshes and the introduction of a cash crop (tobacco) led to the breakup of the large estates of the agas and thus undercut their sociopolitical position. The high labor requirements for tobacco made intensive small farming feasible, and people chose to work for themselves rather than for the agas. But this same process created a favorable situation for the rise of merchants and transporters as a new wealthy class. The integration of Ula into a national system appears to be undercutting the economic basis of small town life, and the more mobile merchants profit from this.

Perhaps to some extent the functional equivalent of the land reform that Turkey never had was the creation of a party structure under Ataturk and especially the period of multiparty competition that has prevailed since 1950. All the accounts of small town politics stress the significance of the rivalry between the Republican Party and the Democratic/Justice Party, and suggest that, in our terms, manipulation of the center by these communities was the prevalent mode of relationship. Mansur gives the example of the efforts of the folk of Bodrum to persuade the government to build them a better road (1972:83-90); their tactics included enticing government officials to town and then showing their displeasure, and a threat by officeholders to resign, eventually they were successful, but not as quickly as they had hoped. Bodrum people prefer to use intermediaries in dealing with the government, for they regard the government as a dangerous "stranger" which must be treated very gingerly (1972:75).

Turkey's experience seems different from that of other Middle Eastern countries. Instead of massive disruption through foreign involvement in the economy and the implantation of radically new technological systems, followed by an effort to create social forms that would neutralize the disruption caused by these innovations, in Turkey the impact of technology came relatively late. It was then absorbed because different political parties compete to carry out the needed reforms. Manipulation and support appear as the preeminant forms of relationship between the central government and the various local communities. Perhaps there would be more to say about "dominance" and "exploitation," but the material from Turkey is not presented in these terms.

D. Lebanon, Jordan and Yemen

In contrast to Iraq, Syria and Egypt, these three countries have not experienced intensive government schemes for modifying the countryside. Indeed, they have largely not experienced the intensive mechanization of agriculture of Phase I and hence not the ensuring disruption. Instead, they have experienced the gradual introduction of new techniques in agriculture, coupled with improved chances for work outside the village.

Peters (1963, 1972) has analyzed a Shia village in southern

Lebanon where the older village elite has been pushed aside by new
leaders. These are the "Professionals," whose claim to leadership
was based on their success in the outside world as businessmen,
doctors and the like, and on their ability to translate this
success into wealth within the village by fostering the cultivation
of cash crops rather than the traditional subsistence crops which
provided the economic basis for traditional leadership. New
leadership led to a new agrarian system, rather than the opposite.

At the other extreme of Lebanon, Gilsenan (1976, 1977)
presents an analysis of continuity of leadership. In the Akkar of
North Lebanon, there is a neo-feudal situation marked by four
strata -- the lords, big landowners who originally entered the
region under the Ottomans; their staff, mostly Circassian in
origin; the shaykhs, who exercise some ideological influence on
behalf of the lords, and the peasants, most of whom are actually
wage laborers on the large estates opened up by the lords. The
more astute lords have been able to maintain their position of
dominance by adopting modern methods of cultivation of cash crops,
and also by the manipulation of ideological notions such as honor
(through the "staff") and Islam (through the shaykhs). The result
is that the general prosperity in the capital did not have much
impact in this peripheral area, despite increases in agricultural
productivity. Gilsenan argues that underdevelopment is a product
of the peripheral position of this area, and of a personal politics
based on the evocation of values such as honor and Islam:

> "There are ways of preserving personal politics
> through underdevelopment, and vice versa, limiting the
> life chances of what amounts to an impoverished and
> subject population; an attempt to keep up the level of
> exploitability through control of resources and avenues
> to income, jobs, and any degree of social mobility"
> (Gilsenan 1977:178).

While doing this lords have become part of the urban upper class
elite which appeared to run Lebanon before 1975.

The picture from the town of Zahleh is not quite so bleak
(Gubser 1973, 1975). Although "big man" politics based on the
culturally defined role of za^{c}im continued to exist and to work
(at least until 1975), there was some tendency for syndicates of
small business men and even unions of workers to be able to play a
role in the politics of the town. What the zu^{c}ama' possess,
however, is particularly their ability to be intermediaries between
the desires and projects of the local population and the potential
of the national bureaucracy based on Beirut. The syndicates used
strikes and other threats of violence to call the government's
attention to their interests and to "force the government to obey
its own laws" (Gubser 1975:276), but they are still less effective
than the zu^{c}ama'. Gubser sees a form of class consciousness
merging through the political action of the syndicates (1975:281),

certainly they imply a different form of linkage between local
interests and national decisions.

These three examples illustrate something of the complexity of
the Lebanese case even though personal links to the center were
important in all three cases. Involvement in the market allowed a
new elite to take power in the Shia village, but simply reinforced
the position of the old one in the Akkar. The lords of the Akkar
often prevented the satisfaction of the needs of the population,
while the zuᶜama' of Zahleh based their position on their ability
to respond to those needs. The growth of a more differentiated
occupational structure in Zahleh concurrently with the increase in
the forces of production permitted the appearance of classlike
pressure groups which challenged the zuᶜama' there, but so far
unsuccessfully. In Lebanon the center made few demands on the
periphery, and local variation seems to have persisted in this
relative isolation.

Something of the same was true for the Jordanian village
meticulously analyzed by Antoun (1979). Although the government
was committed both to development and decentralization, the
villagers of Kafr el Ma remained largely (not completely) free to
regulate their own political life, perhaps because of some
contradictions between these two policies. They were able to
remain at some psychological distance from the regime despite
considerable overlap in values. The element of confrontation and
hard choices, evident say in Iraq or Egypt, is absent here, and
instead there is a gradual erosion of the traditional way of life
as villagers are imperceptibly drawn into the world beyond the
village limits by education, employment and politics. One senses
that these villages would "withdraw" if they could: they distrust
anything that could signify "divisiveness" in politics, such as
parties and elections. On the basis of his field research between
1959 and 1967, Antoun argues for a muted, "low-key" quality to
politics that makes even words like "manipulation" sound like
overstatements.

Politics are somewhat more robust in the Yemeni town of
Manakha (Gerholm 1977), perhaps reflecting the much greater formal
social differentiation there. Men compete for power and the right
to extract some resources from the region's population, but now
find themselves increasingly coopted by the tentative development
efforts of the Yemeni government. These represent a new source of
power, but the town leaders slowly become politically dependent on
the origin of these resources. Roads, labor migration and
education are undercutting the traditional society, but the lack of
class consciousness and the tendency of the local poor to support
their local rich leaders against government officials when there is
a showdown show that Manakha is still largely autonomous.

E. Arabia and the Sudan

Arabia and the Sudan share the problems of the integration

of nomadic pastoral populations. While Saudi Arabia has been largely by-passed by the three phases of agrarian transformation we identified, the Sudan represents a mixed case, ranging from pastoral nomads at one extreme to the Gezira scheme at the other.

Cole (1975) has presented the history of the relations between the Al Murrah bedouin of eastern Arabia with the House of Al Sa^{c}ud. When the Al Sa^{c}ud were competing with their rivals to establish political dominion over the territory of Arabia, the Al Murrah were their allies. After the discovery of oil reinforced the position of the Al Sa^{c}ud as the government of Saudi Arabia, the national polity and economy developed considerably, but the Al Murrah found themselves increasingly left out despite the fact that they were moving into the market economy by switching from camel-herding to sheep-raising. The tribal countryside appears alienated from the multiethnic cities. The Saudi government buys the Al Murrah's loyalty through incorporating most of the men into the well-paid National Guard, and offers them high prestige as noble nomads, eligible for intermarriage with the Al Sa^{c}ud, but has not yet been able to create a modern-type national society in which they can have a place. Schools and medical facilities are difficult to provide for a population that prefers to move around a good deal, and there are still many people who prefer to manage their relations with the government by staying far enough away from it to live in peace -- though close enough to receive the subsidy, buy trucks, and raise sheep for the urban meat market created by the oil growth.

A somewhat different picture comes from Katakura's (1977) study of the Wadi Fatima, between Jedda and Mecca. Here on the one hand the urban merchants have acquired land rights to the farm land and water supplies, and on the other hand, government-sponsored companies have acquired rights to much of the underground water in the area to supply to the nearby cities, so that the expansion of agriculture is strictly limited. The social structure of this area reflects this double penetration.

In Saudi Arabia, the form of political integration involves personal loyalty to the royal house. In the Sudan, on the other hand, it involves a republican/bureaucratic form of government which is attempting to break up patterns of tribal politics in order to create a national of citizens.

The Sudan is the classic site of two contradictory developments. On the one hand, a great deal of the population is historically nomadic. In the past the nomadic populations were linked to the central government in Khartoum very loosely, and usually through their leaders, the tribal elite. Recently, however, some of the nomadic groups, such as the Rufa'a al-Hoi who live between the Blue and White Niles (Abdel Ghaffar 1974) have been brought within the range of government-sponsored agricultural development programs which threaten the ecological base of their nomadic pastoralism. If they accept integration into these

development schemes, then the nature of their relationship to the
government will change. If they move away, they face a different
environment requiring a different pastoral balance. One short-run
effect was to allow merchants to compete with the tribal elite for
power, as the government decreed that elected rural councils would
be the form of local government. The relations which the tribal
elite had nurtured with the family of the Mahdi are being bypassed
as the government extends its own version of political structures.

On the other hand, the Sudan includes some of the classic
grandiose development schemes, such as the Phase I Gezira scheme
and its various extensions (Barnett 1975, 1977). Here government
and private investment has created an entirely new landscape based
on the irrigated cultivation of cotton and other crops. The
communities that live in these schemes, whether tenant farmers (the
elite group) or wage laborers (the dominated/exploited group), are
integrated into the national system by virtue of their involvement
with a bureaucratic apparatus. Currently, massive amounts of
technology are being brought to bear on another ambitious scheme,
the construction of the Phase III Jonglei canal in the southern
Sudan which is intended to save Nile water from evaporation in the
marshes by channelling it quickly north. That this canal will have
an impact on the Nuer, Dinka and others who live in the Sudd is
obvious (Abdel Ghaffer 1977); whatever the economic merit of such a
project it is clear that it will have the effect, whether manifest
or latent, of integrating the ethnically different southern Sudan
more tightly into the national economic and political structure
controlled by the government in Khartoum. Indeed, it has been
opposed by some southerners on those grounds.

The literature on the Sudan tends to stress the gradual
erosion of local community autonomy as the power of the central
government is extended to include nomadic groups or the non-Arabic
speaking groups of the south. The emphasis is on the pattern of
exploitation and domination that this represents. This is
reflected also in Omar's (1976) study of the introduction of
irrigation pumps into the agriculture of the Dongola area in
Sudan's Northern Province. Large stationary irrigation pumps were
introduced into this area with the financial support of local
merchants (mostly non-Sudanese). The merchants also encouraged the
cultivation of cash crops in order to ensure a return on their
investment, and by extending credit, drew the peasants into debt.
This led to "a systematic subordination of the peasants which was
hastened by the establishment of a system of native administration
that worked hand in hand with the rural capitalists to dominate
over the peasant economy." The pre-capitalist mode of production
has begun to give way to a capitalist one:

"New social forces began to emerge as a result of the
enmeshing capitalist mode of production as well as
abortive government policies regarding agrarian reform
and social justice. In Mushu village ... there developed
formations of class nature and consciousness among the

tenant farmers. This led to the uprising of the village tenant farmers and agricultural labourers against the owners of the agricultural scheme" (Omar 1976:33-34).

The increase in the productive forces (i.e., oil production) in Saudi Arabia has created a disequilibrium between urban and rural, and the urban-based state finds ways to extract surplus from the rural nomadic and sedentary populations. In the Sudan, efforts to increase the productive forces are focussed on agricultural development, and so a very different kind of center-periphery relationship is likely to result.

F. Tunisia and the Maghreb

In Tunisia it is easy to see the connection between government development programs and the enhancement of central power. It took a number of years after independence for the government to establish itself firmly; in the early years it had to try hard to retain control of the situation (Moore 1965). The ability of the government to carry out development programs successfully helped to anchor its power.

Phase I in Tunisia, as in Algeria and Morocco, is represented by colonial agriculture. The period from the 1920's to independence in the 1950's was one of the increasingly solid implantation of the colonial package (LeCoeur 1969; Grandquillaume 1976; Pascon 1977; Kassab 1979; Hopkins 1978a) amidst a general pattern of impoverishment of the rural population. The end result of this process can be seen in the precarious living conditions of the hamlet near Jendouba studied by Bardin (1965) and the Ansarin mountain in northern Tunisia studied by Cuisenier (1960, 1975). The period involved here also saw the emergence of the first nationalist movements in the three Maghrebi countries (Hopkins n.d.a.). In Testour the appearance of the Destour party came about because of the disruption caused by colonial agriculture and because the colonial regime had removed all forms by which the population might have participated in the political process (Hopkins 1980).

Consequently when Tunisia and Algeria became independent (Morocco followed this evolution only in part), the first efforts of the government were directed at taking in hand the situation created by colonial estate agriculture (Phase II). The land was taken over from the Europeans, and cooperatives were set up in the place of the European estates. In Tunisia this took the form of the Unites Cooperatives de Production (Ben Salem 1976; Makhlouf 1976), and in Algeria of the "autogestion" sector (Chaulet 1971). This raised the question of the pattern of class alliances that was going to form: would the petty bourgeois intellectuals find their allies among the landless farm workers on the new cooperatives, or among the middle peasants who had already benefited greatly from such policies of independent Tunisia as the abolition of the waqf properties (Zghal 1969)? In the late 1960's, the apparent choice was to seek an alliance between the petty bourgeoisie and the poor peasants through the generalization of the cooperative system. This created a need for cadres trained as economic intermediaries, a function which in a liberal system would have been filled by private entrepreneurs of one kind or another (Ben Salem 1969).

Although Phase II in Tunisia and Algeria was felt particularly on the former colonial estates, the Tunisian government also made an effort in the 1960's to extend production and service cooperatives to small farmers such as those living in the village of "Sidi Mateur" studied by Abu-Zahra (1972), or in the citrus belt of the Cap Bon (Sethom 1977; Simmons 1972). Service cooperatives meant only that a new channel for relations between population and government had been invented, one that allowed for manipulation and the extraction of resources. But the creation of production cooperatives, as in Testour in 1968-69, caused a furor. Testouris were adamant against including their prized gardens in such a cooperative, and appealed to their patron saint to protect them. The old intermediary proved stronger than the new, or so it seemed when the policy was reversed. In Testour and elsewhere in Tunisia at this time there were cases of violence, minor but enough to reinforce the decision to halt the change.

After 1970 the cooperative formula was restricted to some of the former colonial farms. For instance, the Ghanima Cooperative Production Unit (UCP) near Testour had about 70 members in the early 1970's on 990 hectares of rich farm land. This was a production cooperative where people were organized for collective work with the project of the labor divided on an equitable basis among the member-workers (Nash and Hopkins 1976:11). Since its establishment, Ghanima has successfully diversified its activities, adding irrigated gardening and dairying to the basic production of cereals. It was run by a committee headed by a president elected by the cooperative members, in conjunction with a director named by the government. The government continued to make many detailed decisions about production and finance, but the members were resourceful in exploiting the areas left open for them. Near Ghanima was a former cooperative called Rahma. After the dissolution of the cooperatives, Rahma had been rented by a group of its former members who were attempting with some success to farm it collectively. However, the Tunisian cooperatives after 1970, being on state owned land, were under attack from pressure groups in the capital who coveted the land, and the cooperative leaders would need all their political skills to maintain their position.

Phase III in Tunisia as in Egypt involves the abandonment of major efforts to mobilize the people through government-created structures in favor of a technique of economic incentives. Government policy stressed credit facilities, marketing structures, and the introduction (often under government sponsorship) of certain new forms of technology, such as the "Mexican wheat." This is the situation that I observed in Testour, where it seemed that local politics and agriculture were being increasingly tied to the decisions taken at the national/central level, even though the mobilization structures themselves were no more in existence. Production was almost wholly for the market, and this had consequences for the way in which agriculture is carried out. Retail prices in Testour, for instance, were fixed after a telephone call to the wholesale market in Tunis.

In a town like Testour, the result seems to be the creation of two separate classes. Previously the level of the productive forces was compatible with the use of kinship and family to organize most labor in the fields. But the greater demand for labor, coupled with the probability that landowners' children will be in school or employed elsewhere, means that farmers call on wage labor more than before. Thus now on the one hand there are the agricultural entrepreneurs who are borrowing money, buying machinery and establishing connections in the market. On the other, there are the day laborers who work for them. The existence of these two classes (and there are others in Testour) presages a very different kind of integration of Testour into the national community and social formation. Instead of being linked through individual vertical ties, Testour may be linked in the future through collective horizontal ties. For the moment, Testour's stance towards the government is characterized by exploitation, if one looks purely at the economic balance sheet (Hopkins 1978b), or a dialectic between dominance and manipulation, if one focuses upon politics (Hopkins n.d.b.). The various classes in Testour once tried to manipulate the central government into giving them the kind of aid they desired after a serious flood hit the town's gardens in the spring of 1973. At the same time, the formal political structure of the town is decreed elsewhere, and even the town's official leaders cannot be chosen without approval from higher instances of the party.

Zamiti (1977) has traced out the stages by which a group of Zlass nomadic pastoralists southwest of Kairouan has been integrated into the national system. The best valley land was alienated to colonial farmers in 1927, and the population was resettled on the less productive hillsides. After independence, some of the former colonial plantations became private Tunisian farms while others were turned into UCP's. Many of this group worked on the UCP's. After the collapse of the cooperative system in 1969, the biggest landowners on the hillsides were able to purchase pickup trucks, tractors and combine harvesters which they rent to their less fortunate fellows. They extract value from these farmers to the point where the farmers do not have enough to eat to stay alive. They must rely on the World Food Program, but in order to qualify for that they must belong to the party, and thus testify to their political support for the system that extracts surplus from them. This example also shows that programs such as the World Food Program indirectly subsidize the large or middle farmers by allowing them to extract a larger measure of surplus from the small farmers. Thus the process of development has created a class structure where a tribal lineage structure existed before. According to Zamiti, the relationship of this population to the national system is one of political dominance and economic exploitation. His account is generally confirmed by other recent accounts of similar situations in Tunisia, such as Fraenkel's study in the Zouarines area near el-Kef (1975). However, all these areas are among the major suppliers of migrant laborers, and through this mechanism the socioeconomic complexion of the countryside may be changing (Hopkins 1978c).

Algeria has followed a somewhat different evolution, even though the recent history of Algeria is complex enough to make brief exposees more than usually chancy. Shortly after independence there was a political conflict between the government and the unions and farmers concerning the control of the "autogestion" sector (Clegg 1971). The government won this confrontation, and so won the right to centralize decision-making for the former colonial estates. But much of Algerian agriculture escaped completely from central control; for a while this seemed natural for the government was more interested in industrial than in agricultural development. In 1971 the government decided to regulate private agriculture through an effort to redistribute land that belonged to the larger Algerian landowners and to establish a generalized system of cooperatives (Ait Amara 1976; Ollivier 1977). The exact effects of this effort are not at all clear. The program seems to be accompanied by a general disdain for rural life and values on the part of the country's leaders, who see themselves as "giving" to the peasants the institutions they are imposing on them. The "peasants" have shown a lack of interest in the new institutions (Zghal 1977). Perhaps what this means is that Algeria has so far staved off Phase III, while Morocco seems to have moved from Phase I to III without ever going through Phase II. In all three Maghrebi countries, agrarian reform and cooperativization appear as urban projects whose latent function is to link the rural areas more closely to the central government and its institutions, and to create a "tame" peasantry. As the peasants grasp this, they shy away from such projects, and become instead the pawns in a new version of the international division of labor.

Conclusion

My first task in this paper was to establish a general framework within which to understand the relationship between development and the emergence of a certain form of government in the Middle East. Then I illustrated this by analysis of the literature relating to this problem from a number of Middle Eastern countries. Now I offer a few remarks by way of conclusion. These remarks stress the impact of development on local strategies in the Middle East.

Observation suggests that income levels have risen in the last generation in Tunisia, Egypt, Turkey and probably in Iraq and Syria. Of the other cases we have discussed, Algeria needs more analysis than can be given here, Lebanon at the moment is more involved in destructive politics than in constructive economics, and the Sudan and Saudi Arabia present special problems due in part to isolation of much of the population and a nomadic tradition which made the task of national integration that much harder. To say that income levels have risen is to gloss over certain problems, such as the continuing poverty of certain segments of the population, the fact that urban living standards may be rising even faster than rural ones, and the increasing role of labor migration which solves one set of problems and creates another. Development and rising income levels are not synonymous anyway. David Apter (1965:72) noted: "Here then is an interesting puzzle. Development creates inequality; modernization accentuates it." Saad Eddin Ibrahim and I wrote (1977:619):

> "Thus when evaluating development in the Arab world we must ask not only whether total material wealth has increased but also how it is distributed among the population, between cities and countryside; whether the Arab world is less or more dependent on the West, whether Arab women are becoming less or more equal to Arab men; and whether both men and women are less or more literate, participate less or more in making decisions which affect their lives. Development in this sense implies both maximization and equalization of "life opportunities" for the vast majority of individuals in the Arab World."

The rise in income levels is also related to a greater involvement with systems that are no longer so responsive to local control or influence since the decisions are taken centrally by people who are unknown at the local level. We can note this fact, but we should also note that people continue to be resourceful in finding ways to maintain a comfortable degree of local control over everyday activities. Some farmers in one Egyptian village simply pay the fine for not planting cotton rather than get involved; instead they have used government-installed electricity to build up a flourishing chicken raising business geared to the regional market. When migrant laborers return to Central Tunisia, they are likely to invest their money in wells, tractors or trucks, in blithe ignorance of government plans for the area. When it comes to making a living we should never underestimate human integrity.

We can also measure the increase in the level of the productive forces. This represents a wide variety of factors, from dams to tractors and including rural electrification, improvements in road transport and communication systems, the spread of trucks of all sizes, the use of pumps rather than gravity-flow irrigation or man- or animal-powered water-raising devices, tile drainage systems, insecticides and fertilizers, improved record keeping, better storage facilities, and (whatever one might feel about the optimum number) more people in better health and with more skills. All this has created a very different material environment within which people have to work and live.

Another measure would be the shift in systems of surplus extraction. Agriculture is never developed only for the sake of the peasant. To the extent that urban people are interested in developing agriculture it is because they expect to benefit from it as well. There are a range of techniques for this. Rent is the classic one. The importance of rent for the ruling elites of yesterday can be seen in the tendency of royal families and other members of the upper strata to aquire ownership rights to land. King Fuad of Egypt owned 800 feddans when he became king in 1917, and 28,000 feddans when he died in 1936 (Ayrout 1952:42, who adds that he was able to this "thanks to a deft administration.") Reza Shah in Iran did likewise. More proletarian governments have satisfied themselves with state ownership of land, which can also be seen as reflecting classic Islamic conceptions of land tenure. Estate owners later turn to direct exploitation of their estates and hire laborers to do the work; in this case, the initial step of surplus extraction is through the low salaries. Taxation is another common technique of surplus extraction; it can be applied by the government or rich and poor alike and so may represent a second step of surplus extraction for those who have acquired their income by extracting income from wage laborers. A somewhat more subtle technique is a controlled market for harvested crops that allows the government to buy certain crops well below their value on the international market and to realize a profit (some 19th century sovereigns like the Bey of Tunis were also large merchants). There can be complicated patterns of subsidies and fixed prices that leave everyone perplexed.

Most of these techniques characterize Phase I, and are based around the control of the land and its products. Thus the Phase II efforts were directed at negating the patterns of control set up in Phase I, and replacing them by a context of political mobilization combined with different techniques for surplus extraction. The emphasis was less on taxation and rent, and more on government control of prices. To a certain extent, the control of people became a more critical interest than the control of land; hence the mobilization aspect.

In Phase III, the control of capital has become more essential, along with the machines capital can produce and the credit that it allows. Zamiti showed on a small scale how ownership of machinery allowed a local elite to exploit neighbors and kin; the same is true on a larger scale when it is the government that controls the machinery, such as, for instance, the supply of electricity or of irrigation water. The farmers of Testour are content with their wells which eliminate the need for cooperation with their neighbors, let alone with their government. The rise in the level of the productive forces in the countryside tends to offer those who run the governments the opportunity to use the resources at their command to create systems that tie everyone in much more closely.

Faced with tactics of this kind, the reaction of most people

is to seek out ways in which they can control the mechanical
improvements in the countryside themselves. One such tactic is the
use of money earned in overseas migrant labor to purchase tractors
and other machinery (reported from Egypt, Tunisia and Turkey), as
well as to build houses and consume. However, the net impact of
this is to create class differences in the countryside, and to
establish a basis for linkups between classes that extend beyond
the traditional boundaries of a single community. Thus in Tunisia
the national organizations based on economic interests, such as the
General Union of Tunisian Workers or the National Union of Tunisian
Farmers, can play.

The siphoning off of surplus from rural production encourages
class formation in the urban areas, particularly the alliance of
bureaucrats and entrepreneurs who control the government machinery.
This is not the place to engage in a critique of the styles of
class analysis in the Middle East, or to analyze the composition of
these urban-based classes. The point is that in the contemporary
world, the formation of such a ruling class is not limited in its
consequences to a single national unit. Such classes rely very
much on their connections outside the country, as Simmons
(1972:450), Makhlouf (1976:395-396) and Springborg (1977:138) have
shown. At the same time, the rapid growth of a bureaucratic
sector, a kind of state class, has changed the nature of politics
in countries like Tunisia or Iraq. In Tunisia during the 1960's
and in Iraq during the 1970's the government appears to have its
power base primarily in the class of urban government workers who
are the prime beneficiaries of the regime.

Our survey of the situation in a number of Middle Eastern
countries suggests that there are three broad patterns of
relationship between those who man the government and those who
live in local/rural communities. First, there are what Apter
(1965) and others have called "mobilization" systems. These
involve efforts by those in charge of the government to use social
forms to mobilize all the people, to mobilize labor as a factor of
production. Ideology plays a key role in this mobilization
process, and relations between top and bottom are in theory
intense, although Harik (1973:99-102) has shown that there is often
a chasm between the two different levels of the political process.

Second, there are development programs, where the government
is less interested in reaching intensely out to all citizens in the
country, but instead concentrates its attention on particular
projects which, like farm mechanization, often have the latent
function of tying people more closely into the system. Service
cooperatives and credit mechanisms are as much a part of this
pattern as production cooperatives or even collectives are a part
of "mobilization." Development projects are sometimes a way of
paying off one sector or another of the population. Springborg
points out that the agricultural engineers have been able to
acquire property title to new lands in Egypt while peasants have
not (1977:137).

A third option is for the government to do nothing at all, and simply allow the entrepreneurial spirit of the people full rein. This is the case of governments that are relatively weak within their political space, such as Lebanon or Yemen. Whichever of these three patterns is present, it will have clear implications for the kind of intermediary structure that exists between those in the government and those on the ground. In the mobilization system, the intermediaries will be cadres of the government, who may be trained to fill specific tasks within the bureaucracy. In the development system, some intermediaries will be government officials, such as those in charge of the irrigation system in pre-1958 Iraq, but others will be political leaders of one kind or another, and it will be possible to speak of a transition from agas to merchants. In fact, the review of the literature has frequently turned up mention of a category called "merchants" which plays a key role in the development process (Turkey, Sudan). But the merchants are liable to be pushed aside as the ante rises, especially in areas which are conducive to agribusiness operations as in the Iran of the Shah, the Sudan and perhaps in the future, Egypt.

Springborg has sketched in a number of alternative forms of development in agriculture in the Middle East. Each of these has different implications for local community formation, for the style of political communities and individuals in the development process, and for the method of surplus extraction. He lists self-managed collectives, state farms, agribusiness, and agrarian reform cooperatives (1977:134-137). I suppose one should add another -- just leaving the people to themselves with some version of the existing systems of land tenure and labor mobilization. Springborg sees the alternative that faces developers as follows:

> "... government will continue to be confronted with the dilemma of whether to curry favor with the peasantry by pandering to their desire for land and freedom from government interference, or to attempt to stage a Green Revolution by taking direct control of agricultural production" (1977:141).

Like the comment by the Guerreaus on Iraq quoted above, this is too simple and straightforward a choice. The Ghanima case with its Rahma variant from Tunisia can stand as one example among many that there is still room for the application of creative imagination to the problems of reconciling development with social justice.

Footnotes

1. The Middle East is here taken to mean the Arab World, Turkey and Iran. However, two highly critical areas -- Iran and Palestine -- will be left aside in this analysis since to treat

them here would require introducing unnecessary complexities. I
feel that the general patterns analyzed here apply to them as well.

  2. Some clarification is needed concerning the meaning
attached to be phrase "Green Revolution." Whereas initially it
meant a reform of agriculture through the development of highly
productive inputs that were small enough to be accessible to the
small farmer (seeds and fertilizers, rather than tractors and
irrigation techniques), in Egypt the phrase is officially used to
refer to the transformation of agriculture through mechanization
and the reclamation of new lands from the desert.

References Cited

Abdel-Fadil, Mahmoud

  1975   Development, income distribution and social change in
          rural Egypt (1952-1970). Cambridge, Cambridge
          University Press

Abdel Ghaffer M. Ahmed

  1974   Shaykhs and followers: political struggle in the
          Rufa's al-Hoi nazirate in the Sudan. Khartoum,
          Khartoum University Press

  1977   "Anthropology and development planning in the Sudan:
          the case of the Jonglei project" in Sudan Journal of
          Development Research 1(1):26-60

Abu-Zahra, Nadia

  1972   "Inequality of descent and egalitarianism of the new
          national organizations in a Tunisian village" in
          Richard Antoun and Iliya Harik, eds., Rural politics
          and social change in the Middle East. Bloomington,
          Indiana University Press, pp. 267-286.

Ait Amara, Hamid

  1976   "The Algerian model of agrarian reorganization" in
          Popular participation in social change, June Nash,
          Jorge Dandler and N.S. Hopkins, eds., The Hague,
          Mouton, pp. 265-270.

36

Ammar, Hamed

    1960   The sociological approach to problems of community education.   Sirs-el-Layyan, Arab States Fundamental Education Centre

Antoun, Richard T.

    1979   Low-key politics: local-level leadership and change in the Middle East. Albany, State University of New York Press.

Apter, David

    1965   The politics of modernization. Chicago, University of Chicago Press

Ayrout, Henri Habib

    1952   Fellahs d'Egypte. Cairo, Editions du Sphinx

Bailey, F.G.

    1969   Stratagems and spoils. Oxford, Blackwells

Bardin, Paul

    1965   La vie d'un douar. The Hague and Paris, Mouton

Barnett, Tony

    1975   "The Gezira scheme: production of cotton and the reproduction of underdevelopment" in Ivar Oxaal, Tony Barnett and David Booth, eds., Beyond the sociology of development. London, Routledge and Kegan Paul, pp. 183-207.

    1977   The Gezira scheme: an illusion of development. London, Cass

Benedict, Peter

    1974   Ula. Leiden, Brill

Benhlal, Mohammed

    1977   "Politique des barrages et problemes de la modernisation rurale dans le Gharb" in Bruno Etienne, ed., Les problemes agraires au Maghreb, Paris, CNRS, pp. 261-273

Ban Salem, Lilia

1969   "Les cadres de l'economie locale en Tunisie" in Revue tunisienne de sciences sociales, no. 16, pp. 21-40

1976   "Centralization and decentralization of decision-making in an experiment in agricultural cooperation in Tunisia" in Popular participation in social change, June Nash, Jorge Dandler and N.S. Hopkins, eds., The Hague, Mouton, pp. 271-288

Berque, Jacques

1957   Histoire sociale d'un village egyptien au XXe siecle. Paris, Mouton

Besancon, Jacques

1957   L'Homme et le Nil. Paris, Gallimard

Chaudhri, D.P.

1974   "New technologies and income distribution in agriculture" in David Lehmann, ed., Peasants, landlords and governments: agrarian reform in the third world. New York, Holmes and Meier, pp. 157-189.

Chaulet, Claudine

1971   La Mitidja autogeree. Algiers, S.N.E.D.

Clegg, Ian

1971   Workers' self-management in Algeria. New York, Monthly Review

Cole, Donald P.

1975   Nomads of the nomads: the Al Murrah Bedouin of the Empty Quarter. Chicago, Aldine

Cuisenier, Jean

1960   L'Ansarine: contribution a la sociologie du developpement. Publications de l'Universite de Tunis, 3e serie. Memoires du Centre d'Etudes de Sciences Humaines, vol. 7

1975   Economie et parente. Paris, Mouton

38

Fahim, Hussein

    1973   "Change in religion in a resettled Nubian community in Upper Egypt" in <u>International Journal of Middle East Studies</u> 4:163-177

    1975   "The study and evaluation of the rehabilitation process in the newly settled communities in land reclamation areas, part 2, The Nubian Settlement in Kom Ombo, Upper Egypt." Social Research Center, American University in Cairo

Fallers, Lloyd A.

    1974   <u>The social anthropology of the nation-state</u>. Chicago, Aldine

Fernea, Robert A.

    1969   "Land reform and ecology in postrevolutionary Iraq" in <u>Economic Development and Cultural Change</u> 17:356-381

    1970   <u>Shaykh and Effendi: changing patterns of authority among the el Shabana of southern Iraq</u>. Cambridge, Harvard University Press

    1971   "Southern Mesopotamia" in Louis Sweet, ed., <u>The central Middle East</u>, New Haven, HRAF Press, pp. 171-193

Fernea, Robert A. and John G. Kennedy

    1966   "Initial adaptation to resettlement: a new life for Egyptian Nubians" in <u>Current Anthropology</u> 7:349-354

Fraenkel, Richard M.

    1975   "The collectivization experience in Tunisia." MS prepared for the Group Farming Conference, University of Wisconsin-Madison

Gerholm, Tomas

    1977   <u>Market, mosque and mafraj: social inequality in a Yemeni town</u>. Stockholm, Stockholm Studies in Social Anthropology, University of Stockholm, no. 5

Gilsenan, Michael

    1976   "Lying, honor, and contradiction" in Bruce Kapferer, ed., <u>Transaction and meaning</u>. Philadelphia, Institute for the Study of Human Issues, pp. 191-219

1977   "Against patron-client relations" in Ernest Gellner and John Waterbury, eds., Patrons and clients, London, Duckworth, pp. 167-183.

Grandguillaume, Gilbert

1976   Nedroma: l'evolution d'une medina. Leiden, Brill

Gubser, Peter

1973   "The zu^cama' of Zahleh: the current situation in a Lebanese town" in Middle East Journal 27:173-189

1975   "The politics of economic interest groups in a Lebanese town" in Middle Eastern Studies 11:262-283

Guerreau, Alain and Anita Guerreau-Jalabert

1978   L'Irak: developpement et contradictions. Paris, Le Sycomore

Harik, Iliya

1973   "The single party as a subordinate movement: the case of Egypt" in World Politics 26:80-105

1974   The political mobilization of peasants. Bloomington, Indiana University Press

Hinnebusch, Raymond A.

1977   "Rural politics in Ba'thist Syria: a case study of the role of the countryside in the political development of Arab socialism" in Saad Eddin Ibrahim and Nicholas S. Hopkins, eds., Arab society in transition, Cairo, American University in Cairo, pp. 278-296

Hopkins, Nicholas S.

1977a   "The emergence of class in a Tunisian town" in International Journal of Middle East Studies 8:453-491

1977b   "Notes sur l'histoire de Testour" in Revue d'Histoire Maghrebine, no. 9, pp. 294-313

1978a   "Modern agriculture and political centralization: a case from Tunisia" in Human Organization 37:83-87

1978b   "The articulation of the modes of production: tailoring in Tunisia" in American Ethnologist 5:468-483

1978c   "Elements for a social soundness analysis for the agricultural interventions, Central Tunisia." MS, USAID, Tunis

1980   "Testour au XIXe siecle" in Revue d'Histoire Maghrebine, no. 17/18, pp. 19-31

n.d.   (a) "Nationalism and center-building in North Africa." To appear in The uncertain paths: cohesion and change in 19th century Ottoman Turkey and the Maghreb, ed. S. Mardin and I.W. Zartman

n.d.   (b) "Politics and social change in Testour." Paper prepared for the Xth ICAES, India, December 1978

Ibrahim, Saad Eddin and Nicholas S. Hopkins

1977   Arab society in transition. Cairo, American University in Cairo

Ismail, Kamil

1975   Die sozialokonomischen Verhaltnisse der bauerlichen Bevolkerung im Kustengebirge der Syrischen Arabischen Republik: eine Untersuchung im Gebiet von As-Saih-Badr. Berlin, Akademie-Verlag. Veroffentlichungen des Museums fur Volkerkunde zu Leipzig, Heft 26

Karpat, Kemal H.

1960   "Social effects of farm mechanization in Turkish villages" in Social Research 10(7):83-103

Kassab, Ahmed

1979   L'evolution de la vie rurale dans les regions de la Moyenne Medjerda et de Beja-Mateur. Tunis, Publications de l'Universite de Tunis, 2e serie, Geographie, vol. VIII

Katakura, Motoko

1977   Bedouin village: a study of a Saudi Arabian people in transition. Tokyo, University of Tokyo Press

Kennedy, John G.

1977   Struggle for change in a Nubian community. Palo Alto, Mayfield

Khader, Bichara

1975   "Propriete agricole et reforme agraire en Syrie" in
        Civilisations 25:62:83

Kiray, Mubeccel

1974   "Social change in Cukurova: a comparison of four
        villages" in Peter Benedict, Erol Tumertekin and Fatma
        Mansur, eds., Turkey: geographic and social
        perspectives, Leiden, Brill, pp. 179-203

LeCoeur, Charles

1969   Le rite et l'outil. Paris, Presses Universitaires de
        France

Lozach, Jean

1935   La delta du Nil: etude de geographie humaine. Cairo,
        Schindler, Publications de la Societe Royale de
        Geographie d'Egypte

Lozach, Jean and G. Hug

1930   L'habitat rural en Egypte. Cairo, Imprimerie de
        l'Institut Francais d'Archeologie d'Egypte

Makhlouf, Ezzeddine

1976   "Political and technical factors in agricultural
        collectivization in Tunis" in Popular participation in
        social change, June Nash, Jorge Danler; and N.S.
        Hopkins, eds., The Hague, Mouton, pp. 381-411

Mansur, Fatma

1972   Bodrum, a town in the Aegean. Leiden, Brill

Marei, Sayed

1957   Agrarian reform in Egypt. Cairo, Imprimerie de
        l'Institut Francais d'Archeologie Orientale

Mayfield, James B.

1971   Rural politics in Nasser's Egypt. Austin, U. of Texas
        Press

Nash, June and Nicholas S. Hopkins

1976   "Anthropological approaches to the study of cooperatives, collectives, and self-management" in June Nash, Jorge Dandler, and N.S. Hopkins, eds., Popular participation in social change, The Hague, Mouton, pp. 3-32

Ollivier, Marc

1977   "Place de la revolution agraire dans la strategie algerienne de developpement" in Bruno Etienne, ed., Les problemes agraires au Maghreb, CNRS, pp. 91-114

Omer, el Haj Abdalla Bilal

1976   "Rural traders and socio-economic transformation in Dongola area, Northern Province," Bulletin 47, Economic and Social Research Council, Khartoum, Sudan

Pascon, Paul

1977   Le haouz de Marrakech. Rabat

Peters, Emrys

1963   "Aspects of rank and status among Muslims in a Lebanese village" in Julian Pitt-Rivers, ed., Mediterranean Countrymen, The Hague, Mouton, pp. 159-202

1972   "Shifts in power in a Lebanese village" in Richard Antoun and Iliya Harik, eds., Rural politics and social change in the Middle East, Bloomington, Indiana Univ. Press, pp. 165-197

Radwan, Samir

1977   Agrarian reform and rural poverty: Egypt, 1952-1975. Geneva, ILO

Rassam, Amal   (see also Vinogradov)

1977   "Al-Raba'iyya: power, patronage and marginal groups in northern Iraq" in Ernest Gellner and John Waterbury, eds., Patrons and clients, London, Duckworth, pp. 157-166

Richards, Alan

1977   "Primitive accumulation in Egypt, 1798-1882" in Review 1(2):3-49

1978   "Technical and social change in Egyptian agriculture, 1980-1914" in Economic Development and Cultural Change 26:725-745

1979   "The political economy of commercial estate labor systems: a comparative analysis of Prussia, Egypt, and Chile" in Comparative Studies in Society and History 21:483-518

1980   "Egypt's agriculture in trouble," in MERIP Reports no. 84, pp. 3-13

Richards, Helmut

1975   "Land reform and agribusiness in Iran," in MERIP Reports, no. 43, pp. 3-18

Saab, Gabriel

1967   The Egyptian agrarian reform: 1952-1962. London, Oxford University Press

al Sayyid-Marsot, Afaf Lutfi

1977   Egypt's liberal experiment: 1922-1936. Berkeley, University of California Press

Sethom, Hafedh

1977   Les fellahs de la presqu'ile du Cap Bon. Tunis, Universite de Tunis, 2e serie, Geographie, vol. IV

Simmons, John

1972   "The political economy of land use: Tunisian private farms" in Richard Antoun and Iliya Harik, eds., Rural politics and social change in the Middle East, Bloomington, Indiana University Press, pp. 432-452

Springborg, Robert

1977   "New patterns of agrarian reform in the Middle East and North Africa" in Middle East Journal 31:127-142

1979   "Patrimonialism and policy making in Egypt: Nasser and Sadat and the tenure policy for reclaimed lands" in Middle Eastern Studies 15:49-69

Stambouli, Fredj

1977   "Systeme social et stratification urbaine au Maghreb" in Revue Tunisienne de Sciences Sociales, no. 50/51, pp. 69-106

Tadros, Helmi

    1975   "The study and evaluation of the rehabilitation process in the newly settled communities in land reclamation areas, part 1, The newly settled communities in the northwestern Nile Delta." Cairo, The Social Research Center of the American University in Cairo

    1976   "Problems involved in the human aspects of rural resettlement schemes in Egypt," in Amos Rapoport, eds., The mutual interaction of people and their built environment, The Hague, Mouton, pp. 453-482

Vinogradov, Amal   (see Rassam)

    1974   "Ethnicity, cultural discontinuity and power brokers in northern Iraq: the case of the Shabak" in American Ethnologist 1:207-218

Vinogradov, Amal and John Waterbury

    1971   "Situations of contested legitimacy in Morocco: an alternative framework" in Comparative Studies in Society and History 13:32-59

Warriner, Doreen

    1962   Land reform and development in the Middle East: a study of Egypt, Syria, and Iraq. London, Oxford University Press

    1969   Land reform in principle and practice. Oxford, Clarendon Press

Yalman, Nur

    1971   "On land disputes in eastern Turkey" in G. Tikku, ed., Islam and its cultural divergence, Urbana, University of Illinois Press, pp. 180-218

Zamiti, Khalil

    1977   "Exploitation du travail paysan en situation de dependence et mutation d'un parti de masses en parti de cadres" in Du Maghreb, special issue of Les Temps Modernes, no. 375bis, pp. 312-333

Zghal, Abdelkader

    1969   "L'elite administrative et la paysannerie" in Revue Tunisienne de Sciences Sociales, no. 16, pp. 41-52

1977   "Pourquoi la reforme agraire ne mobilise-t-elle pas les
paysans   maghrebins?" in Bruno Etienne, eds., Les
problemes agraires au Maghreb, Paris, CNRS, pp. 295-311

3
Local Leadership in Urban Egypt: Leader, Family and Community Perceptions

Louis J. Cantori and Peter Benedict

The Problem. The substantive empirical problem of the present paper is the neglected nature of the study of local leadership in general in the Middle East but especially that of urban leaderships. Egypt has become by now a country studied by scholars to a greater degree than that of other Arab Middle Eastern states yet even it has only a small but developing body of urban studies.(1) The study of local urban leaderships is lent a policy imperative both by the magnitude of economic development efforts and by the explicit effort of both the Sadat and Mubarak regimes to decentralize and presumably localize these efforts. In fact, the present study was initiated precisely by the need to know more about local leaderships in order to more effectively implement family planning efforts in Egypt.(2)

The theoretical state of the study of leadership in the social sciences is a somewhat disputed one. Thus a psychologist has commented, "The concept of leadership, like that of general intelligence, has largely lost its value for the social sciences, although it remains indispensable to general discourse." He specifically notes that the effort to deal with leadership attributes alone has been abandoned.(3) There is much truth to these comments, at least inasmuch as they reflect a relative academic neglect of the subject of leadership.

The concept of leadership looked at sociologically can be related to status and role i.e. rights and duties on the one hand and action on the other. While the efforts to discuss the attributes of leadership may have been abandoned by the social science literature, their continued importance seems to be two-fold. First, there is the question of defining role from the point of view of a role occupant and from the point of view of a leader's followers, i.e. the community. Second, the concept of leadership begins to take on its political coloration when the concept of authority is added to those of status and role. Authority is related to the question of the effectiveness of leadership but in order to be effective there must be a defined status accompanied by agreed upon role characteristics. The legitimacy of such authority

46

is increased with concurrence upon status and role attributes. It is the quality of legitimacy to which the empirical focus of the present study is ultimately related. The attributes of leadership become those characteristics of leadership status and role themselves but they acquire political meaning when the self-perceptions of these attributes by the role occupant are congruent with those of followers. In the present study, such followers are located both within the family and the wider community.

The preceding distinction is intrinsic to the understanding of Middle Eastern and Egyptian local leadership dynamics. The extended family is the primary unit of membership and loyalty in sedentary Middle Eastern societies. Its importance for the present study is that it both socializes and sustains a leader in his role. In addition, however, the family by reason of its size, prestige and resources also becomes an important instrument of leadership in the wider community.

The present study represents the urban segment of a comparative study of two rural leaders and two urban leaders and their families.(4) The methodology employed is that of semi-structured interviewing by means of a lengthy aide-memoire. This method has been used successfully by Firth in London and Schneider in Chicago, although the questions utilized in the present study were specially formulated for that purpose.(5) The extensive in-depth interviews were tape recorded and were transcribed in Arabic and translated into English. The results yielded a large amount of data - the analysis of which has been assisted by the internal structure of the aide-memoire. Additional informants were also conferred with and in addition there occurred a certain amount of participant observation although the limited field time of three weeks in each rural and urban community was spent largely in interviewing.

The method of sample selection of two urban leaders and their families was essentially that of peer nomination. With the assistance of the prior research experience of the sponsoring organization (the Social Research Council of the American University in Cairo) it was possible to identify and interview a number of leaders in order to discover individuals who could be characterized as leaders. The two subjects discussed in this paper were selected on the basis of their representativeness and their willingness to be interviewed along with their family members.

Urban Contextual Features of The Study

This discussion of the urban contextual features of the present study is limited by the absence of statistical data for such a limited geographical area. Contextual features can of course be treated in an all encompassing encyclopedic fashion or on a more selective analytical basis. The choice of the analytic focus is revealed in the concerns of the present section with ecological features, as well as social/cultural, economic and political systemic features.

The major concern with ecological features focuses upon the question of linkages of the local system to the larger one. The underlying assumption is one of the past historical autonomy of the local system which is to say that the local system has been and continues to be significantly autonomous of the national political system.

The attention to social/cultural, economic and political systemic features represents an effort to plumb the depths of community. The effort is to the answer classical questions of systems analysis: boundary definitions, internal interaction, and interdependence. The thrust of this analysis is to seek the degree to which the social/cultural system, the economic system and the political system overlap and reenforce one another.

The hitta (quarter) of ^{C}Ard Ya^{C}qub is located in the hay' (district) Zeinhoum in the Sheyakha (census tract) of Sayyida Zeinab. It is located in close proximity to the main slaughterhouse (madbah) of the city of Cairo and this proximity gives the estimated 4,000 population of the hitta plus three other hitta surrounding it their common occupational features, namely work involving the slaughtering of animals or the preparation of skins as leather or ancillary industries such as a knife factory. Thus in this urban setting, territory and occupation combine to affirm a high degree of neighborhood.

"Neighborhood" in ^{C}Ard Ya^{C}qub is however even more fragmented and atomized than has been so far sketched. The hitta is in turn divided into about ten hara (streets or segments of streets) each of which in fact receives the major focus of loyalty within the hitta. The hitta itself is very much like other low-income residential areas in Cairo in presenting an exterior image of brown stucco, mudbrick or red brick all gently touched by exterior deterioration and decay. ^{C}Ard Ya^{C}qub is different however in that once one penetrates the interior of these buildings, one can see the evidence of the unusual personal wealth of this neighborhood in the form of such furnishings as refrigerators and televisions.

The area around the slaughterhouse can be characterized as an island in that it was originally settled by people who because of the odiferous and low status character of their occupation found themselves insulated on the outskirts of the city in a previously isolated and underpopulated area.

In recent years, however, the pressure of population has been such as to increase the density within the hitta so that even the cemetery (consisting of dwelling-like tombs) adjoining the slaughterhouse area (which further testifies to its former isolation) has become interpenetrated with dwellings. In addition, the population of the city itself has also expanded to the boundaries of the area, thus reducing its geographical island-like quality.

Linkages between the sub-system of ᶜArd Yaᶜqub and the larger system take on a special meaning the urban context because of the "closeness" in the proximity of the larger system to that of the sub-system. The capital city of Cairo might seem to impinge physically to the point of perhaps being able to smother such a small scale local area. Yet this is far from being the case. For example even communication linkages are less pronounced then in Shanawan, the village studied in the other portions of the present study. Only a single bus line serves the area of the hitta. Socially, the hitta is integrated into the larger system as a result of the fact that while the majority of the population have work connected with the slaughterhouse, increasingly a large number also live in the hitta but have occupations that take them elsewhere.

In economic terms, the slaughterhouse functions as a single economic enterprise linking the local community with the larger one. The enormous salaries of slaughterhouse connected work can be seen in the fact that a scraper of hides receives between LE.5 and LE.7 a day for his expertness (compared to LE.30 a month for university graduates), and it should be added, his willingness to perform such unclean low-status work.

What the foregoing discussion of the weak linkages between the larger system and ᶜArd Yaᶜqub hint at is that the hitta possesses certain systemic features that in fact deliberately work to exclude a role for central government. Foremost among these is the local cultural syndrome that appears to reflect intense hara, and even hitta pride with a underlying sense of fierce familial loyalty. This pride finds expression for example, in the organization of football teams by each hara within ᶜArd Yaᶜqub in order to play one another. In addition, in the past the entire slaughterhouse area used to field a national football team that again seemed to express the competitive sense of localism against that of a national identification.

This antagonistic exclusivism was illustrated in the present study when one of the co-researchers was told that when she entered the hitta if she had been a man she would have been compelled to go to a certain shop in order to explain why as a stranger he was in the hitta.

To a large extent, exclusivism is reflected and in fact probably determined by the underlying social realities of the hitta. It appears that the majority of the population in the hitta are of Saidi or Upper Egyptian origin. This begins to explain the tenacity and ferocity of family identification. The sense of family honor is paramount so that what might remain a situation of personal conflict elsewhere in Egypt, becomes a fierce contest in

Upper Egypt. As a result, conflict in the hitta often becomes a recourse to knives in a way which seldom occurs in areas outside of Upper Egypt. Not only are the people of the hitta of Upper Egyptian origin, but in addition, some of them identify as Arab i.e. bedouin suggesting that they come from sedentarized bedouin background. This became evident in the case of one leader who would not permit his three wives, to be interviewed in the present study. He explained that he kept a "harim" because of his "Arab" ancestry and in fact provided each wife with a separate television, radio and tape recorder so that they would have little need of going out!

Little can be said in strictly economic systemic terms regarding the hitta except to note the syndrome of primary and secondary industries in the area in regards to slaughterhouse activities and the high degree of economic specialization which follows. One of the members of one leadership family studied, for example, is a liver expert! What definitely appears to be the case, however, is that the high incomes of the hitta result in a classic status discrepancy where high incomes do not compensate for low status. As a result, in startling contrast to most communities in Egypt, the interview data reveals the opinion of fathers that sons should not follow in their occupational footsteps. To a large extent in fact they do but there is evidence of sibling differences which follows from educational differences in the drive to break out of the butchery occupation.

The political system of the hitta seems to reflect the essential familialism of the community. The pattern of informal political leadership for example appears to reveal no single personality or family that stands out. Instead, there appear to be a group of leaders who informally play the role of political leaders especially the all important one of settling the fierce conflicts of the community. Related to this for example is the fact that one of the leaders studies was specialized in going to the police authorities as an emissary from the community when members of the community are involved officially in offences and giving their release in his custody in order to settle the dispute by customary means.

In sum, then, what emerges is an exclusivist community whose sense of exclusion is reinforced by a common occupation, by common residential patterns and by a strong sense of extended family identity. The net effect is a self-conscious desire to exclude the role of central government in favor of local values. This appears to be an orientation that is encouraged by the failure of both bureaucracy and political organization to penetrate the community in any significant fashion. The failure of bureaucracy to penetrate the local community is revealed in family planning terms and very human terms by the fact that one of the leaders noted that while family planning was made available in communities near the madbah, he himself had to go to Pyramids Street in Giza (the other side of the city and the Nile River) in order to get a condom in order to practice family planning!

Leadership Background and Self-Perceptions of the First Leader

Salama al-Sa^{C}idi as the first of the two leaders selected for the present study is a butcher employed within the slaughterhouse (madbah) itself by a meatcutting cooperative. Born in the hitta of ^{C}Ard Ya^{C}qub in 1939, he has been married since 1962 to his wife ^{C}Etimad and has three children, Muhammad (12), Amin (10) and Afaf (6) a girl. His own family, as the family name of al-Sa^{C}idi implies, is from the city of Asyvt in the Sa^{C}id or south of Egypt. They have lived, however, for a hundred years in Cairo, at first in the Sayyida Zaynab area and then since approximately 1936 in ^{C}Ard Ya^{C}qub. His grandfather had been a well to do wholesale fruit merchant, but Salama's father had followed the occupation of four of his other uncles and came to ^{C}Ard Ya^{C}qub as a skinner (rayess) of hides in the slaughterhouse industry. Salama thus followed in his father's footsteps and became a butcher. He himself relates how he used to accompany his father to his place of work and at the age of twelve began working. He, however, will not permit his own sons to even visit his place of work. Instead, he is determined that they will not become butchers because of the menial nature of the work and its long hours. Salama's own education did not exceed that of the fourth grade and in fact while he alleges that he is able to read a little bit, he says that his writing is poor.

Salama Sa^{C}idi's leadership position within the quarter (hitta) of Ard Ya^{C}qub is of a second ranked character. It is clear that the major decisions and events within the quarter are dealt with by one or more of five or six more major leaders. Salama's leadership role, for example, is restricted almost entirely to reconciliation efforts. These efforts appear to focus upon the settlement of disputes within families, e.g., husband-wife quarrels or occasionally between families. These reconciliation efforts, furthermore, seem to tend to be localized within his own street (hara). One is tempted in this respect to refer to him as a street or hara type leader. His major contribution appears to be towards maintaining the stability and peace of his own immediate neightborhood. In fact, he is quite explicit in saying that performing reconciliation tasks or acts of charity are what interest him most and not such things a procuring identification cards or ration booklets. In fact it is noteworthy that even when involved in an extreme case of conflict between families, he himself did not write out the reconciliation agreement (a kind of contract between two previous parties to a conflict) even though he was to carry it and become the guarantor of the peaceful relations between the two families.

When queried as to why he and his family "have a word" in his community he states a number of contributing factors. The first is that of the prestige of his family. This prestige is due more narrowly to the fact of its longevity in ^{c}Ard Ya^{c}qub. More broadly, size is a factor. In the area surrounding ^{c}Ard Ya^{c}qub there are approximately 70 families carrying the al-Sa^{c}idi name. There is in the fact of this size an implication of strength - a factor which is probably important in local Egyptian communities generally but possibly especially important in the Upper Egyptian culture and society surrounding the slaughterhouse. Given the tendency of this society to divide in conflict terms into lineage identifications, such a large family undoubtedly has a degree of latent intimidation about it.

Further along the lines of the preceding comment as to the latent power of the family is a comment by Salama that while his family is large, is also "humble." When queried as to the meaning of this characterization, his response was that unlike some families that use such a factor of power to perform "evil deeds" his own family treats people with humanity. This statement suggests the low keyed, low profile nature of Salama's style of leadership. Not doing "evil deeds" suggests a further attribute of his family and leadership, namely a high morality. When the quality of morality is discussed, however, it turns out not be especially religious in character, but rather the assertion is made that at least Salama's immediate family avoids actions which might conflict with law. The conception of morality is further defined in Salama's mind by the practice of good works. When a taamaa (ground fried flat bean) seller's wife dies and under emotional stress the husband gets into a fight and injures someone, Salama takes charge of a neighborhood collection in order to collect the money to pay for a lawyer. Absent in this conception of morality is much reference to religious values or practice. This more perhaps ethical conception of morality is related to a further quality of kindness. Kindness is defined largely in terms of gentleness in the approach to human relations. Sensitivity and courtesy appear to be the elements of kindness present in Salama's mind. What is explicitly present in his elaboration of the term, is lack of force or coercion. Kindness thus appears to be akin to "humbleness" in his characterization of the family. In power relational terms it can be seen as a denial of a quality of power and coercoin of Upper Egyptian village culture. Not that kindness in the most general sense is not present on an individual basis in Upper Egypt, but that kindness is not necessarily a key quality in Upper Egypt in the power relationships between families. The qualities of morality and kindness that Salama sees as governing his family and himself he says he learned from his father.

The ability to be calm he also states as having learned from his father. Calm to Salama means remaining unruffled in the presence of heated debate and bared emotions. Thus, as he described his initial approach to a conflict situation as it might exist between two families, he speaks of the necessity to be reserved in light of the tendency of both parties to a dispute to "tighten up" at the presence of a third party. Only after an initial presence at the conflict can Salama then start exerting his leadership status by use of the formula, "For my sake, will you do this or that," etc.

A very perceptive remark about his ability to be a leader, is Salama's noting of the fact that one reason he is called upon to play a leadership role is simply his availability. For rationing purposes, meat is sold only four days a week in Egypt. Thus in contrast to other occupations, e.g. his contractor brother Amin, he has the leisure for leadership. On the other hand, there is an element of modesty in the statement, because after all, in a neighborhood of butchers virtually everyone has such time available.

Family and Community Perceptions of Leadership

In the preceding, attention has been directed to Salama al-Sa^{c}idi's own perceptions of his leadership. To what extent are these perceptions shared by members of his own family and to what extent are they shared by members of his own community? The importance of the answers to these two questions are two-fold. First, the extent to which the qualities he attributes to himself are corroborated by his family begins to give a clue as to the definition of his leadership role. This is especially important in the case of the family if one assumes, as is the case in the present study, that the family is the fundamental unit of political identification both in terms of political socialization and in terms of its political resources for leadership. Second, the degree to which the community shares these perhaps self-congratulatory perceptions may assist one in the evaluation of the leadership role from the point of view of its ultimate effectiveness. The family member who answered the questions of leadership characteristics most directly was Amin al-Sa^{c}idi, one of Salama's brothers. He stressed that while coming from a large family had some importance, he said, "You see, to be influential and strong one had to have certain abilities and nature - not rely only on my family's size and name." Among these desirable qualities he listed being "strong," "caring," "kind," "courageous," and, in an interesting point of agreement with his brother Salama, to have the time available to devote to leadership tasks. In contrast to these qualities which he attributed to his brother Salama, are those of his eldest brother Ramadan. He said that Ramadan, while the eldest and therefore perhaps the person most expected to play a leadership role from within the family, was in fact too quick to anger to be a leader. In fact, Ramadan's temper was such that he had apparently killed a member of the leading Rawas family and spent time in prison for the offense. The family provided, according to Salama, an apartment in Salama's own building in order to keep an eye on him.

Salama's father Amin, a retired skinner in the slaughterhouse also made the same points regarding the elements of "kindness" and "caring." He also, however, made reference to the manner in which the family itself as a leadership resource perpetuated the leadership role. Speaking of his children, he says that he taught the qualities of leadership to his children because if it is not done, the child, "... will become ignorant. I tell him when I was in such a position I used to do so and so and you have to be like me, so people would say that Amin al-Sa^{c}idi did not die." He also made another comment that is related to a reference made above that the size of the al-Sa^{c}idi family seems to have a latent quality of violent retribution in it. This element of violence is important to note because while Salama, his brother Amin and his wife Etemad suggest that leadership qualities are related to the non-violent resolution of conflict, it should be noted that the stereo-typical view of the slaughterhouse area by other Cairenes is one of its potential for violence involving the knives of the trade being used for other than commercial purposes. Salama's father notes, for example, in some conflict situations he would strike a disputant, especially is that person happened to be younger.

In fact, an important corroboration of this use of violence in the settlement of disputes is provided by the other leader in the urban segment of the present study, Hag Imam Galal. He said that in fact, people went to Salama for the settlement of a dispute if they wanted their position supported by force. In fact, he said that Salama owed his position as a leader to the fact that the family was itself quarrelsome and was feared by people in Ard Ya^{c}qub. The result was not a settlement by reconciliation but one arrived at by virtue of coercion. As already noted above, this is undoubtedly related to the system of clan politics in the ^{c}Ard. If one was a client of the al-Sa^{c}idi family, one went to Salama in order to reap the benefits of such a clientage. Further supporting this idea, is the manner in which the brother Ramadan is referred to be the members of the family. One gets a sense that his disposition to violence is itself regarded as a family resource to be unleashed when necessary.

Leadership Background and Self-Perceptions of the Second Leader

Mustafa Galal Mohammad (the second leader chosen) known as Hag Imam Galal was born in 1933 in Galal Street in ^{c}Ard Ya^{c}qub, Zeinhom. His great grandfather was originally from Zeftah in the Delta but his father was born and bred in Cairo. He was born in the oldest part of the Madbah called Tal al-Akareb (Hill of the Scorpions) where most of the older butchers from the Madbah were born. All the males in his family, great grandfathers, uncles, etc. were butchers. Even his father who was drafted into the army and then entered the secret police had been a butcher and in fact purchased a butcher shop while he was still in government service. He had had nine children, four boys and five girls, of whom Hag Imam was the youngest. His family on his mother's side came from Fayum (southern Egypt) of Saidi and possibly bedouin culture. She had been born in the Madbah also and came from a long line of butchers. His five sisters are all married, three of them to butchers.

Hag Imam has had two marriages. His first in 1954 was an arranged marriage entered into because the mother of his bride to be was to provide a rich dowry. He disliked his new bride from the outset but in spite of this she has born him three boys and a girl. Her father had been a cart owner. In 1958 he finished army service and his father purchased a butcher shop for him. In 1960 he was told by friends of a widow of a very good family he could marry. Her father owned about seven or eight buildings and had been well off financially. While she had only a fourth grade education, three of her brothers had modern occupations and worked for an airline, one as an agricultural engineer and another although also an agricultural engineer was in the army. She had children by her first marriage. Of the sixchildren, five were boys:two worked in industry, one was studying in England, another works as a butcher in Libya, one attends a technical school and the fifth works as a skilled contractor. Again, as in the case of her brothers, a pattern of modern occupations or cosmopolitan experiences can be noted. The marriage with Hag Imam was arranged with his never having met her until the day of the wedding when he thought that she had only two children and not six. Two children were born of this marriage.

Against this family background, Hag Imam has certain life experiences which have influenced him in his development as a leader. An important influence according to Hag Imam was his father who while a secret police officer disliked it and always played the role of a peacemaker in the local community. His father conveyed this negative view of the police when Hag Imam first became responsible for reporting local crimes to the single political party of Egypt, the Arab Socialist Union and his father warned him about what people would say about him. His father was very pious and taught him respect for his elders and correct behavior. While in the army his leadership qualities were recognized and he was put in charge of training recruits.

After discharge from the army, he took up butchery in the shop provided by his father and began as a civil defense official in ^{c}Ard Ya^{c}qub, the first of a succession of formal leadership positions with the Arab Socialist Union. In 1960 he was promoted to Accident Officer for the Shayakha of Zeinhom. His duties in this unpaid position were to settle quarrels, report murders, accidents, etc., i.e. tasks he had watched his father perform. Although elected to the ASU council by popular vote, he refused the position of chairman but instead has become the Political Officer for the entire area. His responsibilities are to report all violations of law and regulations, accidents, murders and settle quarrels. He also observes the working of street lights, street repair, reports loss of persons and generally reports information to the police. As he stated more than once in his interviews, he is like a ^{c}<u>umdah</u> or village headman for his section of the city.

Hag Imam concedes that his father's <u>peacemaking</u> role within the local community has had an important influence upon him as part of a general effort to emulate his father's ways. In addition to his father's influence, he attributes his leadership role to what he referred to as his "brains" in that he knows how to make peace and find solutions.

Courage is also seen by him as an attribute of leadership. So much of what causes him to take action is tied to a sense of morality. Thus he hates what is wrong and feels that the weak must be helped and good people encouraged in case they become discouraged. Underlying all of this is a distrust of executive authority which leads him to refuse ASU positions which might put distance between himself and his community. He stands with the latter because of what he feels to be the frequent abuses of the former. Also contributing to his leadership effectiveness is the fact that while his position with the ASU is without renumeration, he has been able to make the pilgrimage to Mecca five times with grants from it and the police. Hence the honorific title of "Hag" (Pilgrim) in his name. Having made the pilgrimage five times has had the effect of increasing his personal baraka (spiritually) and hence his personal authority. In addition, he had the opportunity to cement personal relationships with police and government officials while on the pilgrimage.

Family and Community Perceptions of Leadership   Neifissah, Hag Imam's second wife, revealed her resentment at the time he spent in his leadership role as detracting from the family. This resentment resulted in a certain resistance to questions regarding his leadership role in the community. She, for example, called this role an "interfering" one and contrasted it negatively with the more private life of others. "Interfering," however, is revealing of a further leadership trait, namely the Hag's sense of community responsibility and good citizenship. Nevertheless, she stated more positively that his leadership followed from his being the son of a righteous man. In addition, a leader should have a good moral character and care for people. As an example, she told how yesterday the Hag had taken steps to have a kiosk removed that was selling bread because the seller was contagious with tuberculosis. The result was an agreement whereby the man's wife would replace him in the booth.

Gamalat, Hag Imam's first wife, also attributes his leadership role to the goodness of his father and his position in the ASU. She made reference to his "white heart," i.e. purity of motives and generosity in dealing with people. One of his sons, Hussein, also concurred in this, saying that his father was helpful and open to the needs of others and this resulted in his being a leader.

Hag Imam was mentioned by other prominent persons in [C]Ard Ya[C]qub as one of four or five "natural" leaders in the area. In fact, when the question of leadership was brought up the first reaction was to consider the ASU committee membership for the area which consisted of 12 members. Even in this context, however, only Hag Imam and another person also identified as "natural" were cited

as being helpful to the community. In short, his ASU connection
was not as important as his personal qualities. He was mentioned
as noteworthy because " ... he tries to help in solving problems
not just talking like the rest." When the people have a problem,
they are said to go to Hag Imam. The reason is that he is said not
to rely on family size and name alone for his authority. Such a
leader must have a strong personality and be courageous but he must
rely more on kindness rather than force.

Conclusion

Three topics can be addressed by way of conclusion. The first
of these is that of an empirical nature, i.e. what is the nature of
leadership in the local urban community based upon a comparison of
these two leaders. The first point is that the two leaders are
quite different from one another. One of them appears more limited
in terms of leaderships role than the other. The geographical area
encompassed by Salama's leadership activities seems limited to that
of the hara or perhaps the hitta. Further, even the leadership
activities of Salama appear also restricted. These appear to
consist largely of quarrel settling and reconciliation. The
leadership of Hag Imam on the other hand is broader geographically
and in terms of leadership activities. The broader geographical
purview is due in part at least to his association with the ASU.
It is possible and likely, in fact, that were it not for the under
authority purview of the ASU that the Hag would have resembled
Salama in having a more limited leadership arena. In addition, the
Hag's actual leadership activities are broader, ranging from
reconciliation, to police reporting, to maintaining order and
discipline on public occasions.

A second topic is that of status. Both leaders appear to
possess ascribed status. Salama's ascribed status seems to be
related to the al-Sa^{c}idi family in terms of its size and reputation in the madbah area. Hag Imam's status appears to have
succeeded to the leadership reputation of his father. While both
leaders may be of ascribed status, that of Hag Imam seems to have
more an achievement quality to it. There is a sense in which
Salama's leadership status having been inherited remains
underdeveloped while that of Hag Imam has expanded beyond that of
his father.

Role definition, as a third concluding topic, is a more
complex subject. As a general proposition, both leaders appear
reaffirmed in their leadership role at two levels. The first level
is that of their extended families. Wives, children and brothers
are all generally supportive of both of them in their leadership
activities. This is true in a general sense (with the exception of
Hag Imam's second wife) but it is also true in a specific sense
that the attributes of leadership listed by the two leaders also
are listed by the members of their families. In addition, many of
these same attributes are also mentioned by non-family members as
well. This widespread sharing of attributes appears to have two

significances. The first is that the attributes themselves operate to tentatively define the role of local level leadership in Egypt. The second is that they also tend to define and legitimate these leaders as role occupants. The general properties of such leadership can be characterized by civic interest, morality, calmness and courage. There are, however, attributes which both leaders do not share or do so in varying degrees. These differences are probably due to their different statuses. It appears that the qualities of humbleness and strength said to characterize Salama are related to family as a status determinant. Strength of numbers and potential for violence seems to characterize the al-Sa^{c}idi family. As Salama himself notes, this could be a force for evil if it was not tempered by humbleness. The status determinant of Hag Imam is less that of family (although family remains important) and more of having inherited his father's reputation and perhaps having built upon it with an emphasis upon even a religious sense of morality. In short, what Salama achieves as a leader by means of implicit force, Hag Imam achieves by moral authority.

This discussion of two urban leaders reveals two very different kinds of leaders. The first of a hara or narrow neighborhood type operates with an imperative for communal peace and conflict reduction. The implicit strength of himself and his family is thus useful for his more geographically limited policy-like task. The second type of leader operates more broadly across an entire urban quarter and attempts to undertake a wide variety of tasks intended to uplift this wider community both materially and spiritually in terms of exhortations for morally correct behavior. He is able to utilize his connections with an organization emanating from the political center (the ASU) to undertake these tasks. This latter factor thus sees him linking the local community to this center but in the process taking this relationship and turning it to the advantage of the local community. One leader thus functions to maintain his community while the other seeks to advance it.

FOOTNOTES:

1. Among such studies on Egypt are those of Janet Abu-Lughod: Migrant Adjustment to City Life: The Egyptian Case," _American Journal of Sociology_ 67 (July, 1961), 22-32, "Varieties of Urban Experience: Contrast, Coexistence and Coalescence in Cairo," _Middle Eastern Cities_. Ira Lapidus, ed. (Berkeley: University of California Press, 1969) and _Cairo 1001 Years of the City Victorious_ (Princeton, N.J.: Princeton University Press, 1971), Andrea Rugh, _Coping With Poverty In a Cairo Community_, Cairo Papers in Social Science, Volume Two, January, 1979; Unni Wakin, _Life Among the Cairo Poor_ translated by A. Henning (London: Tavistock Publications, 1980).

2. Research reported in a present paper was carried out in Egypt under a grant from UNESCO administered by the Social Research Center, American University in Cairo. We wish to acknowledge the two directors of the Center, the support of Drs. Laila Hammamsy and Sa'd Gadallah. Dr. Gadallah was especially helpful in providing both logistical and intellectual support. We wish to thank also our two research assistants on the project, Mrs. Marlene Anawati and Mrs. Laila Stino for assistance that went beyond that of "assistants" and became that of co-professionals. Finally, it should be noted that the present research was carried out before Dr. Benedict joined the U.S. Agency for International Development and that nothing in the present paper reflects anything other than his personal point of view. For references to the Sadat and Mubarak periods see, Raymond Baker, _Egypt's Uncertain Revolution Under Nasser and Sadat_ (Cambridge: Harvard University Press, 1978) and John Waterbury, _The Egypt of Nasser and Sadat: The Political Economy of Two Regimes_ Princeton: Princeton University Press, 1983.

3. Cecil Gibb, "Leadership, Psychological Aspects," _International Encyclopedia of the Social Sciences_, IX, 91-101.

4. The present paper will appear as a chapter in the completed monograph by the present authors tentatively entitled, "Local Leadership and Family in Rural and Urban Egypt".

5. See Raymond Firth, _Families and Their Relatives_ (London: Routledge, Kegan, Paul, 1970) and David Schneider, _American Kinship: A Cultural Account_ (Englewood Cliffs, N.J.: Prentice-Hall, 1968). A preliminary report of the project has appeared as L. Cantori and P. Benedict, _Family Planning and Local Leadership: The Impact of Family and Kinship on Opinion Leaders in Rural and Urban Community in Egypt_, June, 1976, Social Science Research Center, American University in Cairo.

4
Continuity and Change in Local Development Policies in Egypt: From Nasser to Sadat

Iliya Harik

RURAL DEVELOPMENT STRATEGY OF THE NASSER REGIME

The profile of Egypt at mid-century is quite typical of Third World countries: Two thirds or more of the population live and make   a living off the land, more than half of the national labor force is rural,   the   contribution   of agriculture to GNP is one third the total and that of industry less than 15 percent. Land distribution was extremely unequal, where less than one percent of landowners possessed more   than one third of the cultivated land and many of them were absentee landlords. The credit system and extension services were inadequate if available at all. Finally, population pressure on the land was relentless.

In effect, the revolutionary government in 1952 was faced with a situation where agricultural surplus was extracted by wealthy landlords connected with urban centers where underemployment was high and man power productivity very low, with industry growing at a very slow pace.

National leaders felt that a development policy that would help the country break away from the vicious circle of poverty and underdevelopment was called for. The strategy they followed may be summarized in the following terms: (1) industrialization was the major avenue to achieve modernization and for raising the standard of living. Hence, the capital for investment in industry was to be partially diverted from agriculture, voluntarily or through other means of control, since the agricultural sector was the main earner of foreign currency and the major single contributor to the economy.   (2)   Agriculture should be modernized to increase productivity and fulfill the great expectations based on it for national development and provision of food. (3) Opposition forces

Prepared originally for the University of Maryland Baltimore County and Indiana University Conference and reprinted here from the International Journal of Middle East Studies, 16 (1984), 43-66 with the permission of the Cambridge University Press.

to such national targets were to be contained and their power undermined in order to prevent resistance. One of these forces were large landlords whose influence in the government was traditionally great. (4) Small cultivators should be supported and made the mainstay of rural policy without jeopardizing productivity. This was conceived as a measure of social justice and political wisdom. The resultant agrarian reform policy was ideologically compatible with the new regime's outlook, fair from a social justice point of view and politically wise.

It was in this national and economic context that agrarian reform was born in Egypt and it was therefore shaped by these considerations. Consequently, its main characteristics were the following:

I. Maintaining private ownership of land, but organizing agricultural production and marketing by state controlled cooperatives. While cooperative marketing in the sixties became compulsory for the main export crops, cultivation remained a mixed enterprise where the main responsibility fell on the cultivator himself aided by cooperative services and constrained by the consolidation and rotation plan. These measures were obviously aimed at establishing state control of the agricultural sector while meeting the peasant's demand for private ownership and improved income.

II. Land distribution: a fixed ceiling on land ownership was imposed and lands in excess were distributed by the government in small plots to landless and near landless cultivators. This measure followed a golden rule policy by its emphasis on a middle course: abolish very large estates but leave room for reasonably wealthy farmers, support tenants and sharecroppers by bequeathing ownership to them on the land they cultivated and in small plots. (Eventually the ceiling rested at fifty feddans and small plots distributed were around three feddans.) Legislation was passed to give tenant cultivators security in their contracts. This in effect pushed out of the system the extreme minority of about 5000 wealthy owners by disappropriation, and left out the sizable group of landless laborers, of nearly a million and a half by inability to find them land of their own.

III. Productivity was maintained and then increased by means of four major measures: (1) providing the capitalless cultivator with credit, fertilizers, seeds et. al. at little or no interest and collecting state debt at harvest; (2) offsetting the effects of land fragmentation by devising a land consolidation plan, and (3) providing some mechanization through cooperatives and private entrepreneurs, and (4) flood control. These four measures have in effect made it possible for Egyptian agriculture to have the best of two worlds: private ownership of small and medium size estates cultivated by methods of large scale cultivation in basic respects. Land consolidation, crop rotation, partial mechanization and collective pest control measures are the large scale methods of cultivation, while individual labor for planting, maintenance and harvesting were remnants of the old system of household cultivation.

IV. State control of the agricultural sector, which traditionally remained in private hands, was established through the rotational system, accounting and marketing carried out by the cooperative mechanism. Undoubtedly, the most stringent state control mechanism has been the establishment of a completely controlled market for the traditional export and domestically vital crops of cotton, rice and sugar cane, plus requisitions of portions of farmers' output of wheat rice and onions. Purchases of seeds, fertilizers and pesticides were almost completely controlled by the state through the cooperatives.

V. Land reclamation: a valiant but error ridden policy of extending the cultivation land was made and added less than 15 percent of the existing cultivation area, but of extremely lower productivity. This was also a slow process and remained entirely a state sector until recently.

VI. Also to be considered part of the agrarian reform program is the political mobilization of peasants, which though aimed at supporting the national government, was just as significant in checking the local power of landlords and preventing encroachments on peasant gains. Political participation, mainly on local and provincial levels, were encouraged and led to recruitment of peasant leaders for political office. A system of local government was developed in which elected officers and official staff share in decision making on local affairs and bear the responsibility for implementation of national policies.

VII. Finally, any consideration of the rural development strategy in Egypt should take into consideration the extensive services provided for rural communities. These include: expanding the official and technical staff in the countryside, introducing schools, health centers, potable waters, crafts and cottage industry, minimum wage and works projects for agricultural laborers. None of these services can be considered to have reached a level of sufficiency during the Nasser regime nor has it yet. By 1974, about two thirds of school age children were attending primary schools, due to lack of room and inability to enforce the compulsory education law. By 1976, about 25 percent of all houses in Egypt still had no source of purified water, the largest majority of which were in the countryside. Similarly, while electricity has reached the majority of villages, only a minority of households use it domestically. Population per hospital bed and physician is still very high. Nevertheless, the drive to meet these essential needs was started at an extensive scale in the fifties, and was continuing.

The overall view of agrarian reform policies in Egypt seems to conform to what contemporary and classical planners recommend for the rural sector. Its targets have been: increased production (growth orientation), focus on cash crops (acquisition of hard currency), private ownership and profits (incentives), land reform (institutional changes), make accessible to peasants means of production (aid to a depressed sector) social and human services (basic needs).

In addition, the agrarian reform policies in Egypt have also met or tried to meet what more recently has been considered a more relevant and effective development strategy, that is to say, to overcome institutional obstacles in the distribution of power and material resources, and to provide opportuities for decent income earning and access to public services.[1] Agrarian reform in Egypt sought to achieve these goals with considerable effectiveness by land distribution, regulating tenancy, land reclamation, creating work opportunities (in projects such as land reclamation, Aswan dam, drainage works, etc.), politically organizing and encouraging small peasants and the landless to assume local power in place of large landlords. However, reform policies fell way short on population control as the government acted late and ineffectively. Population control aside, one has every reason to expect the Egyptian experiment to be a near ideal strategy for rural development. Indeed, the achievements are undeniable and up to the middle sixties, agriculture continued to experience increase in productivity, services were working reasonably well, living conditions improving, and peasants politically active and occupying leading position in local power structure. This is not to say that all these endeavors were functioning perfectly; they were, however, a going concern and performing in an encouraging way, considering the legacy of the past and the meager experience of rural people in modernization administration.

Obstacles to Rural Progress

Despite the successes described earlier, the state of Egyptian agriculture in the late sixties and early seventies could be seriously questioned. Growth in the productivity of some traditional crops has been in decline, cooperatives have not been functioning properly, extension services practically halted, poverty levels unabated, state policies faltering and political participation in limbo. One thing not expected to improve or let up was the population pressure on the land and indeed it did not.

What went wrong? Land reform has been the subject of many criticisms lately for reasons that are not quite clear. Perhaps expectations are unrealistic and perhaps judgement is sometimes made on the basis of impressions. In a recent article on land reform in Iran, the author concludes that agrarian reform recreated owner absenteeism because he found that five of 1200 people of a reform village rented their land to others and went to live in the city.[2] In Egypt some of the criticisms reflect the biases of those who express them and some are serious and judicious. An assessment of these criticisms is in order here not only to set the record straight but also to gain more awareness of the obstacles to development strategies which face less developed countries.

One explanation of the difficulties in agriculture has focused on the continued existence of large estates. This it is argued has led to continued exploitation and to class struggle, not to mention the detrimental effects of inequality. As is well known, the last measure (in 1969) restricting land ownership placed the maximum holding per person at 50 feddans of land. This constitutes a farm of considerable size which produces a very respectable income, considering multiple cropping and intensive farming. In contrast, there are millions of rural people still landless in Egypt. It is sometimes also suggested that the 1969 law was not followed by release of information showing the number of persons disappropriated and the areas distributed. To this day, the government has not made public [3] any figures on land ownership later than 1965. Some 6000 owners holding about 392,000 feddans should have been disappropriated. This should give ownership to about 80,000 persons, a number not to be belittled, but it would by no means have solved the problem of the landless in Egypt, that would not happen even if land ceilings are lowered to 10 feddans or less. The fact of the matter is that Egypt has 0.3 feddans per rural inhabitant. Land reform was not intended to solve the problem of the landless nor could it have done so. The question of rural over population is a serious question that would be better dealt with as a separate problem, if the discussion is to yield fruitful results.

As for exploitation or diversion of benefits to the interest of large landlords, the question is also murky. It should be made clear at the outset that charges of exploitation cannot be other than political propaganda. The classical exploiters of rural population were money lenders and merchants followed by very large landowners who used to be in league with the other two or one and the same. This phenomenon has been successfully ended by the reforms of the Nasser regime. The fact that there were pockets of resistance and illicit dealings during the Nasser period has been underlined by the Committee formed by the regime in 1965 to deal with infraction of the law. The formation of the "Committee for the Liquidation of Feudalism" shows that the regime was alert to evasion and prepared to deal with it. What is more, the Committee findings show that most of the cases uncovered pertained to acts of violence committed by small peasants who worked their way up by legal and illegal means, acquired land and oppressed their village folks. The large landlords phenomenon in Egypt has disappeared and not only by legal measures of land distribution. Many have left on their own, seeing the climate not favorable. Those who still are wealthy farmers do enjoy a differential advantage because of their connections, skill and position. Such advantage is experienced also in their role in cooperative societies, but any charges of widespread misuse and diversion of resources to themselves has yet to be documented.

As for class struggle, one serious study which made this its focus has turned up evidence only of widespread disputes between tenants and owners, most often small owners.[4] This has been given the misnomer, "class struggle," by the author.

The opposite argument often made regarding the deteriorating rural scene is that excessive fragmentation of land has reduced the farm size much below the minimum level that allows a peasant to make a livelihood. This argument is theoretical since it is made on ground that the practiced law allows all children to inherit, with males receiving twice the shares of females. It, however, ignores the lively market of land. Informal observation and community studies indicate that land changes hands frequently through purchase by and from small owners in particular. Statistical evidence lends support to this observation. Data from the period 1961 to 1974 show that the average holding of small owners (five feddans or less) rose steadily from 1.08 feddans in 1961 to 1.2 in 1965 to 1.5 in 1974 (Table 4.1). The number of small holders has been increasing since the passing of the law of land reform in 1952 but dropped sharply by 1974, by a figure of 393,736 below the 1965 figure. However, the area held by small owners continued to increase throughout the period, which means that this group of peasants have been increasing slowly but definitely, their holdings at the expense of larger landowners.

Table 4.1

Changes in the Holdings of Small Land Owners
(five feddans or less)

Year	Number of Owners	Total Area Held (feddans)	Average holding per owner (feddans)
1961	2,919,000	3,172,000	1.08
1965	3,033,000	3,693,000	1.20
1975	2,639,264	3,948,165	1.50

Note: For complete data see Harik, Distribution of Land, Employment, and Income in Rural Egypt (Cornell University: Center for International Studies, 1979).

Source: Data for 1961 and 1965 have been made public by the various agencies of government. Data for 1974 obtained from the Ministry of Agriculture, The Arab Republic of Egypt, and are still not made public.

Another argument advanced as a contributing factor to the difficulties experienced in the countryside is the shortcomings of the credit system. It is observed first that the cooperatives which extended loans to farmers in cash and kind, failed to collect all their debts owed them and some 60 million pounds were in arrears over the years. A second and more important point is that by advancing loans to all farmers regardless of size of their holdings, the government was engaged in a practice of unequal subsidization. Since every farmer received loans in proportion to the size of his landholding, larger farmers were entitled and received much larger loans from the cooperative, all of which were free from interest after 1961. Statistical evidence shows that all types of farmers regardless of farm size were in arrears on their debt to the cooperative and that the volume of the debt was in direct proportion to the size of the loan. Thus the average debt of the large farmer was much larger than the average debt of the small one, whereas there were more small farmers in debt than large ones, being more numerous.

There is no doubt that subsidizing large farmers was not a functional favor and in fact burdened the cooperative system with additional duties and problems. It exposed the cooperative system to criticism of ineffectiveness because of failure to collect its mounting debts, and of favoritism to large landlords. However, when all is said, this argument does not seem directly related to the ordeals of agriculture and rural affairs since the debt incurred did not in any visible way obstruct agricultural production. Indeed, it could be argued that it enhanced it, for by not denying delinquent small farmers credit as a punishment, it was made possible for them to continue to produce. The debt argument serves only as a point in relation to equality and social justice not very relevant to agricultural production and rural institutions.

In assessing the problem of agrarian reform, it should not escape our attention that rural communities in the last three decades became thoroughly integrated with the national system. The linkages that developed between the countryside and the national government were extensive and close. The command structure, however, remained at the top passing through, and sometimes originating in the provincial government. Grass roots participation was also promoted and encouraged throughout the period at the local levels but did not for all practical purposes go beyond provincial government. That peasants and others voted in plebescites, presidential elections and the National Assembly was a routine matter, the outcome of which was not greatly dependent on the free will of voters. As I discovered in 1966-68, participatory institutions were discontinuous with the national system. The line separating subnational from national institutions was the provincial government. Thus the capacity of municipal councils, cooperative societies or the Arab Socialist Union to reach levels higher than the provincial government level were poor indeed. At the same time, much in these institutions depended for its operation and success on decisions made by the national government.

The implications of this lop-sided dependency on the national government are serious. Above all, the performance and success of these institutions depended on the continued attention and reliable performance by the government. For instance, all the essential inputs for cultivation were extended to cooperatives through the National Agricultural Credit Bank (ACB). Credit, fertilizers, seeds and pesticides had thus to be supplied by the national government through the ACB to the cooperatives. Any shortages or delays in delivery meant that the cooperatives could not perform their functions properly. Similarly, the Bank supplied clerks to the cooperatives to be in charge of accounting. Should these clerks be incompetent or unavailable, the cooperatives' accounts would be in a confused state and members' confidence in the coop system undermined.

Another area where the linkages to the national government were a critical issue was elections to local offices. The national government reserved the right to call for elections of cooperative boards and municipal councils, although they had a tenure period set by law. Thus, unless the national government calls for elections, the same councils and board members would continue in office.

In all three areas -- supplies to the cooperatives, elections to their boards, and elections to the municipal government -- the national government faltered, particularly after the 1967 war. One may say in the case of elections, that the local institutions were victims of benign neglect where a government preoccupied with more weighty national and international issues overlooked to call for elections and allowed local leaders elected in 1960 and 1962 to remain in office long beyond their legal tenure. Resentment among competing local elites mounted and poor performance and corruption was rewarded. Moreover, it was perceived by local leaders in office that the government was not as serious as it could have been about these institutions thus encouraging some to neglect their duties or to resort to irregularities for personal benefit.

Faced with mounting complaints and protests from both competing local elites and offended peasants whose interests were hurt, provincial governors often resorted to peremptory measures of dissolving cooperative boards, without calling for a new election. The consequences were that the official staff were left alone in the administration of cooperative business, without the benefit of advice and assistance from experienced local leaders. Thus peasants were deprived of participation and cooperatives were reduced to government extension offices. Many cooperative boards that were not dissolved acted as if they were defunct anyway in response to mounting criticism. They also shunned getting involved in conflict by shirking responsibility, that is by avoiding to participate in cooperative business. This pattern of withdrawal was particularly rive among members of municipal councils which were in a similar condition as those of cooperative boards. Already by the late sixties, performance of these local institutions was declining rapidly. Such decline could be tolerated in a country where institutions perform part of the business of the day but not where every aspect of agriculture and local administration were bound to local institutions. A practical system devised to meet the circumstances and conditions of rural people was allowed to decline by benign national neglect.

As for the responsibility of the national Agricultural Credit Bank, it could have helped better in the areas of accounting and the provision of agricultural inputs. Failure of the ACB was naturally blamed on the cooperatives and their staff, both official and elected officers. For the cultivator does not deal directly with national institutions but with his local cooperative and any problem that arises is encountered at that level. With regard to credit supply and collection of debts, the ACB could have done better, especially that most large loans to wealthy farmers before 1962 were contracted directly by the ACB.

Had cooperatives developed a national organization and a commitment developed to it, they could have counted on some leverage nationally. But no such thing developed and every cooperative was practically an atom to itself and had to fend for itself. Federations at the Markaz and Province levels were organized, but it seems that they had no real functions and no sense of power. Their record was practically nil. A similar federation of cooperatives was established on the national level in 1969 but was no different from those of the provinces. In short, one can detect a structural defect in the system of local institutions that left them unprotected and with no influence on the national level.

Loading the system. Cooperative societies which were the nerve center of agrarian reform and agricultural production in Egypt were victimized by yet another tendency on the part of the national government. Seeing that the cooperative provided a suitable mechanism for its intervention in agriculture at the grass roots level, the government tended to overload the cooperative system with additional responsibilities. A system devised to administer credit and agricultural production inputs, was charged with the responsibility to develop agricultural mechanization capacity, hiring out cultivation services to members, and above all marketing of their produce. A major burden that may be cited here is cooperative marketing.

Cooperatives were to collect, store, weigh, determine the quality and deliver the produce to the government warehouses in provincial capitals. These new responsibilities were added to the cooperatives without adding new personnel to carry them out. Fearing the burdens of too much work which would keep them away from their fields, elected officers tended to neglect their duties and not show up. Officials found themselves burdened with tasks beyond their ability to carry out. Many of them, especially those under direct control, overworked while others less responsible neglected their duties. This shortage of personnel in charge of cultivators' businesses encouraged bribery and graft. Officials and other officers started to charge extra legal fees for their services. Hence, the reputation of the system was no longer what its friends and supporters would have liked it to be. The loss was universal: peasants suffered delays and were not satisfied with th way their products were handled; officials did not like the extra burdens and performed at a lower level and the national government suffered by not receiving fully what it expected to receive form the local system. No surprise then that the cooperative system was friendless at the end of the Nasser era.

Terms of Trade

Other problems affected the rural sector besides institutional defects. The major one, is a classical problem of agriculture in Third World countries: the terms of trade. Under conditions of free private economy and underdevelopment, the surplus in the rural sector tends to be extracted by urban interests. But in a controlled economy such as Egypt, the surplus is extracted by the national government. Through crop and price controls, not necessarily through taxes that usually tend to be lenient, the national government extracted the surplus from agriculture by buying cheap and selling dear.[5] Moreover, by controlling the growing of export crops necessary for earning hard currency and financing industry and government expenditure, the government cuts down the profit for cultivators. Peasants in Egypt are compelled to plant cotton and rice according to the rotational system, while these crops cost more to cultivate and earn less. Some also argue that control and supply of inputs by the government at government determined rates is another way of exploiting cultivators,[6] though this is a debatable point since some inputs were subsidized and credit provided without interest.

Caution, however, should be exercised in discussing this point, for raising questions regarding the extraction of the surplus in agriculture may conjure up images of 19th and early twentieth century urban landlords. This is certainly not the case. In two decades, agrarian reform in Egypt contributed to the countryside what the countryside had not received in two centuries. For despite the fact that expenditure on agriculture has been only 5 percent of all public expenditure,[7] the inflow of goods and services to rural communities from the national government has been outstanding. Brought into the countryside since 1952 are roads, potable water, electricity, health centers, schools, craft training centers, cooperatives societies, municipal councils, credit for agriculture, land reclamation, a large number of technical and administrative personnel such as agronomists, doctors, nurses, accountants, teachers, etc.

On balance, the transfer of surplus from agriculture during

the sixties is estimated at about 6 percent, though there are differences among authorities on this point.[8] This figure includes price differentials, taxation, and investments allocated to agriculture. It does not, however, include an estimate of losses suffered by cultivators from crop control.

Aggregate figures often conceal as much as they reveal and the loss to farmers from selling to the government may be better appreciated when it is realized that the government profit from cotton during the sixties ranged from 30 percent in 1969/70 to 181 percent in 1966/7. The government share of the income generated from rice has averaged about 74 percent while the rest went to cultivators in the three years of 1968-70.[9] Moreover, it should be remembered that these crops cost the farmer more to cultivate and bring lower prices than other possible crops. It is not surprising therefore to find a malaise in the countryside.

Urban Growth and the Shrinking Cultivation Area. Another serious problem contributing to the difficulties of agriculture and the rural sector in general is the inability of the Egyptians to expand the cultivation area. Ambitious and courageous efforts were made since the fifties to reclaim land from deserts and swamps, and up to 800,000 feddans have been reclaimed, only 200,000 of which are of high yield. In the meantime, loss of agricultural land to urban growth salinity and brick making far outweigh land reclamation. Moreover, land reclamation activities at present have slowed down while the forces eating up fertile land are in full swing. Up to 40,000 acres a year, it is estimated, are lost to urban growth such as expansion of cities, new rural housing, and industrial sites. An awareness of this problem has spurred the government to direct urban expansion toward barren lands of the desert. Ambitious schemes are planned to build several cities in the desert, the feasibility of which has been questioned. Such schemes even when they work, may lead to moving population from crowded urban centers but will do little to stop the growth of a modern suburbia such as one sees between Cairo and the Pyramids of Giza. Moreover, this solution overlooks the fact that housing in the countryside is just as serious as threat to agricultural land as expanding cities. Modest solutions would be perhaps more promising.

In a country like Egypt where the line between the desert and the sown is so clearly demarcketed, it would be useful to attack the desert by the same means it attacks the sown, yard by yard. It is the demarcation line that should be the target of the war on the desert. By creating facilities and providing incentives, villagers and urbanites would be willing to expand outward at the line of demarcation toward the desert, stemming its advance and encroaching on it gradually as has been occurring north of Cairo in Madinat Nasr. People do not like to be transplanted from their communities, and by pushing outward from the village centers to the desert line, villagers remain close to their kinfolks and land. Roads spreading out toward the desert line would greatly facilitate this process. This method, however, does not cope with the problem for the villages that are in the center of the Delta away from the desert line, but it would for a large number of villages on the outer boundaries of the Delta, Fayyum, and in Upper Egypt.

Another serious threat of a more recent origin is the resort to the devastation of fields by brick makers. With the limited amount of silt now coming down the river, top soil is used as a substitute for the silt that is no longer there. Not only are fields lost to agriculture but swamps infested with flies appear in their place. A law has been passed against removal of top soil for bricks but a law does not solve a problem. People need to build houses for which they needs bricks. Until another source for brick making such as clay is made available on economic terms, the rape of th world's most fertile earth continues unabated.

Finally, population growth has contributed to the plight of the countryside and offset to a considerable extent the advantages gained by agrarian reform. Rural population increased from over 16 millions in 1960: to over 20 millions in 1976. In those terms, the share of land per rural individual declined from 0.4 feddans in 1960 to 0.3 in 1976. Industry has not actually absorbed much of the rural labor, contrary to the expectations of the revolutionary regime. Indeed, there has been a slackening of rural out migration into the cities and results of the 1976 census show that provincial towns are now the main beneficiaries of rural out migration not the four major cities. The four urban governorates accounted for 21.93 percent of the population in 1966 and for 21.44 percent in 1976, a net loss of 0.49 percent.[10] The census results also show that the ratio of rural to urban population has remained practically the same since 1966. Some relief has been generated by migration of labor to oil rich Arab countries. Also non-agricultural occupations in the rural areas have grown in importance but we have little information on the rate of their growth and diversity. Despite new opportunities, rural poverty, it has been estimated, increased from 27 percent in the mid sixties to about 44 percent in 1974/75.[11]

In conclusion, one can see that the causes of the slackening pace of rural progress are diverse, some pertain to national causes, some to the administrative weaknesses of the public sector, and some to natural causes. On the whole, the record points up to the problems of socialism in developing countries where administrative talent is limited, scarce and inefficient.

A NEW IMPETUS

As of 1975, the national government turned its attention once again to the rural sector. In its efforts to revitalize rural society and agriculture, it developed a new strategy to cope with the institutional problems linked to the national system. In this plan, local government has been made the focus of institutional reform, which may be summarized by the following points:

1.   Decentralization of authority by a process of devolution from the national to subnational levels.

2.   Providing secure and regular sources of income to sustain the formal measures of decentralization.

3.   Consolidating local authority in the municipal administration and strengthening the representative character of village councils.

4.   Disaggregating cooperative functions and placing most of them in a new structure, the village bank.

The rest of this paper will be devoted to the discussion of the new strategy of local development.

The first order of business was to cope with the structural problems of local institutions such as municipal government and cooperative societies to offset the effects of neglect by the national government. The measures to reorganize these institutions reflect to a great degree the orientation of the Sadat regime.

The Cooperative. The cooperative system continues to function in the seventies, but under stress, criticism, and public discussion about substitute plans. In 1975, the government decided to establish village banks, which are local branches of the Agricultural Credit Bank. The village bank has now been instituted and functioning in most municipal communes. Its functions besides the conventional banking activities is to take over those activities that used to be performed by the cooperative societies such as credit to farmers, provision of agricultural inputs, and marketing of the state crops. What has been left to cooperatives is very limited indeed such as extension work and in all likelihood, they will fade away.

The new system is marked by an extension and upgrading of official personnel administering agricultural work. The new banks are well staffed and there will be no question that they will be able to carry out the diverse activities assigned to them. A second development is the demotion of the representative function in administering local agricultural policy. With the reduction of the cooperatives to few functions such as extension work and agricultural rotation, the elected board becomes functionless and obsolete. The implications of such a development for local participation and democratic practices is to be seriously pondered. Third, and only marginally related to cooperatives, is that new legislation has been introduced in the National Assembly that has the effect of weakening the security of tenants, a step that may generate considerable discomfort to poor peasants and start a period of unrest among them.

The Municipal Government. More promising reforms have

affected municipal councils. Law 52 of 1975 which reorganized local government in Egypt is a scheme aimed at avoiding the weaknesses of municipal government of the previous era. Four main weaknesses may be mentioned here with a view to showing how the new law copes with them.

1)   Failure of the central government to complete the formation of village councils in the country as a whole and neglecting to call for periodic elections.

2)   The head of the village council lacked jurisdiction over officials of line ministries operating in the village council.

3)   Almost complete dependence of village councils on the national and provincial governments for operating funds.

4)   Ambiguity in the representative character of village councils.

The first step in the right direction has been the decision by the central government to reconstitute municipal councils and issue the new law thus demonstrating its resolve to see progress in municipal affairs.   In 1977, marked progress was shown by the activities of many municipal councils, yet many if not most were performing on ordinary or lower levels. Whether this could be attributed to lack of interest by the national government is a mute point.   What is certain is that the government was pursuing its policies of local reform vigorously, taking an attitude that gradualism is inevitable in a country where resources were limited.

Examining the new structure of local government one can clearly notice that the new law builds on what exists with major modifications.   The fact that there is continuity between the pre-1975 and the present municipal system compels us to look at the new structure in terms of the re-enforcement of local reforms of 1960. By re-enforcement we mean the introduction of measures which support existing practices and provide additional means to strengthen the growing tendencies for autonomy in local communities.

One of the major principles of local government autonomy goes back to the 1960 law which made the governor an authority able to make decisions regarding local government. He was raised to the level of a ministerial rank and endowed with considerable degree of jurisdiction. The new law of 1975 has re-affirmed the central role of the province governors by upholding his authority and rank. Recently, President Sadat issued a decree giving governors powers of the President at the governorate level, an indication of the government's resolve to make decentralization work. As a basic step in the decentralization policy (devolution as some call it), has been to shift the center of authority from the national government to the provinces. Provincial government continues to be the major authority with which municipal councils deal and whose powers and resources are most relevant to these councils.

Evidently, the interposition of district authority (Markaz) has not changed this situation markedly.

In addition to instituting provincial government to serve as a reference level which links the Ministry of Local Government to development plans at the municipal level. A new agency known as the Organization for Reorganization and Development of the Egyptian Village (ORDEV) has been created with the express purpose of stimulating local investment and income generating activities. ORDEV has not yet been able to extend its services to all village councils in the Republic but where it has, we have observed a marked difference in the economic growth of activities carried out by the municipal councils. It should be noticed that the new law has provided for local councils to engage in diverse economic activities to generate income and the government has made clear to them that it expects to see them develop their own resources and use them to the benefit of the community. Therefore, economic activities by municipal councils which are aimed at generating income have been carried out also by councils that have not even received loans and grants from ORDEV. The working capital has been borrowed from banks at an interest rate of 9 percent and/or collected from villagers in the form of project shares.

With respect to structural reforms in the municipal councils, three important measures will be noted here.

First, the lines have been clearly drawn between representatives and official leaders in the council. Village representatives are now directly elected while in the past, they were selected among elected leaders of the Arab Socialist Union. In addition, functions of representatives have been clearly defined and distinguished from those of the official staff. The ambiguity in the representative character of the old council has been removed.

Second, authority of the Head Executive Officer (Ra'is al Qariyah) over all line ministries officials in the village, including those of the cooperatives and village bank has been unequivocally established. He was also invested with authority equivalent to that of a department head (in the line ministries at the province level). This expands his authority, increases his prestige, places him above any other village official in rank and enables him to bear responsibilities of local development called for in the new law. Such authority makes the Head Executive Officer (HEO) better able to coordinate developmental activities and obtain the cooperation of other officials working with him. It should be mentioned here that one of the major problems the executive head faced under the old system was the ambiguity of his authority vis-a-vis other officials working in the village council and employees of the line ministries.

Third and perhaps most important is the provision in the new law allowing municipal councils to raise funds, and the allocation

of other funds subject entirely to the jurisdiction of the
municipal council. Seventy-five percent of taxes levied by the
central government on agricultural land are to be returned to the
municipal council. Moreover, a number of legal measures empowers
councils to raise funds and to receive gifts and grants from
foreign donors. Moreover, revenues that are produced locally
revert to a village special fund. A Local Fund for Services and
Development (LFSD) was created to finance local services and
economic projects. In the old system, municipal councils enjoyed
none of these prerogatives and had to struggle to obtain funds from
the provincial government.

It may be readily observed that the new measures meet some of
the problems from which the former municipal government suffered.
These may be summed up as follows:

First, municipal councils have been extended to cover the
whole country and their staff completed. Second, the ambiguity in
the authority of the head executive officer (HEO) as we have
already seen, has been removed. Third, the ambiguity in the
representative character of the local council has been resolved in
theory and there is evidence that the legal format is working.
Fourth, the dependence of the Municipal Councils on the provincial
and national governments for operating funds has been reduced.
Municipal councils are now entitled to raise funds, generate their
own, and receive tax returns levied from their own communities.

The question remains as to whether MC's have been able to plan
on the basis of the new arrangement. The test lies in the capacity
stored in present structures to project entrepreneurial activities
into the future based on capital formed as a result of investment
made available by the new sources of funds. A successful
projection effect is attendant with a growing freedom of economic
and social activities on the part of MCs and hence is a
reinforcement of the decentralization process.

The only light we can shed on the projection effect of MCs at
this point is impressionistic and based on a number of successful
cases. In the first place it may be observed that many MCs have
truly put ORDEV grants to productive use and, in two cases, they
have already started to invest some of the returns in expansion of
existing project or in starting new ones. A third MC has
successfully undertaken entrepreneurial activities on its own
without ORDEV support. In the second place, some head executives
of MCs have been emboldened by the promise in the law regarding
raising and controlling funds and took loans from banks purely as a
business deal. These loans were used to start income generating
projects and, in some cases, have already been paid off from the
returns of the projects. In the third place, in all the MCs I have
visited, regardless of their exploits, I have noticed an attitude
of expectation and readiness to use funds for developmental
projects. I fully expect that by the time the Credit Bank (Bank al
Taslif) succeeds in overcoming the managerial problems in

disbursing to each council its tax share and by the time the ORDEV plan reaches most councils, MCs will have a reasonable amount of funds to invest and to attend to village services on their own.

Needless to say, availability and control over funds is a basic prerequisite for autonomy of any organization. At the practical level, I have noticed that among the successful councils a strong sense of autonomy and of self-reliance has emerged.

One head executive officer who had in 1978 nearly 100,000 pounds in the Local Fund for Services and Development spoke of dispensing with government services, if they do not measure up. For instance, he said that if a physician or a nurse are not performing their tasks properly, he would resort to hiring personnel who could provide those services with his own funds. This would be in lieu of trying to have the government replace delinquent officially, considering the difficulties attendant with such a step.

Similarly, he is contemplating now hiring a dentist for the council villages and building a local pharmacy without going through governmental channels. The same attitude and plans were expressed by two other successful Municipal Councils. In all three councils, the attitude that they were stronger and have more resources than the District Council (al Markaz) was expressed, and they felt that the District Council has nothing to offer them.

In less successful councils, head executives expressed the feeling that true decentralization is realized by provision and control over resources not by supervisory powers over officials. It may be observed that ORDEV has not yet assisted these councils, nor have they started to receive their share of tax returns. Consequently, they feel that they still have not the true means to realize the decentralization plans laid down for them in the law.

Another interesting aspect of the projection effect is the ability of Municipal Councils to draw the public into their enterprises as shareholders. Public participation would not have been possible had the MC lacked financial strength. The public were first encouraged by the success of MCs projects in two councils. In one council, for instance, villagers' main concern was the freedom to retrieve their funds once they bought shares. Confident of his financial position, the NEO made it a rule that any shareholder could sell his share at any time to the MC. Now villagers are shareholders in thousands of pounds worth projects in two councils in Fayum Province. Nowhere else has this phenomenon been observed by this writer, but the idea is now operating in Fayum province and efforts are underway to propagate the idea in other provinces.

Structure and Leadership of Municipal Councils

To the outside observer, it is a big question whether the new structure of municipal councils functions well or whether local leadership exists. In view of the dual characters of the MC structure, it is of particular interest to determine whether the relations between the representative council and the executive council of the municipality is cooperative or obstructive. We shall address ourselves in this section to these questions.

Who does what? The municipal council is constituted of a representative council which is elected and appointed officials who form the executive council. The 1975 law invested the representative council with the responsibility to prepare and pass the MC budget, and with making decisions regarding income generating projects. This means that the representative council is in charge of determining how to spend money from the Local Fund for Services and Development accounts, how to invest, and how to make demands on the national government for particular services such as drainage, roads, schools, etc. The executive council is charged with the responsibility of implementation and of conveying RC requests to the District and Province. The HEO advises the representative council also regarding legality of plans and feasibility. The HEO can refuse to implement a decision made by the RC if it goes against the law.

In practice, however, there are serious impediments to faithful application of law. The RC does not have the staff, resources, or expertise to prepare a budget. They are also less knowledgeable and have less time to devote to initiation of income generating projects. Consequently, it is the HEO who prepares the budget and turns it over to the RC, whose role is in effect limited to approval, not, however, without discussion. Similarly, in questions of income generating projects, the HEO plays the central role in suggesting economically promising projects and the RC in effect agrees, rejects, selects, and/or modifies such projects. The impression gained is that in most cases, the RC approves of suggestion (in almost 95% of the cases) and in addition slightly modifies about 20-40 percent of them. Responsibility for implementation rests solely on the shoulders of the HEO, who puts his official staff in charge, each according to this specialty. There seems to be a consensus that the initiation success or failure of projects depends on the ability of the HEO.

However, it seems that the emergence of project ideas, and sometimes, the overcoming of difficulties, come as a result of communicative process of a group rather than an individual. Ideas come from diverse sources, provincial officials, the HEO, technical officers, members of the RC and even ordinary villagers, sometimes expatriates among them. (Witness in Sohaq, a villager who is now a professor of oceanology suggested the cultivation of fish, already a successful project). Ideas are discussed in meetings of the various committees and council meetings; they are sifted, modified and pursued for further information before a decision is reached.

Role Misconception and Electoral Tensions

During the first year of the representative council term 1975-76, members had, in many cases, an unrealistic conception of their role. Needless to say, they were encouraged in such an expectation by the extensive powers attributed to them in the law and by political consideration. This, they realized, is the period of free elections and relaxation of political constraints imposed by the Nasser regime. The Nasser regime favored officials and officers of the official party, all of whom were practically selected. In reaction to this, members of representative councils brought with them an assertive attitude, sometimes to the point of defiance. Considering themselves the true representatives of the people they sought to assert their supremacy and embarked on making unrealistic demands on officials, especially in the Delta region. Serious friction developed in many municipal councils between the representative council and the HEO. Within a few years, however, this tendency has started to subside and the RCs have since gained a more realistic attitude, considering the practical limitations. They came also to realize that the HEO was not actually an adversary but shared their concerns. It is not possible for this writer to determine how widespread was this trend, except in the Gharbiyah and Beheira provinces. No such thing was reported to me in Sohag or Fayum. All the villages I visited seemed to have reasonably cooperative relations between the RC and the HEO.

Another problem that new municial councils faced was an after-effect rancor of elections. In some cases, and they seem to be few, differences between RC members who belonged to different factions or electoral tickets (lists), led to conflict and obstructed decision-making. HEOs acted as peace makers in these cases. Normal degrees of tension were also reported to have occurred in struggle over the election of head of representative councils.

Leadership

With the expansion of formal organization in Egyptian villages starting in the fifties, leadership emerged in two forms: officials and elected villagers. These worked together in cooperative societies, village councils and the Arab Socialist Union. Small peasants, laborers and other villager started to play leadership roles in such organizations and got used to working with administrative and technical staff appointed by the village.

This pattern of dual responsibility has continued. Some members of RCs have had experience in village affairs in the past as officers in one or another of the existing organizations. Most heads of representative councils that I have met played a leadership role in the past, but the majority of their members occupy an elected office for the first time.

Another change in the background of village councils is the

appearance in large numbers of salaried villagers as representative council members. Those are usually employees who come from rural background but work in public or semi-public organizations at the village and province levels. They include teachers, agronomists, assistant agronomists, accountants, clerks and technical specialists of one kind or another. Some work in villages of their own MC and others outside it. While these salaried cadres are experienced and educated, they do not constitute an economically advantaged group. They tend, however, to be extrepreneurial and, those who can, establish their own business on the side or express their talents in their official work. I was struck by the widespread attitude on the part of village officials in the province in favor of free enterprise and their desire to embark on such pursuits personally.

The official staff in the village are appointed officers who have vocational or higher degrees. The HEOs in particular are people who have had experience in village councils, or as agronomists. These two kinds of professionals seem to make the majority of HEOs; the rest may come from education background, law, administration and the like. Consequently, many HEOs are experienced and capable but, as to be expected, show differences in intelligence, initiative and dedication. Some are less informed about the prerogatives of their office and what they can legally do than others. Naturally, all of them understand the bases, but there are, it seems, some less obvious aspects of the law pertaining to decentralization which are not clear to everyone.

A striking phenomenon in the late seventies was that most officials came from village and provincial backgrounds and served in their own district or province. Evidently, it is a deliberate policy of the government to facilitate life for officials and avoid posting them in remote places away from their homes. Fortunately, educational progress in rural Egypt makes such a step feasible, even in Sohag!

An important aspect of the emergence of local officials as members of representtive councils is that they are able to speak the same language with members of the executive councils.

The prevalence of the small ordinary villager, whether a cultivator, worker or salaried employee still seems to be the pattern that dominates representative councils of municipalities. A few large landowners who stayed behind have made a comeback but in surprisingly small numbers. In places which I have visited, with one exception, they were described as not very interested in the business of municipal council and attended mostly to their private business. Those of them who became involved again in village politics seemed to have also sought offices of upper levels: district, province and/or National Assembly. It is quite possible that their interests in being represented in the village is an aspect of their greater interest in higher level politics.

Why have landlords not returned in a greater force? A few suggestions may be offered here as a tentative explanation. First, the twenty years of the Nasser regime have really undermined their power. The old aristocracy disappeared and the native large landlords were weakened and many of whom had turned to other pursuits away from the village. Second, diversity of village organizations, emergence of new leaders, the strength of the official staff and checks from the provincial government makes their chances limited and possible gains meager. There are now numerous local leaders in a village and the price of their control may be too high. Third, rewards gained from positions local leadership are quite limited now. Fourth, their diminished estates make them turn to private economic pursuits to compensate for their downward mobility in the economic order.

I have observed a near consensus among people involved and express an egalitarian attitude in the form of reckoning with each other regardless of social status differences.

Political and ideological mobilization that prevailed before the seventies has reached a halt. Some of those who were then engaged in such campaigns are not disappointed but expressed the feeling that the requirements of the two eras are different, meaning that no such methods are now necessary.

Some council members are illiterate and inexperienced, others are either negligent or aggressive and such conditions create dissatisfaction and criticism. Often it was affirmed that meetings of representative councils occur regularly but it soon became clear that they may meet only once a month, or in the rainy season (Delta), not at all. Sometimes an HEO barely manages to have a quorum to have representative council pass the business of the day. None seemed though to think that these questions seriously hampered the work of the executive council. Apparently, such failings are not widespread or severe so far, but should they become so, the business of municipal councils would be seriously compromised.

At present, one should pay attention more to the manner in which the representative council and executive council work than to formal rules and regulations. It seems that contact between members of both councils, especially between HEO and representative council was maintained regularly and informally as much as formally, if not more. The HEO attended representative council meetings and talks with members individually on a regular basis.

I have mentioned previously that representative councils tend to do things differently from the text of the law. Their involvement in municipal council business is one of sharing in decision-making with HEO, who plays usually the dominant role. However, representative councils perform informal roles consistent with their character as representative bodies. They provide the linkage between the executive council and villagers. Being more in touch with people and sharing their problems, they can transmit requests, information, and grievances to village officials very quickly. As one representative council member put it: "An idea would be floating among the people of the village; What we do is translate it into decisions." They are also keenly aware of problems in the villages, apparently in most cases pertaining to social services and agricultural problems such as drainage, irrigation, fertilizers, spraying, roads, drinking water, schools, mosques, and the like. It is not surprising, therefore, that most issues pertaining to village services are initiated by representative council members and resolutions regarding which are also passed by them. In contrast, most economic, technical and income generating projects come from the HEO.

Of great interest is the invaluable role representative council members play in self-help projects. This affects mostly infra-structure and service activities like draining a swamp, paving a road inside the village, contributing land to build a school, building a mosque, etc. In self-help projects, representative councils take the leading role in propagating the idea, getting public support and in implementation. It seems also that the suggestive and encouraging leadership of an HEO is of special importance in this regard.

Let us look, for example, at self-help as a means to circumvent persisting legal impediments to local autonomy. A municipal council has the right to impose levies locally but this is subject to approval by the Governorate. To avoid delays and possible rejection, and municipal council decides to raise funds as voluntary contributions by villagers. Once the representative council approves of one, it becomes like a "levy" and is collected locally without interference from the outside. Without the approval and active participation of the representative council such measures would have not chance of passing. Because of their local influence and contacts representative councils are a major factor in winning the cooperation of the public with officials. In short, the significance of representative councils is not in literally conforming to the letter of the law nor in their regular attendance of meetings but in their informal role as representatives, intermediaries and expeditors.

Allocation of Resources

Who benefits from resources, services and projects discharged by municipal councils? One of the interesting things about officials and representatives at various levels is their egalitarian attitude and keen awareness of the need to ameliorate the conditions of the village poor. Curiously, this attitude is spontaneously elicited even among individuals who express strong anti-Nasserist attitude as among others.

There are legal constraints against misuse or gross favoritism. Funds that are provided by ORDEV as well as the regular village budget are subject to annual auditing by the government accounting office and by ORDEV officials. Despite this, it is possible for an municipal council which is so inclined to make choices that would favor a few. I have not noticed any such favoritism, nor was it possible for me to do so under the circumstances.

In trying to assess the allocation of resources in the villages I visited, the only available indicator is an examination of the revenue generating projects and services made by municipal councils.

The services commonly performed by municipal councils consist of building youth centers, housing for officials, community housing and planning, schools, warehouses, mosques, consumers cooperatives, introducing electricity, water fountains, fire fighting units and performing such things as drainage, land reclamation, and health services. Most of these activities, it is obvious, are of use to the general public and are not likely to benefit a special individual or group in the village.

Among income producing projects one finds milk refrigerating units, dates packaging, carpentry, hat making, rug making, furniture material, olive canning, mint distillers, raising silk worms, bees and chickens, engaging in animal husbandry, investing in trucks, tractors and taxis. Some of these projects produce revenue to the municipal council, some to both municipal council and private citizens in partnership and some to villagers alone. A milk refrigerating unit for instance, will make it possible for villagers to market the milk they produce and contribute to the revenue of the municipal council from the service charge. The same may be said of date packaging and olive canning. Investing in a taxi or tractor is sometimes made by both municipal council and villagers in partnership and both benefit from the returns.

Naturally, not all villagers have savings to enable them to invest and therefore this includes those of middle to upper bracket income groups more than poor folks. This is particularly true of raising bees where only economically and socially advanced villagers will venture to undertake. Almost all the economic projects involve a pecuniary or employment benefits to villagers. In carpentry, for instance, when a municipal council takes an order to make furniture for a customer, not only will it generate income for itself but also involve employment of villagers and training of the youth in carpentry. Similarly, in a distilling unit, the municipal council finds an outlet for the product of a number of peasants. A particularly important service for villagers, regardless of how poor they are, is the breeding of chickens. municipal councils usually raise chicks until they are almost a week old or so then sell them to villagers to raise. Hardly any villagers fails to benefit from this service, since they raise chickens in their homes.

As for people that are employed in revenue generating projects of the municipal council, about a thousand were seasonally employed in Biyahmu, Fayum province.

Taking a look at Zawyat al Karadisa in Fayum, we find the unit distillery employs 5 workers and uses the produce of 50 small cultivators. Pickling and canning of olives project employes 200 and finds outlet to the produce of 5 farmers. (Tree growing villagers are generally more wealthy farmers.) As for beehives there are 200 units in the municipal council and 200 for villagers. Council technicians extend services to private citizens on how to raise bees. The municipal council tractors serve about 300 cultivators. As for investment, there are 40 villagers now who have invested in tractors and taxis; 20 shareholders in 2 tractors and 20 in 2 taxis. Many more have done so in Abu Gandir, Fayum province, but we have no precise figure.

Despite the egalitarian and distributive nature of municipal council allocation of resources, one can detect that some people benefit more than others. It would be remiss to call such a phenomenon exploitation simply because the better-off can benefit more. Exploitation did exist before 1952 where cultivators were given survival wages or shares by owners, and low rates for their products by merchant-money lenders.

We suggest that the current situation does not reflect exploitation but another phenomenon that we shall refer to as differential advantage or the variable ability of individuals or groups to make better use and reap greater benefits than others from available opportunities.

In the cases at hand, we can distinguish a number of actors who enjoy a differential advantage. First, we notice that individuals make a different use of resources. The better-off, the more educated and expert officials benefit more than ordinary villagers from existing services and projects. For instance, only the wealthy villagers can hope to raise bees, because the economic success of such an enterprise requires raising at least 20 beehives, which is a large investment. Village officials such as agronomists often enter into partnership with such farmers and undertake such projects on their own.

Second, some villages in the municipal government benefit more from municipal council activities than other member villages. This occurs because some villages have a better location or ability to respond. The village in which the combined services unit is located often reaps more benefits than other villages of the municipal council. Another kind may occur in a village that does not have a combined services unit but, because of the education, cohesion and initiative of its people, can divert resources to itself.

A third case in which differential advantage occurs is

regional. Some areas are better located and stand to benefit from proximity to the central cities. One finds that middle and lower Egypt benefit more from public services and opportunities than upper Egypt. Similarly, some provinces are fortunate to have dynamic governors who make major contributions to development in their provinces. The cases of the Fayum governor in the later seventies of Beheira in the sixties are good examples. Differentials occur within the same province too, for instance, three municipal councils in Fayum are superior and must be tops in the country; others range from the moderately successful to the failure. Factors that make for success are: (1) the initiative of the executive staff, especially the HEO, (2) a cohesive community not torn by factional struggle, (3) municipal council that has a combined services unit and (4) the educational and living standards of villagers.

Regional and community differentials are possible to deal with and to reduce. One fruitful method would be to hold seminars and conferences to disseminate ideas of successful municipal councils among the less successful. Such seminars should be guided by provincial officials but the main participants should be executives and few representatives of municipal councils. Second, ORDEV and Governors could devote more attention to less capable councils, educationally and financially.

Differential advantage among individuals is another question. It is not as easy to ameliorate, nor is such an effort developmentally advisable. A rigid adherence to equitable distribution of resources in a poor country prevents capital formation and investments which are major factors making for development in local communities. Those who are able to benefit and produce should be encouraged because through their entrepreneurial exploits the public benefits and villagers find employment. Their productivity after all will be part of the gross national product of the nation. A rigid egalitarian policy will prove counter-productive.

CONCLUSION

It is perhaps clear form this discussion that the contributions of agrarian reform to peasants' welfare and political advancement have been drowned by ideological biases among intellectuals at the initial stages, and by the ills of collective marketing, controls and benign neglect in later stages. Regardless of where a person stands on this issue, one major development cannot be denied -- agrarian reform as a broad package brought with it government hegemony over agriculture and rural society. Whether students focus on village communities, regions, classes or the market community, they will find that in countries such as Egypt these sectors have incontrovertibly become integrated with the national system and can be understood best in that context. The fact of the matter is that rural people are no longer face to face with the landlord, the money lender, the merchant or urban population, such classical conflicts are no longer prominent. A great deal of land is still under rent in Egypt, not necessarily by large owners but more often by small ones, and this gives rise to much disputation in which government regulations and interference also play a major role. The villager now lives within a larger context -- the state. He is face to face with its officials, its teachers, doctors, police, its plans and rules, its designs and its intractability His problems thus have a state focus: his succor and his deprivation can be equally attributed to the state.

In as far as we have seen here, the Sadat regime in Egypt did not introduce a new comprehensive scheme or strategy to face the problems of the countryside. It has reconsidered some of the local institutions and tried to modify them in a direction that may provide such institutions with greater strength, and greater ability to serve but without much progress for participation and representation. The basic strategy identified at the beginning of this paper for the sixties is still in effect. It calls for relying on resources from the countryside to feed the urban population, finance industrialization and earn foreign currency. Changes in the national approach to the economy may have diversified the government's sources of income to cope with these issues but the government has not come up with a national plan that reduces the rural burden. For instance, crop and price controls were still in effect in 1983.

It is the irony and paradox of socialist regimes which are based on humanitarian ideals and principles of equality and justice that they fail to come face to face and honestly with the distributive question. Despite ideological commitments, governments find that distributive policies constitute a serious constraint on capital formation and consequently adopt a policy of etatism which has all the ideological trappings necessary for a self-proclaimed socialist system and at the same time all the effects that prevail under capitalism as far as the poor are concerned. Just as is the case with agrarian reform in Egypt, most distributive policies were limited by the small size of the population they covered, by price and crop controls and by self-defeating employment practices. The question has to be faced squarely: how in a generally weak economy are welfare, equality and development to be pursued. Does the government really want to aid and develop and agrarian sector that is depressed by limited land and water resources and burdened by surplus of labor, or does it want what bourgeois regimes in the past practiced in the way of extracting the surplus from cultivators? What, if any, is the government's policy toward the non-agricultural sector of the rural community which is growing rapidly in size? Ideological justifications and claims that sacrifices are needed for the development of the national economy serve only to camouflage the issue, not only of rural problems but of urban ones as well.

FOOTNOTES

1.   See, for instance, Milton J. Esman, Landlessness and
Near-Landlessness in Developing Coutnries (Cornell University:
Center for International Studies, 1974) and Harik, The Political
Mobilization of Peasants, Bloomington: Indiana University Press,
1974.

2.   Daniel Craig, "The Impact of Land Reform on an Iranian
Village," The Middle East Journal, Vol. 32, No. 2, (Spring, 1978),
p. 146.

3.   For complete data on land distribution in 1974, see my
monograph, Distribution of Land, Employment, and Income in Rural
Egypt, (Cornell University, Center for International Studies,
1979).

4.   'Abd al Basit al Mu'ty sal Sira' al Tabaki fi al Qaryah al
Misriyah

5.   Two unpublished papers deal with this question in detail:
John Waterbury, "Administered Pricing and State Intervention in
Egyptian Agriculture," Conference on Politics of Food held in Rome
by the American Universities Field Staff, June 1978; and Karima
Karim, "Tawzi 'al Dakhl Bayn al Hadar Wa la Rif, 1952-1975," Third
Annual Conference of Egyptian Economists, Cairo, 1978.

6.   See Robert Mabro, The Egyptian Economy, 1952-1972, Oxford:
Clarendon Press, 1974, pp. 76-79; also Waterbury, op. cit.

7.   USAID, Near East Bureau, "Egypt: Recent Socio-Economic
Data," October 1977, p. 17.

8.   Mahmud Abdidl Fadil, Income Distribution ..., p. 120;
Radwin, op. cit., p. 76; Waterbury, op. cit.; Karima Karim, op.
cit.

9. Karim, op. cit.

10. CAPMAS, al Kitab al Sanawi, 1977.

11.   See Samir Radwin, The Impact of Agrarian Reform on Rural
Egypt (1952-1975), Geneva: The International Labor Organization,
1977.

5
Local Patterns of Leadership and the Development of the Aswan High Dam Lake

*Nirvana Khadr**

INTRODUCTION

This paper deals with the changing role of leadership in the development of the fisheries in the Aswan High Dam Lake of Upper Egypt. The filling of the lake after the completion of the Aswan High Dam in 1964 created radically new ecological possibilities. The story of the social organization of fishing in the new lake combines traits of continuity with the emergence of new institutions as competition over the exploitation of the new resources took shape. In this paper I am concerned with the changing role of the leaders of the fishing organization.

There are three types of people associated with the Aswan High Dam Lake. Our focus here will be limited to the socio-political structure of the Saidi fishermen, who number more than 7,000. The other people of the lake, who will not be discussed in this paper, are the old Nubian communities and the Eastern Desert nomads, the Ababda and the Beshari (for more details, see Fahim 1981).

The Aswan High Dam Lake (formerly called Lake Nasser) is a man-made reservoir with a length that exceeds 300 kilometers in Egyptian territory and over 150 kilometers in the Sudan (where it is known as Lake Nubia). The heavily indented shoreline has a length of over 4,000 kilometers. The inlets along the side of the lake are referred to as khor -s.

Fishing in the Aswan High Dam lake produces about 1/8 of Egypt's fish catch. The Aswan High Dam fishermen specialize in fishing in the lake and never fish in the open waters of the Nile. The social organization of fishing reflects the ecological description of the lake. Because of the various constraints on the lake such as difficult environmental conditions (the harsh arid area) and the use of primitive fishing techniques, fishermen are scattered in small camps all along the khor -s on both the east and west shore of the lake.

*With the editorial assistance of Dr. Nicholas Hopkins.

In addition to the ecological constraints, the social organization of the fishermen was also affected by the various original tribal affiliations, which introduced conflict among the various groups. In particular there was rivalry between one group from Qena Governorate and groups from two different communities in Sohaj Governorate. These two basic constraints, ecological on the one hand, and socio-political on the other hand, led the government, in collaboration with the leaders of the fishermen, to divide the fishing areas in the lake among the three groups.

Because of the nature of the socio-political process in the lake area, I consider the historical method to be the best way to reveal the continuous process of interaction between the government and the fishermen. The historically derived socio-political process will be important for the future perspectives of fishery development in the Aswan region.

Before moving on the main body of the paper I shall briefly define certain concepts. The concept "development" is generally too ambiguous. But as a maximal definition of "development" I shall refer here to James N. Kerri (1977) and C.S. Belshaw (1974). Kerri (1977:35) describes development as:

"...the process through which we attempt to maximize the efficiency with which we explore and exploit both the material (human and natural) and the nonmaterial resources that form part of our social, ecological, and cultural environments so that an equitable and just distribution of these resources among the members of the population is maintained."

This definition of development implies both organization (the key element in the Aswan High Dam Lake fisherman case) and satisfaction (Belshaw's "performance"), as well as an increase in the quantity and the quality of the goods and services produced (Belshaw's "growth"). Above all, such a definition raises the issue of equitable distribution of resources that is often ignored and very difficult to maintain. We shall see in this paper how the ability of the traditional fishing leaders to adapt to new circumstances was more effective than the efforts to build a socialist system, and how change towards more equitable distribution has almost failed. This case may remind us of Bailey's (1969:220-221) repetitive change or the reverse of a process.

Other concepts include "patterning," defined by Peters (1972:196) as something more than an arrangement. It involves a number of components weighted in relation to a problem. Some components remain close to the nucleus while others remain on the fringe. In brief, the ordering of assets (or components) into a pattern "produces a structure." Peters' definition may be useful when we reach the description of the continuous process of interaction between the government and the fishermen below.

"Leadership" is not studied here in its static form. It is analyzed in a dynamic situation where the leaders of the fishermen are faced by a regional policy of planned change. This situation encompasses both 'authority' (i.e., status, the subordination of consciousness to a legitimate rule) and 'power' (i.e., the relationship between exploiter and exploited). Terms such as shaykh al-qabila and raiyyes saiyyadin refer to leaders or to powerful figures. The shaykh al-qabila represents all the fishermen originally from one of the Upper Egyptian communities, while the raiyyes saiyyadin or fishing chief is a leader of a fishing group and of a fishing base on the lake. Individuals in either of these positions can play the role of sawwaq, the broker or entrepreneur linking fishermen on the lake to tradesmen in the city.

Today the prestige and wealth of a fishing chief comes not only from his membership in the Aswan Fishermen Cooperative Society, nor from his ownership of boats and fishing gear, but also from his property in terms of the number of salted fish store rooms located in Aswan City. Formerly, the fishing chiefs and even Al-Haj were considered to be only supervisors and protectors of the salted fish production; however, as the price of salted fish is not controlled by any governmental pricing system, the returns on the open market are quite profitable to the chiefs and to Al-Haj who thus become tradesmen themselves.

Other terms such as 'araqa (those who sweat) refer to the least powerful figures among the fishermen of the lake. They are laborers without capital who are recruited in the home fishing villages to work for lengthy periods of time in the isolated lake camps under the supervision of the fishing chiefs. Even lower than the 'araqa are the rajil illa ruba' or "man minus a quarter," referring to teenagers and new apprentices on the lake, whose income is reduced, and the sabi, the boy who helps the fishermen by carrying things and by doing the necessary household chores in the fishing camp.

The remainder of this paper is divided into three parts. Part II discusses the lake fishermen before the construction of the Aswan High Dam. Part III is an historical overview of the major organizational components or assets that developed after the construction of the Dam and that have modified the nature and role of local leadership among the Lake fishermen. In Part IV, I will summarize the analysis and stress the importance of finding alternatives to the current situation that are available to the concerned authorities whether local, regional, or national, for the sake of the development of the Aswan HIgh Dam Lake.

THE FISHERMEN BEFORE THE CONSTRUCTION OF THE DAM

Before the construction of the High Dam, fishermen were rare along the Nile in Nubia. They used to fish only during two main seasons, in the spring from January to April and in the summer from July to August. The system of fishing was based on the iltizam, a kind of tenure system that established fishing rights and claims over fishing territories The Nile waters were divided into iltizam Number One (south of the old Aswan dam including the Alaqi area) and iltizam Number Two (North of the old Aswan dam). The iltizam was a one-year contract between the Government and the fishermen. The latter paid rent on a quarterly basis, a set sum every three months. The disparity between the regular payments and the irregular fishing income restricted these contracts to those with sufficient capital to bridge the gap. These contracts allowed the family to establish themselves as virtual "fishlords" in the area with indebted laborers or araqa performing the actual work of fishing. The contract-laborers would then engage or commission individual fishermen with boats and gear. These men in turn employed helpers on their boats. In the long run there was a certain tendency for them to become supervisors based in Aswan.

As early as 1935 the Abdel Tawab family of Aswan had established a virtual monopoly over the fishing rights for Aswan Governorate both south and north of the old Dam. The records for the years 1924-1926 show that the Abdel Tawab family shared the fishing rights in those years with several other families or individuals. But from 1935 through 1960, theirs was the only name cited. Even though the old Haj Abdel Tawab died in 1950, the areas south and north of the dam continued to be maintained by his sons Mohammed and Ahmad who signed the last iltizam contract for the three year period from 1958 to 1960.

THE FISHERMEN AFTER THE CONSTRUCTION OF THE ASWAN HIGH DAM

The Cooperative

The year 1960 marks not only the beginning of the construction of the Aswan High Dam but also the development of the new Socialist system in the Aswan area and the establishment of a decentralized "local authority". The old "fishlords" were attacked at this time by the representatives of the new Socialist institutions. The Aswan Fishermen's Cooperative Society was among the newly created socialist institutions. It was intended to protect the 'araqa fishermen (the poor and powerless laborers who did the actual fishing), and to establish a more equal distribution of income and resources to their benefit. The Cooperative was also meant to circumvent the power and wealth of such people as the Abdel Tawab family. We will see that it did neither.

Ironically, Ahmad Abdel Tawab, the son of the person who had monopolized the region, was appointed by the government as the leading chairman of the temporary administrative board of directors at the initial formation of the Cooperative. The government was forced to choose him because of his expertise in the Southern fishing areas, in fish marketing, and in the processing of salted and smoked fish. Abdel Tawab, an old "fishlord," thus became the first member, first chairman and first person to invest capital in the new Cooperative. His share of L.E. 200 far exceeded the L.E. 30 invested by the four other members. It amounts to 87% of the total capital.

It is important to note that these five people, the first investors in the cooperative, were later to become the most powerful figures in the Lake area. Only Ahmad Abdel Tawab was of elite background. The other four investors were all originally Abdel Tawab's 'araqa fisherman laborers whom he used to send to Nubia to fish for him and whom he could still control and require to follow his instructions.

These former clients are today's most important leading figures among Lake Nasser fishermen. The Qenawi Al-Haj has become the most important figure for the Qena fishing group and is today the chairman of the board of directors of the Cooperative. T.N., a current member of the Cooperative's board of directors, represents the Jehena fishermen group from Sohaj Governorate. T.N.B., who is currently the treasurer of the Cooperative and who represents the Qenawi fishermen group, was another former client chosen by Abdel Tawab to be among the first five investors in the Fishing Cooperative Society. Last but not least, B.N., the current representative of the Balliana Sohaji group and also one of the Abdel Tawab's clients, was the only one of the four who had any independent financial means. Besides fishing he had accumulated some wealth through trading in animals between Egypt and the Sudan as he maintained food contacts with his Sudanese maternal relatives.

Clearly then, when the Cooperative was first formed, the chairman of the Cooperative was in a strong position as the board consisted of his own clients who were still loyal to him. This loyalty did not, however, last. It was not long before Abdel Tawab's former workers were able to consolidate sufficient power and independence to seize control of the Cooperative and to establish their autonomy. They began to recruit boat fishermen from their own home villages on their own account as labor for their fishing operations which they were not capable of financing themselves. This resulted in the emergence of separate groups of fishermen each corresponding to one of the investors, and reflecting his home village.

To a certain extent the socialistic objectives of the formation of the Cooperative were achieved. However, the initial leadership was able to establish an oligarchic domination. Though the Cooperative should have operated on the principle of socialist justice and equality to defend the rights of the poor, the initial members decided to restrict membership to those who were owners of boats and other fishing gear. The oppressed and exploited boat fishermen, suffering the hardships of the wilderness in the lake and owning nothing but their physical effort were subsequently barred from membership in the Cooperative.

In 1962, according to Law No. 2373, the Fishing Cooperative Society came under the supervision of the General Egyptian Organization for Aquatic Resources, Ministry of Agriculture, and in 1964 the Cooperative obtained a basic governmental long term loan of L.E. 8,476.376 to enable it to develop effectively as a productive enterprise. The board of directors was expanded and its temporarily appointed members grew from five to eleven.

The six additional members appointed by the government to the Cooperative Board were officially 'araqa -s. But they were also close relatives of the original five members. It is clear that Al-Haj and T.N. had the greatest influence in the selection of the new members. Al-Haj succeeded in bringing in a paternal cousin, a brother, and an affine. T.N. brought in his paternal cousin and his wife's brother. The only other leader influencing the structure of the new membership was B.N.; he brought in a brother's son. All board members, with the exception of the chairman, supervisor, secretary and treasurer were required to be boat owners and with property in fishing gear and equipment. The chairman had to be chosen from Aswan. All the top administrative members had to reside in Aswan and each received a monthly compensation of L.E. 24.

The Cooperative had developed into a very powerful monopoly controlling almost completely the production and market distribution of fish from the Lake. The development was especially significant after the 1967 war which closed off alternative fish supplies from the Red Sea, Suez, and Port Said. In order to undercut the Cooperative's monopoly, the government decided to create its own institution, the "Southern Fishing Company." The Company was originally conceived as an operation specializing in fish transportation and marketing. It, too, was established as a branch of the General Egyptian Organization for Aquatic Resources (Ministry of Agriculture) in Aswan. This event marks the beginning of the second historical period, from 1968 to 1976.

Company versus Cooperative

The establishment of the Southern Fishing Company threatened the powerful Fishermen's Cooperative Society. Within a year of its establishment in 1968 the Southern Fishing Company seized the full responsibility for the Lake Nasser fish transportation system from the Cooperative and began to supply fresh fish to the consumers' cooperatives throughout Egypt. Under this new system all the Fishing Cooperative's motorboats were turned over to the governmental Company with compensation. The network of transportation on Lake Nasser linking the fishing camps to the urban system thus came under the full control of the government. In spite of the structural changes instituted by the governmental company, the fishermen still had the autonomy to organize their own fishing, and continued to market salted fish.

After the seizure of the network of transportation on Lake Nasser, the Company moved to expand its power. The main objective of the Company was the absolute control of the area known as Khor al-Allaqi, as a fishing territory of its own. This area was contested by fishing groups from Qena and Sohaj (see Fahim 1981:87).

The first tactical step taken by the Company was aimed at the Cooperative's administrative board. The Cooperative chairman, Mr. Abdel Tawab, had become a powerful figure. He was a rich capitalist and had access to all fishing territories and markets. To persuade him to act in the interest of the Southern Fishing Company as opposed to the Cooperative would not have been easy. So the Governmental Company, using its government influence and in coalition with Abdel Tawab's former clients, moved to expel him and bring in a weak chairman. To justify this, Abdel Tawab was blamed for the conflict on the lake and for his failure to arrive at peaceful solutions to the various problems of the fishermen.

The Company succeeded in its objectives. The resignation of Abdel Tawab became effective in 1971. The members of the Cooperative board of directors and the government made sure that the new chairman was pliant and subject to influence. He was to be compensated and materially rewarded, something that had not been necessary to ensure the participation of Abdel Tawab, the former elite chairman.

Until then, the Cooperative board members -- Abdel Tawab's former clients -- believed that the interest of the Company chairman in overturning Abdel Tawab was in conformity with their own interests. They did not yet realize that the Company's major intention was to establish its exclusive right to fish in the Khor al-Allaqi.

The next strategic step taken by the Company was to encourage the formal delineation of the Lake by the Cooperative into three fishing sections, formalizing what had been an informal and sometimes contentious division into zones:

1.   Northern Lake Nasser, from the Dam to the 80 kilometer mark, was assigned to the fishermen from Jehena (Sohaj Governorate).

2. Middle Lake Nasser, from the 80 to the 145 kilometer mark, was assigned to the fishermen from Balliana (Sohaj Governorate).

3.   Southern Lake Nasser, from the 145 to the 300 kilometer mark, at Adindan on the Sudanese border, was assigned to the fishermen from Jaziret Matera (Qena Governorate).

Each section was assigned a leader who represented that section to the Company as well as retaining his membership in the Cooperative board of directors. These were the same individuals already mentioned. This added designation gave these leaders special prestige among their fishermen.

Further appointment of members from the Cooperative's board of directors was made possible by the Company chairman who thought that by appointing either directly or indirectly three leading raiyyes figures as employees in the Company it would gain their loyalty and support for the Company's secret intentions for the Khor al-Allaqi. Thus the Company appointed T.N., representative of the Jehena group controlling the Northern section of the Lake, as assistant in the Unit of Fishing Nets. Also, B.N., the representative of the Balliana fishermen group which controlled the middle section of the Lake, was appointed as an assistant and broker in the Unit of Fishing Products.

The leading figure offered a Company job was Al-Haj, representative of the Jaziret Matera group, which had the largest number of fishermen on Lake Nasser. The Company named him as its major contractor for the production and marketing of salted fish. This appointment was definitely the highest prize. It eventually led to Al-Haj becoming the richest and the most prestigious of the fishing leaders. It gave him tremendous access to other fish production centers and governmental affiliations that have helped him to amass his current wealth. In exchange, Al-Haj helped the Company move into Khor al-Allaqi. Such an arrangement would not have enticed Abdel Tawab, for he was already wealthy and there was no need for a strong exchange of interests between him and the Southern Fishing Company.

Today, Al-Haj and his relatives personally own the harbor pontoon on the Western High Dam Lake, the new three-floored building which houses the Cooperative offices, fish production shops in Aswan, in Upper Egypt, and in Cairo, and a salted fish processing plant in Aswan City. In addition, although illiterate, he became the present Cooperative Chairman. Whatever the formal requirements of the Cooperative may be Al-Haj, although illiterate, appointed and not elected, and engaged in more than one career, was still chosen to be the chairman of the board. He stands at the node of many networks, ranging from the marketing of salted fish to the recruitment of boat fishermen in the home villages.

Other working employees recruited by the Southern Fishing Company were temporary poor migrants from other Upper Egyptian governorates or peripheral members in the Fisherman's Cooperative Society. These marginal members of the Fisherman's Cooperative Society included leaders whose identity and background prevented them from being integrated into the Cooperative.

Most people who were engaged by the Company were considered public sector employees. They earned only around ten pounds a month, but enjoyed the prestige of being public sector employees as opposed to the 'araqa -s (boat fishermen) who worked as oppressed laborers in the Cooperative. In addition to their salary, the

Company's employees participated in a profit sharing system whereby 60% of the earnings of the Company were distributed to the workers.

Apart from the fixed governmental salary and incentives through the profit-sharing program, the Company employees also used to increase their income by dealing with leading fishermen in the Cooperative. Much of the catch and many fishing nets and significant belongings of the Cooperative often disappeared. It was an open secret that many of the Cooperative fishermen used to sell these items to the Company employees in the remote reaches of the Lake. This was possible because there was no one in the Company to restrict the field employees or to prevent them from moving easily within the lake and in Aswan. They were much less supervised than the boat fishermen who lived under the constantly onerous and oppressive conditions of the fishing base leaders or "fishing chiefs."

Company workers were not, thus, as oppressed and as exploited as their counterparts in the Cooperative. First, the boat fishermen were immediately made indebted to the fishing chiefs so that they might be better controlled; second, unlike the Company workers, the boat fishermen never received any monthly salary. The income of the boat fisherman was based on the annual production of the fishing base and was payable only every ten months, depending on his success in catching fish. Such an oppressive financial device enabled the Fishermen's Cooperative Society leader to control the boat fishermen far more effectively than the Southern Fishing Company's measures. This factor of lack of supervision together with mismanagement and corruption at the higher levels of the Company eventually led to the Company's demise.

The introduction of the national Southern Fishing Company in 1972 in the Lake area had a contradictory effect on the powerful fisherman leaders. Intended to decrease their autonomy, it failed to compete with their rigid control of the work hierarchy on the Lake, and so reinforced their position. In fact, the Southern Fishing Company became a positive asset to the power of the leaders of the Lake fishermen.

Another asset for the leaders was the creation of formally approved tribal fishing zones in the Lake by the government. Here again, although this measure was intended to enhance Company control of the area, yet it gave the leaders representing each section a special prestige among his fellow fishermen.

Another asset of direct positive effect in favor of the Lake fishermen leaders' status was the appointment of three of the leading fishing chiefs to jobs in the Southern Fishing Company. Although the Company sought only to coopt the loyalty of the fishermen leaders, yet such appointed positions in the public sector represented quite a high prize. It gave the leading fishermen tremendous access to other fish production centers and to other markets. Such as asset, among others, made them wealthy and allowed them to develop other projects either directly or indirectly related to the fishery development of the lake.

A major asset in favor of more powerful fisherman leaders was the widely dispersed organizational and government administrative structure in the Aswan region. Until 1975 there were more than four central national authorities all responsible for the development of the Aswan High Dam Lake area (see Chart 1 in Khadr 1975:153). Such an uncoordinated administrative structure made its members always dependent on a central authority located somewhere in Cairo and not in Aswan. This distance contributed to both physical and psychological problems. It meant lack of government control and lack of supervision in the area.

Unfortunately, when the thought of a more independent and decentralized government authority -- the Lake Nasser Development Authority -- developed at the end of 1975-76 it was almost too late to restructure the lake area in favor of absolute government control. The continuing dispute over the fate of the Khor al-Allaqi is illustrative of the consequences of this division of authority. Eventually, in May 1978 a new and promising national administrative structure was introduced to Aswan. The new institution was called the High Dam Lake Development Authority and was under the direct supervision of the Ministry of Reconstruction and New Communities which is the national authority directly responsible for any such development project in Egypt.

CONCLUSION

I noted in the introduction of this paper that "development" implies both material and nonmaterial resorces. The material resources, in our case, include such components as the physical environment and demography of the lake. The social resources include such components as economy, genealogy, and ethnicity. Both resources in the Aswan High Dam area have stimulated the accumulation of assets that could then develop the reverse of the expected governmental socialist political structure among the Aswan High Dam Lake fishermen. The result of the contradictory socialistic institution came close to being a feudal system with unequal distribution of resources.

The fishing leaders deserve credit for the effective organization of fishing on the Aswan High Dam Lake under changing and sometimes difficult conditions. To do so they have drawn on the pre-Lake organization of fishing around groups drawn from particular villages or regions and organized into boat drews and fishing camps. Competition between the three groups helps maintain this structure. But the leaders have also taken advantage of the new opportunities offered to them to cooperate among themselves with the support of the national government, first in the form of a cooperative, then in the form of collaboration with the Company. The key to their continued power, however, has been their knowledge of fishing conditions on the lake, and their ability to recruit boat fishermen from distant villages and to establish a social organization that allows them to exert effective control over their dispersed clients. This organization of fishing on the Lake has sometimes been referred to as "tribal." "Tribal" is a misnomer in the case of the Aswan High Dam Lake fishermen leaders. They have used it only for their individualistic rather than for the common tribal interest of the whole group. "Tribal organization" was used as another asset in favor of the leaders' rather feudal power structure.

Organization is one of the factors of development, together with growth and performance. It is also the gear of integration between material and nonmaterial or social assets needed for the development of a powerful political structure. In this case, however, organization has been used effectively by the members of the board of directors of the Aswan Fishermen Cooperative Society, enabling them to maintain their position with regard both to their clients, the boat fishermen, and to the efforts of the government to control Lake fishing. The effectiveness of their organization was, paradoxically, at the cost of social justice, and the lot of the 'araqa boat fishermen is still pitiful, while the various fishing chiefs enrich themselves. Development has helped the few, and the majority have been left out.

Therefore, before other projects in the Aswan region's High Dam Lake area are undertaken, the various socio-political, ecological and technical constraints should be solved under conditions of efficiency and social justice.

Although the Aswan High Dam Lake fishermen leaders may be criticized for their political structure, yet their Aswan fishermen Cooperative Society represents a good case of confrontation between a successful local organization, on the one hand, and a slow-moving national organization, on the other, both facing the same objective of "development" and prosperity in the region. Whatever the damage to proper and equitable distribution of wealth, income, and resources among the Aswan High Dam Lake fishermen may have been, the Lake fishermen leaders have managed until 1978 to act on stable, competitive, efficient, and organized grounds towards development projects (i.e., increasing fishery production; the purchase of new motorboats, participation with an international agency in a development pilot project, and so on). Comparatively, the national efforts were exhausted from 1963 until 1978 by continuous administrative and structural changes and too many competing authorities, all responsible for the development of the lake area, but none committed to the pragmatic and applied implementation of development projects.

BIBLIOGRAPHY

Bailey, F.G.
      1969   _Stratagems_ _and_ _Spoils:_ _A_ _Social_ _Anthropology_ _of_
Politics. New York, Schocken Books

Belshaw, C.S.
      1974   "The Contribution of Anthropology to
Development." _Current_ _Anthropology_ 15(4):520-526.

Fahim, Hussein M.
      1981   _Dams,_ _People_ _and_ _Development:_ _The_ _Aswan_ _High_
Dam _Case_. New York, Pergamon Press

Kerri, James N.
      1977   "Applied Anthropology, Urbanization and
Development in Africa: Dream or Reality?." _Human_ _Organization_
36(1):34-42

Khadr, Nirvana
      1975   _Patterns_ _of_ _Local_ _Leadership_ _Among_ _Lake_ _Nasser_
Fishermen. Unpublished M.A. thesis, American University in Cairo

Peters, E.L.
      1972   "Shifts in Power in a Lebanese Village." In
Rural _Politics_ _and_ _Social_ _Change_ _in_ _the_ _Middle_ East, ed. by R.
Antoun and I. Harik, Bloomington, Indiana University Press

6
Syria: The Role of Ideology and Party Organization in Local Development

Raymond A. Hinnebusch

A "RADICAL" ARAB REGIME AND LOCAL DEVELOPMENT

The political model adopted by a national leadership inevitably shapes in critical ways the strategy and outcome of local development efforts. Syria, ruled by the Ba'th Party since 1963, is conventionally regarded as one of those Arab states which have adopted a "radical" approach to social and political development. In fact, however, there is little consensus on either the precise nature of the contemporary Syrian state or on its implications for grassroots development in Syria. The original architects of the Ba'th political system, self-proclaimed revolutionary-socialists, ostensibly set out to build a powerful revolutionary state along Leninist lines centered on an ideological "vanguard" party made up of militant political cadres drawn from and leading the masses. Such a "revolutionary-mobilization" system, combining the concentration of decision-making power in the hands of a strong leadership at the top, with voluntaristic mass activism at the base, was seen as an ideal tool for carrying out a revolution in Syria and for mobilizing mass support and participation in the enterprise.[1] The performance of such Leninist models elsewhere does suggest that, to the degree the Ba'th leadership succeeded in actually forging such a revolutionary state, it would wield a powerful instrument for reshaping society at the grassroots level. Notwithstanding this revolutionary blueprint, however, many observers have been unprepared to acknowledge much resemblance between it and the actual practice of the Syrian regime, indeed, the dominant view of the regime tends to stress the military character of its rule and is very skeptical of its ability to mobilize the masses to carry out revolutionary change. One common interpretation sees the Ba'th state as essentially "praetorian," i.e. a military dictatorship based almost exclusively on force and lacking the political institutions needed to engage mass participation or support.[2] A variant interpretation challenges the assumption that regimes like the Ba'th are modernizing in orientation, seeing traditional personalistic and primordial loyalties and motivations as dominant rather than revolutionary ideology, newly built political organization as

facades for patron-clientism, and the masses in such regimes as
still essentially unmobilized.[3] Yet another interpretation does
see regimes like the Ba'th as genuine expressions of the efforts of
the "new middle class" to carry out development and reform, but
sees this as largely happening "from above," through the state
bureaucracy, and although acknowledging that a tutelary effort is
made to "awaken" the masses, sees the enduring gap between elite
and mass and the bureaucratic style of the regime as precluding
much mass mobilization and participation.[4] Certainly, to the
extent these more critical interpretations of the Syrian regime are
closer to reality than its own self-conception, one should expect a
much more modest capacity to implement rapid major change in the
local community.

This essay will explore the linkage between the particular
type of national regime which has emerged in Syria under the Ba'th
and the nature of local development under this regime. An analysis
of national level ideology, strategies, conflicts and structure
will be undertaken to assess how these -- the potentialities and
weaknesses inherent in them -- have shaped the goals and actual
performance of the regime at the grassroots level. Then the
analysis will turn to structures and performance at the local
level. Such local level performance can rightly be regarded as a
critical acid test of the national regime's overall performance,
for the efforts of the state to penetrate the villages and
quarters, mobilize human energies and support and extract
resources, are crucial to development plans conceived at the
center. A study of how and what the Ba'th regime does -- or fails
to do -- at the local level can help to lay bare the very structure
and dynamics of the Syrian political system, as well as reveal the
consequences of this particular "road to modernization" for the
vast majority of the population living in the quarters and
villages. Thus, in the analysis, two general issues will be of
concern. First, given the evidence available, and particularily
that on the regime's local development performance, how far, if at
all, has it succeeded in its avowed aim of creating a
revolutionary-mobilization system and how far are the views of its
critics closer to reality. Second, especially insofar as the
regime bears some resemblance to the revolutionary-mobilizational
model, what are the costs and benefits, particularily at the
grassroots level, of its effort to use radical ideology and party
organization as instruments of rule and development.

POLITICS AND DEVELOPMENT STRATEGIES IN SYRIA: THE CHANGING VIEW
FROM THE CENTER

The Roots of Ideology and Leadership, 1943-63

The evolution of the Ba'th experiment after the seizure of
state power in 1963 makes sense only against the background of the
party's prior development. The Ba'th Party was founded by men --
like Michel Aflaq, Salah Bitar, and Akram Hawrani -- who were, for
the most part, professionally educated sons of traditional middle

class merchant and medium land-owning families. Their political commitments were shaped by exposure to European ideas of nationalism, liberalism, and social democracy, by the nationalist struggle against imperialist domination and division of the Arab world and by disillusionment with the leadership of the great traditional notables who inherited power in Syria after independence. These first-generation Ba'th leaders were romantic nationalists, populists, and reformists, expressing the claims of the middle class to a share of power, rather than revolutionaries repudiating the whole social order. In the later forties, seeking to spread nationalism in Syria and to challenge the policies of the ruling traditional elite, they began to develop a party base. Many of the first Ba'thists were teachers and their primary appeal was to youth, hence the party first took shape as loosely linked halaqat (circles) of teachers and student-disciples. From the beginning, the party's main following came from rural small town and peasant youth who came to the city for education and were recruited by Ba'thist teachers. Through these students, who returned to their villages to proseltize, the party began to build a modest peasant base and a scattered network of young followers in the villages. The party also developed a corps of doctors working in rural areas and lawyers defending the rights of peasants in court -- thus Akram Hawrani built his peasant following in Hama. By the mid-fifties, the party's leading role in the nationalist agitation against Western interference in the Arab East was winning it a big following in the cities as well, especially among students and younger army officers. In this period the party began to emerge as a relatively modern type of organization with a sizable voluntaristically-recruited base -- something quite novel in the region. Nevertheless, there were definite limits in this period to the party's development as a potential instrument of political leadership and change. Under the "old Ba'thists," it never had a strong leadership team able to work together well and forge a disciplined movement with clear strategies. Its origin in scattered halaqat, intense personal rivalries, the rather broad nationalist-reformist ideology attractive to people with the most varied orientations, and a leadership style, either too idealistic and aloof from practical work with the masses (Aflaq), or too engrossed in intrigue within the army and parliament (Hawrani), were all obstacles to the shaping of the party into an effective organizational weapon. Moreover, even at the height of its success in the late fifties, the party remained a minority force. Its base did not extend much beyond the rising generation of newly politicized "moderns," a politically very strategic, but numerically limited segment of the population, for it had yet to make a large scale mobilizational breakthrough to the vast majority of the population -- peasants still mostly "encapsulated" in their villages under the leadership of landlord or traditional za'im. Also, in its claim to lead the new political forces in Syria, it faced competition from other middle class political movements, such as the Syrian nationalists and the communists.

By the late fifties, a second rank and generation of Ba'th

leaders, students of the party founders, were beginning to emerge, who by the time of the seizure of power would be ready to challenge their mentors for control of the party. By origin, this new political elite-in-formation was essentially rural petty bourgeois, sons of peasants or rural small town tradesmen, upwardly mobile through acquisition of some modern education translated into careers as small professionals (rural teachers and doctors), petty officials, and junior army officers. Many came from deprived peripheral religious minorities, conditioned to rely on sectarian solidarity for protection, but simultaneously committing themselves to broader loyalties to a secular nation in which they could enjoy equal status. Such a stratum need not become revolutionary, but in the special conditions of post-independence Syria, it did so. Carriers of the grievances of the village against the landlord elite and of the minorities against the Sunni establishment, exposed by their teachers to nationalism and socialism, stimulated by education to rising expectations, then frustrated by the scarcity of modern careers in traditional Syria, embittered and humiliated by the Palestine disaster, increasingly influenced by the rising prestige of the USSR and of Marxism as a critique of the old ways, a small but growing and disproportionately influential number of these young moderns began to see revolutionary socialism as the only effective way to modernize society and economy, break ties of dependency, and forge a strong national state able to stand up against imperialism and Zionism. The 1958 merger with Egypt and the subsequent breakaway period did not diminish the appeal of revolutionary socialism, but they did check the momentum of the revolutionary movement: the Ba'th Party was partly dissolved and demobilized at Nasser's insistence and divided over issues connected with unionism, the party lost much of its urban following when it quarreled with Nasser, and its leaders split over how to deal with him. The disillusionment surrounding the UAR and its failure undermined the older Ba'thists and their nationalist-unionist centered ideology and caused radical ideological ferment among rising second rank leaders. By 1962, roughly three alternative leadership groups still associated with the Ba'th movement had emerged, the "old Ba'thists," several groups of radical intellectuals on a Marxist tangent, and a group of Ba'th army officers of village origin subsequently made their stand with -- or use for their own purposes -- one or the other civilian group. Thus, in March 1963, when Ba'thi officers seized power for the party in a sudden coup d'etat, it lacked a strong united leadership group agreed on doctrine and strategy, its organization was in disarray, and its popular base largely demobilized. It did have a cohesive group of young officer-partisans in control of the army, a corps of revolutionary intellectuals ready to try out their ideas at the heights of state power, and a nuclei of former partisans scattered throughout the countryside. Despite this inauspicious beginning, the young officers and militants who emerged at the top, products of the intense politicization of the last two decades, were determined that, far from being just another in a long line of coups, March 1963 would be the start of a revolution -- of some kind -- in Syria. To make this a reality they would have to build political organization, linking up with and expanding their scattered strongpoints across the country.

The Struggle for Power and Policy, 1963-65

For the first 2-3 years of its rule, the Ba'th Party was preoccupied with two main tasks. First, it took an effort to stay in power, for in the fragmented Syrian political arena of the early sixties, it was only one of several forces vying for power and, at this time, by no means the largest. Its rivals, the Nasirites, the traditional Sunni establishment, the Ikhwan al-Muslimin, liberals and communists had -- at least together -- wider popular support at a time when the Ba'th's former rural base was demobilized and fragmented. Indeed, given its relative popular isolation in the first two years after the coup, it was only its grip on the army that allowed the party to hang on to state power. The party's second task was to reformulate Ba'th doctrine so as to adumbrate the shape of its projected revolution and provide a coherent strategy for building a popular base. These problems immediately led to cleavages between the more moderate old Ba'thists and the more radical second generation leaders who had now emerged in top positions.

At the historic Sixth National Congress in late 1963, the radicals succeeded in taking the lead in a revision of Ba'thi ideology which, in principle, committed the party to a revolutionary-socialist program. 1) It was decided that henceforth the party would base itself exclusively on the workers, peasants, and "revolutionary intellectuals," leading them in a class struggle against the landlords and the bourgeoisie who the party professed to consider socially bankrupt. 2) A socialist transformation would be launched, aimed primarily at large property, through nationalizations, land reform, co-operatization and the assumption by the state of leadership in the mobilization and investment of capital for development. Private ownership of the means of production and the hiring of labor even on a small scale was, in principle, declared to be exploitation, but, in practice, it was conceded that smaller property could only be socialized gradually and through persuasion. 3) A Leninist style single party-state, operated on the basis of revolutionary ideology and run by militants recruited from the masses, would undertake to break mass ties to traditional leaders and mobilize the people to participate in socialist transformation and national development. 4) Arab unity and national liberation, it was held, could come about only through the export of revolutionary-socialism from Syria so as to mobilize for development and the battle against Zionism and imperialism all the human and material resources of the Arab world which were being kept out of it by traditional Western-linked regimes. As a practical strategy for building a power base, this program meant an attempt to outflank on the left the party's rivals who controlled much of the arena of participation and thereby to expand that arena through a mobilization of the (largely rural) peripheries under Ba'th leadership on the basis of a revolutionary program designed to appeal to the deprived majority. By breaking the control of their traditional rivals over land and business, re-distributing land and career opportunities, and by using party and mass organization as a new form of "political technology" to by-pass traditional local gatekeepers and penetrate villages directly, party leaders could put down the popular roots needed to survive. At least for the core group of radicals, men like Salah Jedid and the "Three Doctors," Zuayyin, Atasi, and Makhous, this was more than mere slogans or tactics for staying in power, but a genuine vision of revolution.

The old Ba'thists did not accept it on many grounds. They rejected the decision to "write off" much of the upper and even middle classes and sought some accommodation with "national capitalists," Nasirites, and liberals, with whom by background and outlook they had an affinity and whose cooperation they deemed essential for Syria's development. They were far less disposed to confront traditional influentials in the villages and quarters and were repulsed by the radicals' readiness to use force and class agitation against their enemies. The conflict was also, of course, over personal power. For three years the two sides carried on an intra-party struggle which was finally resolved in February, 1966, when the old Ba'thists were purged in an intra-party coup.

The Ascendancy and Decline of the Radicals, 1965-70

For about four years the radicals kept the upper hand inside the regime and were relatively free to try to translate their ideas into practice. They had some success, but paid a high price. The land reform was implemented in earnest and finally completed under their leadership. Industry and foreign trade were nationalized and their profits, added to significant aid from the Soviet Union, invested in an ambitious development program (The Euphrates Dam, an oil industry, agricultural supply and processing industries, textiles, infrastructure.) By these measures they weakened their opponents on the right and won (often grudging) support on the left. The party apparatus was forged and a set of mass organizations began to penetrate society. In the cities, the regime presided over an atmosphere of austere egalitarian leveling, and a growing ruralization as peasants streamed in to take advantage of new opportunities. Intense class and political tensions flared up in periodic strife or rumblings in the army. Party cadres training in arms and grassroots leadership began to build a popular militia, and the regime armed and set on their feet several contingents of the Palestine Liberation movement. Thus, the radicals did begin to build a popular base and to impart a sense of drive to Syria's development effort. Nevertheless, they were unable to sustain their course and by 1970 had so exhausted their political capital that they could be easily displaced by an emergent alternative leadership based on the army under a prominent party officer, General Hafiz al-Asad. An explanation of this development may give some insights into the dynamics of the regime.

The precariousness of the radicals' leadership from the outset can hardly be overstated. Their inability to reach some accommodation with the other contingents of the "nationalist-left," especially Nasirites (owing to conflicts over Arab unity, social radicalism, and Ba'th insistence on its leading role in Syria) deprived the Revolution of many natural sympathizers among the politically mobilized middle strata and among part of the peasantry. The split with the old Ba'thists cost further such support. In the effort to stay in power, and as a result of intra-party quarrels and purges, the gates of the party were opened to many on the basis of personal and sectarian connections, diluting the ideological solidity of the party base. The ideological re-direction led by the radicals at the Sixth National Congress was accomplished not solely by a mass conversion of partisans to the new prophecy, organizational tactics played a role, and many less politically conscious or more opportunistic elements simply went along with slogans which seemed to serve their desire for power or revenge against the old order, but who would quickly turn color in the seventies when the political winds shifted. To win out in the struggle with the old Ba'thists in 1966, Jedid, the radical leader, had exploited personal ambitions and weaknesses as well as sectarian connections. He put together a winning coalition but, overly reliant on such links, it turned out to be quite fragile. (For example, his alliance with the flamboyant, but politically primitive and undisciplined Selim Hatoum backfired disasterously.)

The style of leadership and relative inexperience of the radical leaders was probably incompatible with the demands of their messianic ideology. In principle, they were committed to popular mobilization, but they had been catapulted into power by military coup, not at the head of a peasant army or workers movement. Some had had experience in village work in the fifties, but had then gone on to become officers and professionals, distancing themselves from political work at the bases; they came to power lacking the tempering experience of years of struggle at the grass roots level which may be necessary to forge a revolutionary leadership. To be sure, many were filled with intense emotional revolutionary zeal, but too many lacked the asceticism and self-discipline needed to direct such sentiment into constructive work. (A case in point is the radical trade union leader, Khalid al-Jundi, who seems to have been discredited through personal misconduct.) Anxious to convince the masses of their sincerity, they engaged in demagogy and reckless overbidding on the issue of Israel, with disasterous consequences. Many could never overcome an ingrained penchant for factionalism, or resist the temptation to identify the revolution with their personal power position. (For example, the conduct of Salah Jedid and Amin al-Hafiz in their very damaging quarrel in the summer of 1965). Finally, in part because the radicals never were fully in control, in part because they came to power by military coup, lacking an organized popular base, they were ultimately unable to institutionalize revolutionary authority in a party center able to give unified and stable direction to the mobilization drive. Central party institutions did count for

something and party loyalties and organizational strength did help
to hold the regime together against outside attacks and the
tendency to splinterism within. But the politics of appointment,
transfer and dismissal in the army and that of intrigue between
factions cemented by personal, sectarian, and patron-client like
bonds operating intertwined with the politics of elections, voting
and assemblies, meant that authority was always in danger of
slipping away -- into the hands of key unit commanders or rival
factions. Hence, the unified leadership needed to build a strong
disciplined party base was often lacking. Further the role of the
party base could be nullified by the actions of a few army
commanders, and ultimately the army -- or more precisely various
cliques of party officers -- proved the surest base of power.

The radical's revolutionary strategies also had their built-in
costs. Their social approach -- leveling, discrimination in favor
of partisans, rurals, and members of minority sects, a tacit "scorn
of expertise" especially among rural officers, alienated the upper
and good parts of the middle classes, especially those of Sunni
origin. Many left Syria, taking with them education, skills and
capital needed in the modernization drive. In the countryside
itself, agrarian stagnation prevailed throughout the sixties owing
to drought and the drying up of landlord-merchant credit at a time
when the state-cooperative infrastructure meant to replace it was
still only being forged. But the most damaging consequence of the
radicals' policy was the defeat in the 1967 war. This disaster
sapped the radicals of the will to fight, disillusioned and
sensitized the lukewarm to the the costs of a revolutionary course,
split the party over strategies to cope with it, and gave
credibility to the challenge raised by General Asad to the radical
leadership. Asad's program called for first priority for recovery
of the occupied territories, hence, detente with the internal class
enemy and the traditional Arab states, and an end to the
revolutionary-socialist struggle in the interests of Arab national
war unity. Moreover, in the interim, the liberation of Palestine
would have to wait. The radicals wanted to continue, even deepen
the revolutionary course (hence their call for yet another land
reform) and were sure that detaching the recovery of the occupied
territories from the goal of recovery of all Palestine meant giving
up completely on the latter; hence their call for intensified
support for the fedayeen and mobilization of the entire population
around the theme of national resistance to capitulationist
solutions. But in 1970 General Asad won out in a quiet military
coup. Perlmutter, writing in 1969 that Syria was incapable of
sustaining, physically or politically, the most messianic Arab
nationalist party of modern times, predicted the demise of the
Ba'th.[5] Today, to be sure, the Ba'thists remain, but their
messianism is far less in evidence.

Ba'th Realists, 1971--?

By social origin and political generation the "realists" are
identical to the radicals, and sometimes they are even the same

men, changed, a decade later. But the rise of Asad has nonetheless meant the ascendency of the military, the bureaucrats and the technocrats over the radical intellectuals, the triumph of realism, caution and political astuteness over reckless idealism and vision.

Asad's coup eliminated the first ranks of the party leadership, men whose careers were too closely identified with radical policies or who refused to compromise on them. Into their places moved the second rank, either men with careers to make and protect who welcomed the closing of the gap between ideal and reality and switched sides readily in the changing political climate, or men who sought to "save" the regime from the "right," and allowed themselves to be mollified by assurances that there would be "no backtracking on the socialist-nationalist gains of the revolution."   Thus, Asad was able to preserve much of the base built by his predecessors, and by concessions to the "progressive opposition" (the National Progressive Front and a quota of state jobs) and the urban upper and middle classes (a certain political and economic liberalization) broadened it. In this way, the Asad regime seemed on the way to building a workable cross-class, urban-rural coalition heretofore lacking as a stable base for the Syrian state.

Ostensibly, the Asad regime has not demolished the work of its predecessors. In fact, it has profited from and developed some of it further; earlier development investment has matured and further investment through the state is being pushed ahead. The party and popular organizations have grown, although their purpose is now more to stabilize than to mobilize.   Nevertheless, two orientations, present but submerged under the radicals, have come to the surface under the current leaders and are effecting slow, subtle, but important changes from within. The first trend is a pragmatic-technocratic orientation which puts priority on economic growth over socialist purity and nationalist self-sufficiency; hence, the resurgence of previously waning capitalist forces and the decision to encourage a role for foreign contractors and Arab oil money. In agricultural policy, while radicals preferred to let large tracts of land expropriated in eastern Syria lay uncultivated since the state lacked the means to do so rather than rent them out to investors for fear of encouraging capitalist forces, the new leaders, taking a more liberal attitude toward private investment, have rented them out to raise production and help finance war and development, and have generally encouraged a revitalization of agrarian capitalism.   Asad has made efforts to attract back to Syria emigrated specialists and to curb the brain drain at the cost of permitting a creeping economic liberalization. This combined public-private economic strategy has resulted in a substantial economic growth and some access to needed foreign technology and skills, but at the price of a serious inflation which is having deleterious effects on the modest strata from which the party has recruited its support. The second emergent trend could be called "neo-patrimonial."   It can be seen in the decline of ideology, the replacement of ideological factionalism inside the regime by a less

intense rivalry between shifting patron-client, sectarian blocs,
the subordination of a collective party leadership to a dominant,
virtually unchallengable "Leader-President" with his charisma and
cult of personality, and , especially since the 1973 war and the
influx of oil money, an unleashing of corruption and privatistic
concerns among the elite at the expense of public interests. Thus,
by the later seventies, the longer term consequences of decisions
taken by the realists at the beginning of the decade were vaguely
discernible: the Palestine cause still supported, but subordinated
to Syrian reason of state; the socialization experiment not so much
reversed -- for the public sector is still expanding -- as
undermined by corruption and the resurgence of capitalist forces,
and the drive to create an ideologically energized mobilization
system largely exhausted. For many, the Asad regime brought
relative stability and security after two decades of enervating
conflict and change. Yet these trends may be slowly undermining or
at least metamorphizing the Ba'th regime as it alienates a growing
number of old supporters, without picking up many real new friends.
Thus, the emergence of a left opposition on the campuses, old
Ba'thist breeding grounds, and signs of decay at the party bases --
the dismal 11% turnout in the 1977 parliamentary elections can
perhaps be explained by the alienation or indifference of those
responsible for mobilization, the party militants. On the other
hand, the resurgence of rightwing revolt in the cities in the late
seventies shows the continuing weakness of the regime in the urban
areas and the erosion of support resulting from "neo-patrimonial"
practices; it also points to the vital importance, for the regime's
survival of maintaining its rural base.[6]

LINKAGE, CADRES, ORGANIZATION, AND MOBILIZATION

The strategy of revolutionary mobilization and state-led
development initiated by the radicals (and not wholly repudiated by
their successors) required the creation of a new type of party
organization hitherto hardly developed in Syria, the formation of a
new type of local leadership -- militants or political cadres, and
the creation of a development bureaucracy. In the sixties and
seventies, the regime invested a considerable amount of time and
effort in building this new political-administrative
infrastructure; but how well has it turned out?

Local Political Leadership

Any assessment of the Ba'th's development experiment must
examine its ability to create a pool of local leadership a "sub-
elite" able to lead the revolution in the villages and help
translate national development projects into local realities. What
was needed was a new type of "militant" drawn from and close to the
village community, but committed to party goals. Bureaucratic and
technical cadres, skilled in the management of things and of law
were equally indispensable, but they were not enough. Men with
motivation, and the ability to lead and organize people were also
needed if the regime was to win the mass support and cooperation

needed to give reform real roots and set development going from below as well as from above. Such cadres were all the more needed because the regime decided it could not work with traditional local influentials who had too much at stake in the status quo and were too often committed to older leaders and their ways.

The Ba'th has indeed made an effort to forge a corps of local leaders recruited from the masses. The party and subsequently the mass organizations, especially the Revolutionary Youth Union and the peasant union, were designed, in part, as recruitment infrastructures to select and socialize large numbers of ideologically receptive cadres from village and quarter. There is good evidence that the regime has succeeded by any quantitative measure in so tapping its potential mass base. The recruitment infrastructures reach most villages, providing ladders of mobility for many not particularily well placed persons lacking wealth and status. The main target groups, lower and lower middle class rurals, appear to have been quite responsive to these recruitment efforts. The party probably has more than 100,000 members (i.e. 4% of Syrian adults and 1 out of every 13 adult males). The peasant union has graduated thousands of typical middle and poor peasants -- not officials or local zuama -- from its leadership training schools. The youth union prepares thousands of high schoolers for admission to the party.

The "quality" of these cadres is another question. Theoretically, recruitment infrastructures, with their provisions for screening, periods of candidacy, probationary service and indoctrination, are supposed to weed out undesirables and maximize commitment to the revolution. In practice, they were too often by-passed in the days when the party had to expand to survive, or in periods of intra-elite conflict, when the outcome sometimes depended on flooding local branches with supporters regardless of their qualifications. Apart from this, it is questionable how far any amount of candidacy procedures or indoctrination can ensure ideological commitment, this can perhaps only be generated and measured in periods before the revolutionary party takes power, times of intense conflict when the personal risks of commitment separate the "true believers" from the "opportunists," and strong partisan solidarities are forged in "battle." The Ba'th did have two decades of political work before the power seizure when the choice of membership incurred an "opportunity cost" and during which remarkably strong party loyalties do appear to have been forged, but it was not a period of intense personal danger requiring great self-discipline or sacrifice. At any rate, many of the older comrades recruited before the power seizure, tended to fall by the wayside in the continual outbreaks of factional conflict inside the party. Thus, the bulk of the current membership may have been recruited subsequent to the power seizure and as much on grounds of personal or sectarian connections or career considerations as belief in ideology and program. Finally, since 1971, intensity of ideological commitment has probably ceased, even in principle, to be an important recruitment criteria.

A study of recruitment motivations of party youth conducted by the writer in 1974 suggested that "careerism" (a desire for upward mobility and status often sought through privileged personal connections) accounted for about one-third of recruitment. Another one-third was explained by a "personalist-localist" sort of motivation (a desire for solidarity with local influentials and friends).[7] The resulting deviations from the ideal role of (disciplined, politically conscious, active) militant, of which all too many party members have been "guilty" are cataloged in party documents: a "personal style of work," negligence and weak discipline, "feverish craving for benefits and posts," "revolutionary chattering"(!), i.e. idle talk of goals without looking for the instruments to carry them out, "sick" (tribal or sectarian) relations, etc.[8] In short, the Ba'thi militant seems to display many of the very traits of his society he is ostensibly committed to change. This is not, however, to say that ideological commitment plays no important role, in the writer's sample, it did seem to account for another one-third of recruitment motivation, the importance of which was indicated by its association with higher levels of political efficacy and participation. The study suggested that the party is seen by some rural youth as leader of a nationalist, socialist revolution, defender of the underprivileged, and an anti-traditional modernizing force in the villages, and worthy of support on this account; thus election to membership does often seem to involve a definite value choice. On the whole, the Ba'th has been able, at the least, to build a body of followers politically loyal to the regime and to the general Ba'th orientation, and, stretched throughout society, cross-cutting sectarian and center-periphery cleavages, this has been crucial to the consolidation of the regime and to the integration of state and society. On the other hand, while its local leadership is, at its best both close to the common people and receptive to change, the recruitment system has had very limited success in inculcating the asceticism, discipline, and cooperative team spirit needed to provide a truly dynamic leadership in the villages.

Political Organization

The easiest task of research on the Syrian experiment has been the verification of the existence of the organizational apparatus. It does indeed exist, with offices, work plans, and lines of authority stretching from center to village, i.e. it is not a mere paper organization. Exactly what it does and how well is another more difficult question.

At the center is the party's regional (country) command with its series of functional offices for various sectoral and popular organization affairs, e.g. Maktab Fallahin (Peasant Office), Maktab Shebab (Youth Office), Maktab Amal (Worker's Office), each with derivitive bureaus at lower levels. These offices, including in their membership under the direction of a member of the Regional Command, representatives of the relevant popular organizations and state bureau, seem designed to function as bodies for coordination, under the aegis of party authority, of decision-making and implementation in a given sector, e.g. peasant affairs and agricultural development in the case of the Maktab Fallahin. At the governorate level, the branch party organs, which have considerable power, perform analagously on a more limited territorial basis, and, being closer to the local communities, are in a better position to tailor national programs to the special needs of their area, and to follow up on implementation. The branch secretary (Amin Fara') is typically a local politician, while the governor is a bureaucrat and outsider to the area; as such branch party organs appear designed to exercise dual control over local bureaucratic offices and to keep them closer to the local party's constituency, while the governor is presumably more responsive to his ministerial superiors at the center. Branch party organs also seem to be concerned with initiating local development and popular organization projects. At the district (mantiqa) and village levels, the party organizations are supposed to be centers of grassroots leadership and recruitment. Few villages seem to lack their party cell. In addition to the hierarchy of offices flowing downward, there is, in "democratic-centralist" fashion, a series of assemblies running upward, formed through a mix of election from below and co-optation from above, culminating in the authoritative Regional (Qutri) and National (Qaumi) Congresses from which the central party leadership is elected.

Alongside the party apparatus, stand its auxiliaries (munathamat shabiyyeh), led and sometimes organized from scratch by party members who, subject to party discipline, keep the organizations inside the party line. These organizations, too, have their dual lines of offices running downward and representative assemblies running upward. The most important for mobilization are the youth, peasant, and trade unions, but there are also womens, student, professional and artisan unions, and a party militia. These organizations are supposed to mobilize a wider proportion of the population than that incorporated into the "vanguard" party, and to get people involved in regime programs relative to their particular interests. Thus, peasant union cadres are supposed to help in the cooperatization process, watch and assist in state agricultural supply and marketing operations, and participate in village improvement projects.

Both party and popular organizations are obviously mechanisms of control, but they do give the appearance of serving as elite-mass communication channels as well, and may even to some extent perform representative functions for local people, mediating between and helping to generate some common interest between elite and mass. The cycles of assemblies from base to center do seem to pass upward discussion, and their resolutions do appear to express very real and concrete peasant concerns.[9] Through the interlocking party Maktab-popular organization structure, the motions, at least, of a consultative process are gone through. Peasant cadres "represent" their constituencies on a plethora of party and state decision-making committees, mediate between individual peasants and state agencies and represent peasants in the agrarian courts. The access points do appear to be there; it is quite doubtful however, that peasant leaders carry much "bargaining clout" in regime councils. It is true that Ba'th leaders do seek peasant support for their policies and rule, hardly likely to be forthcoming if peasants do not perceive the regime to be responsive to their needs. But the crucial ability to hold leaders accountable by removal is (except at lower levels) hardly operative, and lower ranking party members and peasant leaders are too dependent (subject to discipline and removal) to overtly challenge policies unless they find encouragement in high places. The popular organizations have yet to become significant power bases able to compete with the party -- much less the army.

We can get a little closer to the actual operations of this apparatus by examining the strategies adopted and problems encountered in creating and running it, taking the peasant union as a case study. Creating the local organs of the union, the critical linkage point between state and society, was crucial for mobilization. The village had to be penetrated and the wall of negative solidarity traditionally offered to government broken through. This could not be done by outsiders or by officials claiming to speak for peasants, as these would have met passivity or evasion, nor by enlisting the local zuama who would have turned the village union into a disguise for a traditional village faction. The key was thought to be local recruitment of politically receptive younger small and middle peasants. Sometimes the ground for this had been previously prepared by past party work in the village, but often it started from scratch. Local party units and union work teams from the governorate level selected promising peasant candidates and sent them for training and indoctrination in union schools. Returned to the village, the new cadre was in a potentially promising position to bridge the center-periphery gap. Committed to regime goals through training and control from above (the possibility of promotion or dismissal), he would also have local ties, be able to articulate upward local needs and enjoy local confidence. He would continue to work his land rather than turning into a full-time official, and could be kept locally accountable by village social pressure and, with the establishment of the local union, by competitive elections. In practice, local peasant leaders did have certain resources with which to build local leadership. Whenever possible, the land reform became the focus of the organizational effort, providing a concrete benefit which could dispose peasants to the regime and its local representatives, state services were funneled into the village in part through the union, and it was given the job of representing peasants in the courts and with the bureaucracy. Ideology may also have been a resource for local leaders, for Syrian peasants, especially younger ones, do appear receptive to the nationalist and populist propaganda disseminated through the union.

However, as organization documents make clear, things did not always work out as anticipated. Identification with the regime was not necessarily an asset for local leaders, especially when supply and marketing functions were performed inefficiently or leaders were called upon to enforce unpopular policies (e.g. enforcement of state marketing when free market prices were higher). Ideology also was a two-edged sword; it embodied ideals and standards of conduct, but when party or state leaders were manifestly engaged in corrupt practices, the natural result was cynicism and withdrawal. Inspite of rules excluding persons owning land over sixteen hectares or who did not personally work their land from membership, local notables did manage to "infiltrate" and "capture" a number of local unions and, so leaders claim, worked to sabotage the experiment. Sometimes the local union turned out to be a mere paper creation or a disguise for a traditional village faction, dominated by one or a few families, boycotted by the rest. Cadres were sometimes only superficially oriented to ideology and used public programs to build personal followings and to benefit a few at the expense of others. Many simply showed no initiative in getting peasants to try new practices or undertake self-help projects. In the late sixties, rectification committees fanned out over the provinces to deal with some of these problems; paper unions were dissolved and new ones created only after members from all kin groups could be recruited. But in the seventies, many of the same problems are reported to persist. At higher levels as well, the organization did not necessarily function as an innovative or efficient machine. Patronage-like concerns "sidetracked" the work of the union, i.e., some leaders paid more attention to doing individual favors than to working for broader union programs. The "individualistic spirit" and "personal relations" often prevailed, a single leader trying to dominate an organizational body while others remained passive, or energy being expended in factional rivalries at the expense of team work for organization goals. Ignoring the nizam (internal rules), lack of systematic work methods and planning, and the supposed bureaucratic sins of sitting in offices at the expense of field work, idleness, and arrogance are other "deviations" reported. The new organizations like the peasant union do seem to differ from traditional patron-client networks in their relative development of modern organization and goal-orientation and in the lack of great asymetries in the personal resources of leaders and followers, but characteristics of the patron-client network have clearly creeped into the system. Similarly, as voluntary organizations recruited from local communities with formal arrangements for an upward flow of opinion and some scope for election from below, they differ from conventional bureaucracies while showing traits of bureaucratization. On the whole, while they undoubtedly do give the regime access points to the village useful for control, communications, recruitment, and a modest diffusion of innovation, they appear incapable of carrying out the revolutionary transformation of the village for which they ostensibly were created.[10]

Development Bureaucracy and Techno-Administrative Cadres

When the Ba'th came to power, Syria did not possess an efficient rational state bureaucracy, much less a development or service oriented one. Yet, the party imposed itself atop the state machine that it found to hand, determined not only to impart a revolutionary and developmental orientation to it, but to greatly expand it and its functions through nationalizations and an ambitious development plan. A whole new set of development ministries and agencies and a large public sector have indeed emerged in the last decade. A greater development orientation than heretofore does seem to have been imparted to the bureaucracy, and, among younger officials recruited from the village and close to the field, a greater service orientation to the local community. Nevertheless, the bureaucracy remains the Achilles Heal of the Ba'th's development effort.

The political policies and practices of the Ba'th regime itself have often been detrimental to the effort to build a development bureaucracy. Political discrimination against the urban bourgeoisie, contempt for expertise displayed by some rural politicians and officers, slashing of bureaucratic salaries and the ability, in any case, of many other (often nearby oil) states to offer higher salaries, a consequent brain drain, the flooding of the state machine with unprepared rural partisans, and the first claim accorded the army on the best graduates, have all been obstacles to the recruitment of quality personnel in sufficient numbers. The Asad government has made efforts to attract back emigrant experts and two new universities and a score of technical institutes are beginning to produce graduates in significant numbers. But the problem has yet to be solved because of the continuing lack of an effective personnel policy which could put the "right man in the right place" and reward him according to performance. Political loyalties and personal connections often appear to count for as much or more than skills and hard work in appointments and rewards. Hence, the performance motivations and skills needed by a development bureaucracy do not appear to have been strongly generated. The result has been costly for development. Industry suffers from a lack of technicians and quality management, while in agriculture co-operatization and agricultural extension have all been hampered by the scarcity of agronomists and accountants. Moreover, the whole public sector suffers from a growing problem of corruption, an increasing tendency toward embezzlement and influence peddling at the expense of the public treasury. In general, the record of the Ba'th Party in forging and leading a state machine which is both politically loyal and motivated and capable of undertaking development -- a function performed by revolutionary parties elsewhere -- does not seem impressive.

Mobilization and Development at the Base

What has been the actual performance of the regime's new

infrastructures in mobilizing effective support and participation for development, i.e., what difference have they made? Quantitative performance (membership figures) has not been bad. Besides the party's 100,000 militants, the popular organizations each have their own bases. The peasant union may have "mobilized" about 40% of the economically active adult peasants in about 3000 village unions, and claims to be expanding at the rate of about 30,000 new members each year. This indicates that a good part of the peasantry -- especially younger, more active elements -- is being involved. Nevertheless, many older, more traditional and many poorer peasants are far less so, and the Ba'th has failed to unionize agricultural laborers, a striking hiatus in its effort. The case of the urban working class is similar; by the early seventies, about one-half of it had been organized, but many workers in micro-industries and about three-fourths of the crucial private construction industry remain ununionized. Of course, thousands of unemployed, tiny peddlers, beggars, vendors, domestics, and service workers remain outside any organizational framework.[11]

But what do these figures mean in the villages for real change? It does seem that in many villages, the party and popular organization leaders -- an alliance of educated youth with small and middle peasants -- do constitute a genuinely new local leadership, having good relations with their neighbors and intimately involved in day to day matters of importance to villagers. That a portion of the peasantry has been drawn into the Ba'th's effort at change seems to show that some peasants are breaking out of their age-old passivity and are no longer exclusively committed to the traditional political game of clan rivalry, face, and honor. To this writer, at least, politically active Syrian peasants appeared much less "traditional" than those described in much of the ethnographic literature on Middle Eastern countries. In some villages (in particular ones visited by the writer in Hama, Latakia, and Raqqa) where the former power of landlords or tribal chieftains was especially repressive, the breaking of their hold through land reform and the fostering of new peasant leadership appears to have been a very liberating change, clearing the way for the development of peasant dignity and initiative and uprooting much of the old dependency and servility. While there is little evidence of a major transformation in values or social organization, the regime's efforts could be said to have removed major obstacles to the development of the village and at least stimulated the process of change.

The ability of the regime to engage at least some peasant participation also seems to have been important for the success of some of its programs. For example, in one Aleppo village visited by the author, traditional clan conflict had previously set villagers against each other, making cooperation impossible. The youth of the local party, because of their recruitment from all clans, were able to play an important role in defusing this conflict and uniting the village for some modest local development.

Conflict resolution in a segmental society is an important function
which in this case depended on a national political penetration of
the village. Efforts at creating cooperatives in many villages
also depended on this penetration, for the motivation to make such
new forms of social organization work cannot really be generated by
bureaucrats and outsiders if at least part of the village cannot be
enlisted. In a Raqqa village visited by the writer, it was the
peasant union leader who carried through the cooperative experiment
in the face of adversity and the hostility of the former tribal
chieftan. Local party leaders and unionized peasants also played a
role in land reform, after years of trying to carry it out by (a
not always sympathetic) bureaucratic and legal apparatus, the
radicals put the job in the hands of local cadres who finished it
quicker and in a way more favorable to peasants and less to
landlords. The agrarian relations law had been on the books since
1958, but it was only with the spread of the new political
organizations in the middle sixties that it began to be
implemented. Previously, the social inequality of employer and
peasant, the inability of peasants to pursue their rights under the
law on an individual basis, and the incapacity or indisposition of
the bureaucracy to aggressively defend peasant rights had made it a
dead letter, now the peasant union educates the peasant as to his
rights under the law and represents him in the courts. With the
spread of its influence in the countryside, the landlord can no
longer count on having the local functionaries in his pocket. The
role of party and peasant union also seems critical to the
functioning of the cumbersome supply and marketing infrastructure
created by the state, if the amount of time spent by local cadres
in checking, straightening out oversights and following up on
delays is any indicator. The bureaucracy may need this kind of
local control to effectively service village needs, and while it is
extremely difficult for the outside observer to judge how effective
it is, even sporatic success in the exercise of such peasant power
makes a difference for both social and political development at the
grassroots level.

It is important, however, not to overstate the party's
mobilizational drive. In many villages, traditional zuama or
landlords remain rival centers of power, sometimes evidently intent
on derailing the government's efforts. In all villages a good part
of the population remains aloof either by choice or because they
have been ignored by the regime. In some villages, the party
appears as little more than a small coterie around the
schoolmaster. In one studied by the writer, politically interested
peasants were so divided by years of political conflict, attaching
them to different parties -- communists, Hawrani socialists, the
Syrian nationalists, various shades of Ba'thism -- that the local
group in power was paralyzed and isolated. This case suggests that
the continuing inability of the Ba'th regime to overcome the
fragmentation of the political arena in the urban center may have
its paler reflections in the rural periphery. Another weakness of
the party's mobilizational effort was illustrated in a rather
conservative village studied by the writer where local party

leaders actually seemed to take on the color of their environment, segregating their wives and conforming to the norms of the traditional part of the village rather than taking the lead in cultural innovation. The weakness of the cooperative movement is another excellent indicator of the modest dynamism of many local leaderships.[12] After twenty years of cooperatization in Syria, only one-fourth to one-third of eligible peasants belong to full-fledged cooperatives, although a more sizable number receive many of the services provided by cooperatives through the peasant unions when the former do not exist. Moreover, many of the cooperatives do not function well and at least part of the explanation for this is the weakness of the cooperative spirit among peasants which the party's mobilizational effort is ostensibly charged with generating. A comparison of the Ba'th performance with that of China were local cadres led peasants into production cooperatives and communes in a few years, or even Egypt where most peasants were cooperatized by the bureaucracy, makes the Ba'th's performance look pale indeed. A dynamic local leadership should be able to get peasants to adopt scientific agricultural practices, work harder, save and invest, but as yet there is little evidence that the regime's political infrastructure has made any big difference either for its ability to stimulate local production or to extract a surplus for national development. The story of an Alouite village recounted by Ismail where peasants spent state loans on furniture and clothing suggests, in fact, that the opposite may sometimes by taking place: that the diffusion of greater political power to the village effected by the Ba'th effort may have merely enhanced its capacity to make consumption demands.[13]

THE CONSEQUENCES OF BA'TH DEVELOPMENT STRATEGIES

The ostensible purpose of the effort to create a "mobilization system" was to generate the political power needed to reshape state and society. By now, it should be possible to make some tentative assessments of the consequences of this effort, particularly as it has impinged on the development prospects of local rural communities.

Although the outcome seems to have diverged considerably from the original revolutionary blueprint designed by the Ba'th, the social structural and institutional configuration of the Syrian countryside has indeed been changed in at least three important ways.

First, the traditional "feudal" structure has been destroyed. In the wake of the land reform, the great "latifundia" are gone, and the vast asymmetries between the social resources of landlord and peasant greatly reduced. Nevertheless, the Ba'th slogan, "The Land to He Who Works It," remains far from realized. The old class of landlords still controls large portions of the best land worked with hired labor, and a significant rich peasant stratum - "owner-managers" using hired labor or absentees letting their land to sharecroppers -- still exists. Moreover, many city folk also own small or medium property, rented out or sharecropped.[14]

Second, the small and middle peasantry, heretofore of modest weight in the rural social structure, has become an important social force, expanded and buttressed by land reform, protective legislation and state aid. The land reform has transformed a considerable portion of the landless peasants into small proprietors. These and other small peasants have been linked to a state-cooperative network for the provision of production requisites and the marketing of the crop which, by the seventies, seemed to be working tolerably well and to have reduced peasant dependency on the merchants and moneylenders who used to cultivate "empires of debtors" and ultimately appropriate the land of the small peasantry. In addition, although cooperatives are still limited in numbers and effectiveness, they have enabled a modest but growing number of smaller peasants to purchase farm implements or make land improvements beyond the means of individuals, thereby enhancing their livelihood and security. For the stratum of peasants below these, those with share cropping contracts or those who must deal with contractors for irrigation or plowing services, the enforcement of agrarian relations legislation has made a difference, providing security of tenure, easing personal dependency, and reducing the return to the owners of land and other inputs relative to that for labor. On the other hand, while the poorest stratum of the peasantry, the landless agricultural laborers, has been considerbly reduced by land reform, those without land have been largely neglected by the regime. It is tempting to explain the failure of the regime to unionize the rural poor by its petty bourgeois social roots; as long as many rich, even medium peasants hire labor, the organization of laborers could touch off anti-regime sentiment where the Ba'th can least afford it. Moreover, current leaders, anxious to encourage investment in agriculture, do not want the social strife unionization could unleash.[15]

A third major change in the countryside is the greatly expanded role now played by the state. The state has linked itself through credit, supply, and marketing arrangements directly to the peasant producer. Its political-administrative infrastructure penetrates the village and its socio-economic legislation has far greater real impact on local life than heretofore. State policies favoring a widening of openings for rurals in education, state employment, and in the new factories it builds, have meant a wider range of opportunities for villagers. The state also plays a direct role in agricultural development -- in land reclamation, seed and water source development and agricultural extension services. It has created industries for the manufacture of agricultural production requisites, and state agencies or factories buy and process an important part of the harvest. Through these activities, the state is extracting a modest surplus from agriculture and reinvesting it.[16]

In general, a mixed socio-economic structure -- combining

state, cooperative, private small-producing and medium sized agrarian capitalist sectors -- has emerged in place of the pre-revolutionary feudal-latifundia-capitalist system. This change has been accompanied by at least two important social benefits for the average villager. There has been a significant redistribution of resources which, formerly siphoned off to fill the foreign bank accounts or pay for the private pleasures of a small class of landlords, are now more likely to stay in the village or be extracted by the state to pay for development or defense. Second, the emergent social structure appears to be a more open one: the old caste lines have been broken, people of modest origin are moving up in the social system, and the old social climate of feudal dependency, servility, resentment and repression in the village has been greatly diluted.

The economic consequences of the regime's development efforts, including these structural changes in the countryside, also appears to be mixed. There is evidence that by the late fifties Syrian agricultural development based on modest investment in extensive expansion had reached a limit and that further development would require investment on a far greater order, probably through the state, and structural change -- of some kind -- in the village. This reorientation did begin in the sixties under the Ba'th regime, but the immediate effect of the agrarian upheaval of that decade was agricultural stagnation. Nevertheless by the seventies there were clear signs of a new, albeit modest, expansion in Syrian agriculture. The land reform may be a factor in this: landlords must invest to maintain their incomes from reduced holdings, and in the more liberal climate of the Asad regime, a new medium size agrarian capitalism may be emerging. Rich peasants have greater opportunities to expand, and small proprietors may now have more incentive and means to develop their lands than they did as sharecroppers. State investment has probably had an effect: the Ghab project is finally complete, new reclamation is at least coping with salinity, a new miracle wheat has been introduced, with good results, and the Euphrates Basin development project should provide the base for a substantially enlarged modern irrigated agro-industry in the coming decades. Yet, it must be observed that, by comparison to the country's goals and potential, economic performance in the countryside has fallen well short. One expert suggests productivity is but 40% of its potential under conditions of modern organization and technology. The cooperative movement, limited in extent and efficiency, has not become a major generator of peasant investment or a conduit for diffusion of new methods and technology. State farms and development projects are marred by inefficiency and poor management. Agriculture is not yet producing the sizable surplus needed for industrialization.[17]

In general, both the shape and the direction of the emergent socio-economic system in the Syrian countryside remains fluid and unclear. The policies of the regime appear to have destroyed the potential for modernization via some form of large scale agrarian capitalism -- English or German style -- and the regime has been unwilling or unable to move very far toward a Stalinist development strategy. This may spare Syria's peasants much misery, since these approaches have made the peasant bear the heaviest burdens of modernization, but, in the absence of the ruthless but successful methods of capital accumulation and social reorganization pioneered by these systems, Syria's rate of modernization is likely to be more modest. A less rigorous "socialist course" combining state entrepreneurship and cooperative agriculture similar to some Eastern European models, appears to have been favored by a majority of the regime elite, and may yet emerge as a workable "third" path to modernization in Syria, but the realization of this model would require a continuance of the ideological impulse of the last decade and this shows very serious signs of having nearly exhausted itself. If so, the outcome of the Ba'th efforts may be, ironically, not socialism but some form of capitalism, perhaps resembling the early Japanese model with its combination of state entrepreneurship and small and medium sized agrarian capitalism. In that case, the fundamental social consequence of Ba'thist policies will have been to clear the way for the emergence of capitalism through the destruction of the patrimonial social structure inherited from Ottoman times.

Political Development

What consequence for political development has the Ba'th experiment had? It seems clear from the evidence considered that the Ba'th has fallen well short of its avowed aim of creating a revolutionary state along Leninist lines in Syria, yet the effort to do so has made an important difference for the kind of political system which has emerged and for the outcome of local development efforts. Briefly, it seems in two respects to have enhanced the capabilities of the regime and to have contributed to the creation of a stronger more stable state in Syria.

First, the regime's mobilizational drive has transformed it into something quite different from the conventional narrow-based military dictatorship. The military-police base of the regime is hardly unimportant; but it is not the exclusive key to its persistence. Equally important as an explanation for the relative strength of the regime has been its ability to use ideology and party organization to put down organized roots in the villages and thereby build a rural base which has given it some popular legitimacy and helped contain its largely urban opposition. The very reliability of the regime's repressive instruments, indeed, is due in part to their recruitment from this village base. To be sure, this effort has not been enough to submerge many of the deep cleavages in Syrian society or to unify it behind the regime. Besides the concentrations of opposition in the cities, traditional resistance or indifference to the regime persists in the village; communal cleavages remain sharp and have even been aggravated as a result of the incorporation of representatives of the minorities into the national elite on a disproportionate basis. Yet, the ability of the regime to overlay these cleavages with an organizational network linking the political center with strongpoints fostered in the village seems to have been crucial to holding this historically fragmented society together, containing the tendency to political mobilization on a communal basis, and, in the long run, to bridging the great urban-rural, communal, and center-periphery cleavages characteristic of old Syria. This has permitted the emergence of -- by Middle Eastern standards -- a relatively stable state. In this way, performance at the local level has had important consequences for the whole political system.

Second, while the Ba'th has certainly failed to carry out a revolution in the Syrian village, or even to significantly exploit it for the sake of one at the national level, it has left a by no means negligible imprint on the countryside. Its political organizations do appear to be too infected with traditional and bureaucratic behavior traits and too lacking in ideological discipline to mobilize the village population for social transformation. Nevertheless, they do appear to be effective enough to have given the regime a penetrative capability much superior to that possible through the conventional instruments of elite-mass linkage in the Middle East -- the classic bureaucracy and patron-client network. Moreover, its political organizations have helped permit it to carry out a serious program of social reform and economic change in the countryside. Ideology and party organization in Syria have made for a more effective state.

Nevertheless, the effort to build this state has had its costs. In doing so, the Ba'th has alienated important parts of the politically aware population which has refused to accept the claim of the Ba'th -- or that of the particular party faction ruling -- to sole power and legitimacy. This has seriously hurt the ability of the regime to enlist public cooperation in its development effort. Thus, in a sense, Syria has paid the cost of the effort to forge a Leninist system, without getting many of the advantages of such regimes.

What effect has Ba'th rule had on that other dimension of political development, participation? It would be difficult to argue that there has been a serious "participation revolution" in Syria. The big decisions which affect the little man -- war vs. peace, socialism vs. capitalism -- have resulted more from the ideological preferences and interests of elites, intra-elite conflict, and the need to cope with constraints and threats (e.g. defense against Israel or the need for greater investment) than from popular preferences articulated and aggregated through political institutions. The acts of a few commanders of military units often appear to have counted for more than those of thousands of less strategically-placed persons, and few institutional checks on elites appear to exist.

Does this mean that, in spite of all the talk about participation and "popular democracy" the Ba'th has created nothing more than another military-bureaucratic state where popular wishes count for nothing? Plausible arguments to the contrary can be made. First, it does seem that there has been a redistribution of power at the local level, and a widening of the arena of participation there. The Ba'th notion of "self-management" by locals is not entirely chimerical and does seem to mean local power and political experience for a still limited but larger number of persons than heretofore. Social change and political organization have created new political forces in the village competing with the old, have, as Harik argues for the case of Egypt, but perhaps more so, pluralized political life there. Further the mobilization initiatives of the Ba'th have broken through the "encapsulation" of the villager, displacing traditional "gatekeepers" and opening access to the larger political arena. The redistribution of wealth, spread of education, the greater personal independence of the peasant, all spell a wider and less asymmetrical distribution of the basic resources needed for political participation. Rigid stratification and segmentalism, sure depressants of mass participation in the political macro-arena, are being broken down in Syria; the masses, so emerging from the "cave" of non-participation cannot easily be wholly denied the sun. These changes, plus the creation of new political infrastructures, mean more direct elite-village access points, a larger number of activists than heretofore and a widening of the recruitment pool for elites.

Logically, these changes at the "base" should have repercussions -- on decision-making and elite responsiveness -- at the "top," hard though it is to trace or prove it. Perhaps greater activism at the base translates into both a greater need and opportunity for elites to use support there in intra-elite conflict -- for which something must be given in exchange. It can also be argued that leadership recruitment makes a difference for common folk, i.e., that having ex-villagers in high office is an improvement over the rule of landlords. Thus, if army officers play a dominant role in national politics, at least it is a peasant army, not an aristocratic or elite-professional force cut off from the people. And the former village socialization of the new elite as well as the persistence of its local connections may count for something in the decision-making process. On the whole, there seems little reason to doubt that the Ba'th experiment has led to a wider and more equal diffusion of political resources. Such change is very likely to have some informal, indirect, impact on elite decisions, and on the outcome of intra-elite conflicts -- in the end, on who gets what, the essence of politics. The Ba'th has made far less progress, however, toward the creation of a set of institutions -- commonly accepted rules of decision-making and leadership recruitment -- which could channel in an orderly manner the use of the political resources now more widely accessible to Syria's emergent mass citizenry. Until it does, the "crisis of participation" will remain on Syria's political agenda.

CONCLUSIONS: AN AUTHORITARIAN POPULIST REGIME

The political regime emergent in Syria falls short of the Leninist totalitarian model in its capacity to mobilize the population for modernization and social transformation. Yet, it is not simply the traditional Mamluk state in new clothes; those interpretations of the Ba'th regime which see it as largely paralyzed by traditional behavioral traits do understate the effect of its modernization drive. Nor is the Syrian regime a mere military dictatorship; those interpretations which stress its military-bureaucratic character, to the neglect of ideology and party organization probably underrate the scope of political participation in contemporary Syria. The intent of the foregoing argument is not to deny the repressive military bureaucratic or sectarian dimensions of rule in Ba'thist Syria, but to show that ideology and organization has given it another dimension. This dimension has made an important difference for both regime and village, enabling the Ba'th to organize a popular base and carry out social reform in local communities. The regime may thus perhaps be best conceptualized as "authoritarian populist:" authoritarian in its concentration and unrestricted use of political power, populist in many of the basic purposes to which this power has been put.

FOOTNOTES

1. The definitive ideological document on the Ba'th's strategy of political organization is National Command, Some Theoretical Points of Departure (Damascus, 1973).

2. Avraham Ben Tsur, "The Neo Ba'th Party of Syria," Journal of Contempory History 28 (1968): 165-175.

3. Robert Springborg, "Baathism in Practice: Agriculture, Politics and Political Culture in Syria and Iraq," Middle Eastern Studies, Vol. 17, No. 2, April, 1981, pp. 191-209.

4. Morroe Berger, The Arab World Today (New York, 1964) pp. 361-414.

5. Amos Perlmutter, "From Obscurity to Rule: The Syrian Army and the Ba'th Party," Western Political Quarterly, April, 1969.

6. Among the best sources on political developments at the center are: Tabitha Petran, Syria (London, 1971); Itimar Rabinovitch, Syria Under the Ba'th, 1963-1966 (New York, 1972), Nikolas Van Dam, The Struggle for Power in Syria (New York, 1979) and Michael Van Dusen, "Syria: Downfall of a Traditional Elite", in Political Elites and Political Development in the Middle East, ed., Frank Tachau (New York, 1975).

7.   Raymond A. Hinnebusch, "Political Recruitment and Socialization in Syria: The Case of the Revolutionary Youth Federation," _International_ _Journal_ of Middle East Studies, 11, 1980, pp 143-174 provides greater detail and documentation on the recruitment process.

8.   Parti Socialiste Arabe al-Baas, Commandement National, _Programme_ du _Parti_ Damascus, 1965 discusses the ideal party militant and his duties and lists various deviations which must be combatted.

9.   For example, the union has asked that investors be given licenses only on condition that they have fulfilled their contract obligations to sharecroppers, as certified by the local peasant union, that legislation be promulgated prohibiting the seizure of peasant crops for payment of debts to "usurers," that the state sugar factory pay more for sugar beets delivered to it by peasants, that the agricultural bank accept a sharecropping contract as sufficient collatoral for a loan, and that a third land reform be issued reducing the ceiling on property to that cultivable by the effort of a single family. (See e.g. _Muqararat_ _al-Mutamar_ _al-Thalith_ _lil-Ittihad_ _al-Am_ _lil-Falahin_ Damascus, 1970)

10.   For a more detailed discussion of and documentation on the peasant union experiment see my "Local Politics in Syria: Organization and Mobilization in Four Village Cases," _Middle_ _East_ _Journal_, Vol. 30, No. 1, Winter, 1976.

11.   "Local Politics in Syria," p. 6.

12.   On these village cases, see "Local Politics in Syria," and also my _Party_ and _Peasantry_ in _Syria_, _Cairo_ _Papers_ in Social _Sciences_, Volume 3, Monograph 1, Cairo, November, 1979.

13.   Kamil Ismail, _Die Sozialokonomischen_ Verhaltnisse der _Bauerlicken_ _Bevolkerung_ _im_ _Kustengebirge_ _der_ _Syrischen_ _Arabischen_ _Republik:_ _Eine_ _Suchung_ _im_ _Gebiet_ _von_ _As-Saih_ _Badr_ (Berlin, 1975).

14.   _Party_ and _Peasant_, pp. 48-49, 57-60.

15.   _Party_ and _Peasant_, pp. 49-55.

16.   _Party_ and _Peasant_, pp. 55-57.

17.   _Party_ and _Peasant_, pp. 60-63.

7
New Institutions and Processes in a Traditional Setting: Examples from Al-Karak, Jordan

Peter Gubser

Development from the top often involves the introduction of new institutions into traditionally-oriented societies. Critics frequently contend that the new institutions are ill-suited to the social, cultural and political constraints of these societies, and that these new institutions will not constructively contribute to the development of these societies due to these very constraints. The contention in this paper, however, is that the success/failure of new institutions is not as simple as the above criticism implies. To judge the potential viability and effectiveness of new institutions in local "traditional" settings, one must probe the level or state of development and change in any given society; one must examine the nature of the institution and its appropriateness for the functions which it is supposed to fill; one must look at the central government's commitment to the new institution and the manner in which the government expresses this commitment; also, if possible, it is quite valuable to view the evolving socio-political organization of the community and the history of the institution in order to see how the above factors alter and, in turn, affect the success or failure of the institution.

To demonstrate this approach, the author proposes to describe and analyze the experience of two of the new institutions which were introduced into the traditionally-oriented society of the District of Al-Karak, Jordan. The focus will be on the municipality and the agricultural co-operative, the former being established only 83 years ago and the latter starting in the 1950s. We will find that the success or failure of these new institutions cannot be arbitrarily posited, rather it depends on the very factors outlined above.

BACKGROUND

Al-Karak District of Jordan is located in the land area which abuts the southeast quadrant of the Dead Sea and stretches to the major north-south Amman-Aqaba road on the edge of the Syrian (or North Arabian) Desert. To the north and south, the district is cut off from its neighbors by precipitous valleys, the Wadi Al-Mujib and the Wadi Al-Hasa. The major land area and where the majority of the population resides is the central plateau region which averages 770 meters elevation. The district's capital, Al-Karak town, is located in the center of this high area on top of a small mountain. The balance of the people live along the edges of the steep valleys and in the low area on the edge of the Dead Sea. In the 1960s, the District's population numbered around 60,000, of which 8-9,000 were in Al-Karak town.

In the low area, precipitation is virtually nil. In the plateau region the average is 35 millimeters (mm) but with great variation from year to year with highs of 50 mm and lows of 10 mm.

The economy of the district is largely based on sedentary agriculture with some diversification appearing in recent years. The agriculture of the area is primarily of the dry land variety, wheat being the major corp. Barley, lentils, olives, melons and grapes make up the balance. In the low area adjacent to the Dead Sea, irrigation is employed to raise cash crops, mostly tomatoes and other vegetables. Sheep and goat raising, partially based on a semi-sedentary mode of livelihood, is the only significant form of animal husbandry.

Commerce, construction, services (including government services) and some small manufacturing make up the bulk of the balance of economic activity. In terms of employment of persons resident in the district, these secondary activities only absorb around one-third of the work force, the remainder being in the agricultural sector for most of the year.

With respect to income for the area, the phenomenon of emigration has become increasingly significant over the past two decades. In-country emigration assumed importance first. Karakis moving to Amman for jobs in the private or public sector, including the army, have provided a source of remittances for their families back in their villages and the town. Of more recent significance, especially post-1973, has been temporary emigration to Saudi Arabia and the Arab (Persian) Gulf countries Some Karakis go on fixed contracts arranged through the government while many others have arranged their own jobs independently. Whatever the case, most eventually send remittances to their families at home.

This emigration is considered to be a mixed blessing. On the one hand, it has provided greater income for the area. On the other, however, it has deprived the district - and in terms of out-country movements, all of Jordan - of skilled people and, at times, has caused disruption due to large-scale movements of a number of skilled people in one profession during a short period.

Turning to the socio-political characteristics of the district, one may consider the tribe and its segments to be the most important groups. Structurally, the tribe may be described as a corporate territorial group with pyramidal and segmentary qualities. Starting from the base of the pyramid, the smallest segments would be the nuclear and extended families followed by sub-lineages, sections and finally the tribe itself. These tribes vary in size from 3,000 members to a few hundred.

At the next level of the tribal system is a series of alliances. These are semi-permanent arrangements binding the groups together for relevant political functions. At the top of these alliances are two which encompass the large majority of the district's tribal population, the Eastern (Sharaqa) and Western (Gharaba) Alliances, the latter of which includes the Christians and is the most powerful. In recent decades, the importance of the alliances has declined as the power of the central government has grown. However, they still play a role in the formation of municipal councils, parliamentary elections and the distribution of government services.

Although other minority groups are present in the district, only two are relevant in the context of this paper: the Christians and Palestinians. The former, who are primarily Greek Orthodox, have lived in the town and district for many centuries, are organized into tribes similar to the Muslim tribes, and are part of the Western alliance. They are the sole residents of a couple of villages, share other villages with Muslims, and are a significant bloc in Al-Karak town. They constitute about ten percent of the District's population and thirty percent of the town's.

Before and after the turn of the century, a few Palestinian families, mostly from Hebron, moved to Al-Karak where most of them became merchants, traders and craftsmen. AFter the 1948 Arab-Israeli war a larger number of Palestinians took up residence in the districts. Two small groups settled in the rural area, becoming farmers. Another group, mostly from the Bir Saba/Gaza area of Palestine moved to the town where they eventually came to dominate the retail-commercial activity.

Another part of the structure in Al-Karak is the central government. From a general standpoint, it may be said that during the period between World War One and Two, the government presence in the district was confined to the basic infrastructure of the state (governor, police and courts) and minimal services (health and education). In the past three decades, most central government departments have opened local offices and a much greater level of services is increasingly provided.

In terms of district politics, again from a general stand-point, the expansion of the central government has considerably altered the basis of power. In the pre- and interwar years, a leader's position was largely dependent on his abilities and assets in the tribal and alliance context. In the subsequent period and in an evolutionary manner, a Karaki leader's position is becoming equally or even more dependent on his ability to deal with the central government, at the least to be able to operate without the government's hindrance and at the most to be able to participate in the allocation of resources in the government's hands.

THE MUNICIPALITY

The Municipality concept as employed in Jordan is essentially an alien import of a whole system. In Al-Karak District, its record is quite mixed. Only in the last couple of years can it be said to have finally worked effectively and this as a consequence of change in the society and adaptation of the institution since its introduction by the Ottomans in 1885. In summary, the following will indicate that: (1) traditional tribal relation- ships continue to operate in the selection of municipal council members; (2) the formalization of power, i.e., the establishing and filling of official and authoritative positions, did not conform to the traditional political style and the alien "modern" institution consequently did not adequately fulfill its prescribed functions; (3) as the society developed, the norms necessary for the successful operation of the new institution, as adapted, enjoyed more success; and (4) the role of the central government throughout the period was erratically crucial to significant aspects of the municipality's operations.

In terms of responsibilities, the municipality reflects the Western European model. The legal duties of the municipality and its governing council were and are to provide basic utilities, roads, town planning and some welfare. For these purposes it taxes houses and shops, charges for water and electricity, and collects sundry fees. The central government provides some regular financial aid and grants long-term credits for civic projects. Major projects, tax rates, resolutions and business other than daily housekeeping must be approved by the central government. This latter has been and is in the hands of the local governor (appointed by the central government from outside the district) and/or the Ministry of Municipality and Village Affairs.

Al-Karak Town - Early Period

When Al-Karak District was under the authority of the Ottomans (1890-1916) and Amir Abdullah's Amirate (1920-1950), the actual selection of Al-Karak town's municipal council members reflected two major factors: the power position of the tribes in the dis- trict and the tribal population in the town itself. Thus, although the Majaly, the pre-eminent tribe of the district and the leading member of the Western Alliance, have never had more than six or seven extended families resident in the town, except for a short time after a 1910 revolt against the Ottomans and after the recent 1976 municipal elections, a Majaly has always been head of the mu- nicipal council; and from 1918 to 1976 Duliwan Pasha Al-Majaly, one of the paramount tribal leaders and brother of Rafifan Pasha (the top leader of Al-Karak District until his death in 1942) held this position. On the other hand, the Habashna, a relatively weak tribe, has a larger proportion of the population of the town than any

other tribe and it consistently has a tribal member on the council.
The Christians, who form a significant proportion of the town's
population and are strong in the district (and are part of the
Western Alliance), claim consistently 2 or 3 of the 8 or 9 seats.
With respect to the major alliances, the Western Alliance, with one
quarter of Al-Karak town's population, rarely has had more than one
member. The Palestinians, invariably in the person of one of the
more established Hebronis (see above), are allotted one and occasionally two places, reflecting their numbers and economic
importance in the town. The semi-sedentary groups and tribes of the
district's periphery (who are not members in the two major Western
and Eastern Alliances), of whom there are very few in the town and
who lack power in the district, have never held a council seat.

For the earlier period, the data on the operation of the
municipality and its council is relatively scant. It does indicate
in general terms that before the late 1950s, although the council
did provide certain minimal municipal services, it was noted for
its desultory and mediocre performance. Its members used the
council as a means of gaining prestige, political in-fighting,
obtaining funds through petty corruption and allocating very
minimal resources. Also, very few of the important decisions for
the municipality were made in connection with this formal body, but
rather through one of the following three methods. First, a few of
the leaders, always including Rafifan Pasha (until his death) and
Duliwan Pasha, formulated proposals and presented them to the
council for formal approval. These discussions leading to
decisions would take place solely in the "traditional" tribal
contexts, usually leaving out significant segments of the municipal
council because they did not qualify to participate in this august
level of decision-making. Second, the central government, as part
of its general development program, submitted measures for which it
expected and obtained passage. Third, the more usual method was
for the district leaders (Majaly plus significant allies) and
central government personnel to work in concert, for their
relations with Amir Abdullah's government were usually excellent.

The Villages - Intermediate Period

Subsequent to King Hussein's ascension to the throne in 1951
and his establishment of firm authority after the tumultuous 1950s,
the central government eventually started taking a more activist
role in the rural areas, albeit with considerable inconsistency.
During this period, more municipal councils were established in
Al-Karak District. They have experienced a very mixed history,
with only a partially positive result in the most recent years. To
indicate the trends we will use a couple of brief case studies to
exemplify the evolution in the institution and the society.

In the large village of 'Ay and Al Mazar in Al-Karak District,
quite active political struggles, each with similar patterns, were
centered on the municipal councils which had been newly established
at the time. In 'Ay, a number of small tribes which traditionally

had been dominated by more powerful ones in the village attempted to gain the presidency of the municipal council in 1966. In the election, neither side won a clear majority and in the ensuing negotiations both were adamant in their claim to the council's top office. Unable to resolve their differences their hostility increased until it spilled into the streets, with members of rival tribes throwing stones and eventually shooting at each other. The governor of Al-Karak arrived the same day with a detachment of soldiers. He remained in the village for twenty days, but could not persuade either side to compromise. He then appointed a special committee with himself as president to run the municipality. In the 1967 national parliamentary elections, 'Abdul-Wahhab At-Tarawna, one of the successful candidates, whose tribe leads the Eastern Alliance which in turn controls the area where the village is located, turned the dispute into a campaign issue. Seeking the support of the traditionally dominant leaders in 'Ay, he declared that, if he won, he would have the council reconstituted and their man named as its president. After he was elected, he fulfilled his promise, but within six months, the losing faction felt itself oppressed and violence again flared up in the streets. The governor returned with another detachment of soldiers and again set up a new special committee with himself as president to conduct municipal affairs.

In Al-Mazar, the Qatawna and Nuwaysa have always been dominated by the Tarawna, leaders of the Eastern Alliance. However, because they are the second largest group in the village, the Qatawna felt that they had a right to the presidency of the municipal council in some form of rotation. The consent of the Tarawna not being forthcoming, the Qatawna's anger grew. Over and above these emotions, the Qatawna vociferously objected to a project formulated by the president of the council, 'Abdul-Karim at-Tarawna, and his supporters to open a new street which would necessitate tearing down a few Qatawna houses. Rancor turned to violence when King Hussein visited the district in 1968. The municipal council had decided to provide a large lunch for the officers of the King's guard, but it failed to do so. The Qatawna accused the Tarawna of destroying the honor of the municipality and of the village as well. As in 'Ay, the opposing sides started throwing rocks at each other, forcing the local policy to call in reinforcements from Al-Karak town. The governor used his office to try to re-establish good relations between the two tribes, but finding this impossible, he dissolved the council and replaced it by a special committee with himself at its head.

In both 'Ay and Al-Mazar, the disputes were caused by similar forces related to the change occurring in the district. The traditional minor tribal alliances are breaking down. In the period before any central authority was exercised in the district (pre-1880) and in the period before 1950 when central authority was weak, these alliances had a raison d'etre, i.e., they constituted a form of protection against stronger forces inside the district (in this case, the Majaly and their allied in the Western Alliance) and

outside the district (bedouin tribes and smaller semi-settled
tribes of neighboring districts). Thus in the more recent period
when no outside force to unity them existed, the minor alliances in
the village contexts split into their basic tribal groups. The
traditionally dominant tribes and their leaders are thus being
challenged by those over whom they had held sway. Some members of
the newly-educated group or stratum of Al-Karak district like to
explain this phenomenon in terms of class struggle. The
protagonists, however, see it solely as a struggle for political
power among the tribes. From another standpoint, with the
establishment of municipal councils in the villages, new objects
for political competition were created. Whoever controls the
council and its presidency is in a very obvious way recognized as
the leader of the village. Not only does the winner enjoy the
symbols of office, but he also has very real legal control over
village affairs. He has the commanding say in designing projects,
hiring men, and the disbursements of funds. Previously, rival
shaykhs claims superiority, but unless one could persuade his
opponent's followers to turn to him, there was little he could do
to prove his claim. Material resources in his hands were usually
minimal. But the president and members of a council possess
recognized symbols of power and control material benefits.
Finally, disputes degenerating into violence indicate that the
villagers have not yet adjusted themselves to these new forms of
competition and methods of distributing power and authority.

Al-Karak Town - Intermediate Period

Returning to the situation in Al-Karak town, one finds
continued frustration with the operation of the municipal council
in the 1960s, but due to developments in the town itself (primarily
the education of the population) the 1970s finally saw the
municipality taking firm root in the local context and the
potential that it may be able to perform its functions.

In the 1950s and 1960s with only occasional breaks, the
membership of the municipal council continued to be dominated by
the "traditional" political forces in Al-Karak. As in the former
period, it corresponds to the power balance in the town and
district, with a majority of members from the Western Alliance
(both Muslim and Christian), one or two from the town's minority
commercial groups, and one from the Eastern Alliance. The actual
choice of members was not made by town-wide elections as in Al-
Mazar and 'Ay, but by private negotiations among the various
political leaders. The Jordanian statute on municipal law (1955)
provides that if the number of candidates equals the number of
seats on the body, they shall be considered duly elected. Thus,
for example, when the 1966 council was formed, forty men entered
their names as candidates, but the town leaders and the governor
met, worked out a compromise among all sides, and obtained the
withdrawal of all but the required number to fill the council. The
two most powerful voices in these election agreements were those of
Duliwan Pasha Al-Majaly and, increasingly, of the governor.

Duliwan Pasha was the perennial president of the council and a major power in the Majaly tribe. The Majaly have long enjoyed a high standing with King Hussein and the central government; many from the tribe have held high positions in the civilian sector and the military. Equally, many have held important cabinet posts. As a consequence, Duliwan Pasha wielded considerable influence which he used partially to maintain the traditional balance and forces in the council. The governor may legally intervene in many of the affairs of the municipality and in the 1950s and 1960s felt it necessary to exercise this right with regard to both the selection

The predominance of traditional methods and criteria for choosing municipal council members in the contemporary period caused distinct difficulties in meeting the growing demands, needs and expectations of the town's increasing population during the period from the mid-1950s to the mid-1960s. In any political system there is invariably a difference between the qualities a man must have to win the political support of others in order to gain a specific office, and those necessary for efficiently carrying out that office's defined duties. In Al-Karak town, this problem became acute in the aforementioned period. Because the council members who were chosen on the basis of tribal leadership think and compete almost solely in terms of tribal politics and traditional prestige, and because the nature of traditional tribal relations has little in common with demands of municipal and civic development and construction, these men tended to have minimal aptitude and were usually ill-equipped to perform the work of councilors. The new demands of the town's growing and more education population caused frequent disputes within the council which stalemated its activities and often ended in its dissolution. Consequently, although the legal term of a council is four years, the average between 1950 and 1968 was only two.

To exemplify the above, the history of the council between 1962 and 1968 is presented below. In 1962 a new council, chosen by the traditional methods of compromise, was made up as follows:

Municipal Council 1962-4

Name	Alliance or Origin	Qualifications
Duliwan Al-Majaly	Western	Tribal leader
Ibrahim Al-Madadha	Western	Tribal leader
Ahmad Al-'Asasfa	Western	Civically active and tribal leader
Khalaf Al-Ma'ayta	Western	Tribal leader
'Ahmad As-Su'ub	Eastern	Tribal leader
Muhammad Zayn 'Abu Al-Faylat	Hebroni	Civically active and group leader
Tuma As-Suyagh	Western-Christian	Tribal leader
Ghassan Al-'Amarin	Western-Christian	Civically active
'Isa Al-Kuwalit	Western-Christian	Tribal leader

With only three men interested in civic progress, the council
proceeded in its usual inactive manner with considerable internal
bickering and devisiveness. In the spring of 1964, a flash flood
cut the water supply to Al-Karak town, forcing drastic rationing of
what little water was brought in by truck. The municipal council,
split as it was, took no action despite the crisis situation, until
finally the three civically active men resigned, causing its
dissolution. At this juncture, the governor intervened and
appointed a special committee to run the municipality. It was
composed of the following members.:

Special Committee 1964-6

Name	Alliance or Origin	Qualifications
Dulwan Al-Majaly	Western	Tribal leader
'Abdal-Wahhab At-Tarawna	Eastern	Tribal leader former MP, civically active
Sulayman Al-'Akasha	Western-Christian	Civically active
Muhammad Zayn 'Abu Al-Faylat	Hebroni	Civically active and group leader
Yusif Al-Habashna	Western	Tribal leader

As may be seen from the above list, the governor created the usual
tribal balance, but at the same time ensured control by civically
active men. 'Adbul-Wahhab At-Tarawna and Sulayman Al-'Akasha did
most of the work with steady support of Muhammad Zayn. Yusif Al-
Habashna attempted to block most projects while Duliwan Al-Majaly,
an octogenerian by this time, merely looked on. The committee
quickly re-established the water supply and reorganized the whole
system, water was delivered only to given points in each quarter of
the town, but by 1966, over 85 percent of the houses had their own
supply. The municipality's administrative staff was increased
three-fold, making services more readily available and more
efficient. Long-needed streets were opened and surfaced and the
municipal library was expanded. In two years, many neglected needs
were met.

In 1966, a new municipal council was chosen through
traditional negotiations, but also with strong intervention by the
governor. It appeared as follows:

Municipal Council 1966

Name	Alliance or Origin	Qualification
Duliwan Al-Majaly	Western	Tribal leader
Dr. Mahmud Al-'Alawy	Western	Civically active educated middle stratum co-operating with the establishment
Mahmud As-Su'ub	Eastern	Tribal leader
Mahmud Al-Habashna	Western	Tribal leader
Yasin Al-Mahadin	Western	Civically active
Myhammad Zayn 'Abu Al-Faylat	Hebroni	Civically active and group leader
Mikha'il Ash-Sharayha	Western-Christian	Civically active
Sulayman Al-'Akasha	Western-Christian	Civically active
Tuma As-Suyagh	Western-Christian	Tribal leader
'Abdul-Wahhab At-Tarawna	Eastern	Civically active

The tribal balance was kept, but civically active members were in the majority. However, one of these died and 'Abdal-Wahhab at-Tarawna resigned when he was elected to the national parliament in 1967, leaving the body equally divided between the two groups. The civically active members, frustrated by lack of what they perceived to be positive action, complained about the make-up of the council and seriously discussed its dissolution once again. However, due to the progress made under the previous committee, the council retained its form for the balance of the 1960s.

Apart from showing the disparity between the qualities required for becoming and for effectively serving as a councilor and the inappropriateness of an alien institution in a traditional, tribal-dominated society, this example also indicates three tendencies with respect to the role of the central government in the local context. Central authority through the office of the governor was becoming increasingly crucial to the conduct of local politics, especially as they relate to the new institutions (e.g. municipality) and changing demands form the population. Equally, the governor was pushing the direction of local politics towards reform which is exemplified by his forcing a balance in the council in favor of the civically active. Finally, the civically active men in this period were becoming dependent in practice and in their thinking on the intervention of the government to obtain their desires. Thus, in 1954 and 1964 the governor set up special committees to reform the municipality of Al-Karak town and in the late 1960s with the degeneration of the regular council once again, the civic activists started to pressure him to intervene a third time. However, they did not have the power of the Majaly tribe and Duliwan Pasha Al-Majaly in the central government, noted above, and consequently did not succeed as was the case in the 1966 crisis situation.

Al-Karak Town - Modern Period

The mid-1970s witnessed another change in the fortunes of the municipality, a change which was nation-wide in its scope and somewhat revolutionary in its impact. In the militarily-occupied West Bank, the municipal elections of spring 1976 brought to power a whole new group of men who may be described as much more educated (often in technical fields) and more "radical" in their politics. (Many openly support the Palestinian Liberation Organization, in direct defiance of the Israeli military authorities.) The traditional town leaders either had to take back seats on the council or were not elected at all. On the East Bank of Jordan, a similar phenomenon occurred in the fall of 1976. In council after council, a new group of men was brought to power, a group which is younger, much more educated (again many in the technical fields), and which contains many who were active in the officially-banned political parties during the tumultuous 1950s in Jordan.

This new wave was also reflected in Al-Karak town where the people elected a progressive, technocratic council made up of members of the educated middle stratum. The elections, which were preceded by a quite active period of campaigning and included advertisements by opposing electoral lists in Jordan's national newspaper, took place on November 17, 1976. The Minister of Municipality and Village Affairs promised honest and fair elections throughout the country. From all accounts, this tended to be the case and was certainly so in Al-Karak town.

Of the 1,445 registered voters (only males over 21 can vote), 80% turned out in the town. The successful list, the Solidarity Block, with the percentage of the vote each candidate received, appears as follows:⁵

Name	Percentage of the Total Vote	Alliance or Origin
Hamady Al-Habashna	76	Western
Mazin Al-Qasus	63	Western-Christian
Jamil Al-Mahdin	64	Western
Yunia Al-Madadha	69	Western
Fa'iq Al-Damur	67	Eastern
'Isma'il Al-Ja(abry	67	Hebroni-Palestinian
Rafiq Al-Sunna'	63	Western-Christian
Myhammad Al-'Alawy	64	Western
Average Percentage	67	

Most of the balance of the votes went to the opposing list which termed itself the National Bloc. A smattering of votes were picked up by independent candidates.

As may be noted from the above winning list (which consists of

progressive technocrats of the educated middle class), it is
balanced in the traditional manner with the great dominance of the
Western Alliance tribes (including Christians) and a
Hebroni/Palestinian. Notably, however, no Majaly is present on the
council. As indicated earlier, the Majaly tribe only has a very
few families in the town, but is very much the dominant tribe in
the district. The lack of a Majaly on the council chosen by free
election is a further indication of the erosion of the larger
alliances' political power in the town and district.

The opposing ticket, the National Block, was equally balanced
in the alliance, Christian and Palestinian senses. Also, at its
head, was a son of Duliwan Al-Majaly (then in his 90s, but Mayor
until this election), Bahjit Al-Majaly. This ticket essentially
represented the old guard and many of the traditional tribal ways
of conducting political affairs, despite the inclusion of some
younger, more educated individuals on the list.

A number of trends came together in the mid-1970s to allow for
this rather radical change in Al-Karak town and its municipality.
The traditional style of tribal authority has been gradually
breaking down as the central government has slowly come to the
fore, especially with its ability to distribute material benefits.
This is not to say major tribal leaders do not still have power in
the capital. They do, but they are increasingly exercising power
as much for their ability to deal within the norms prevalent in the
capital as for their positions within the tribe. A second parallel
factor is the growth of an educated group within the town. The
phenomenon is the fruit of extensive government efforts to provide
public education for the whole population. This educated group
started to have influence in the town in the 1960s. By the 1970s,
as it matured, it was in a position to take over control of the
town's municipality and dominate aspects of regional politics. (In
the 1967 parliamentary election, the last to be held in Jordan, one
member of this group ran for office. Although he lost in the
district, he polled more votes than any other candidate in the town
itself which indicates the growing importance of this group even at
that date.) It should be noted that this group is not the same as
the "civically active" individuals mentioned previously. The
latter were tribal leaders, etc. who could see beyond their tribal
affiliations and who attempted to work for the benefit of the town.
They essentially would be part of the traditional upper stratum.
The new group which came to power in 1976 does not belong to this
stratum (although a few are sons of it or from collateral branches
of it), but are of the newly-formed educated middle stratum.[4]
Not incidentally, some of the individuals on the successful 1976
list had been members of the officially-banned political parties of
the 1950s, notably the Ba'th Party, branches of which currently
rule Syria and Iraq. Most had joined the parties during their
youth while still in high school. Again most had dropped out by
the end of the 1950s or early 1960s as the government asserted
considerable control. Some served short periods in prison. They
thus had been activists in their youth, but conformed to some

societal and government strictures as they became older. A few
subsequently worked for the central government's offices in town.
That the central government and King Hussein allowed people with
such political records to run for and be elected to office is not
atypical. King Hussein has often appointed to positions of some
authority, individuals who had once erred in the eyes of the
central government. Thus, the central government neither put the
new group in power nor prevented it from obtaining power. But the
government did allow the change to occur.

From another standpoint, it is noteworthy to observe the
considerable change in Al-Karak town's society which has permitted
the new institution, the municipality, to be integrated into the
political system as an effective body. The key to this change is
the central government's provision of education to as broad a group
as possible. The products of this schooling by 1976 came to form a
significant percentage of the electorate. This growth in education
then allowed a new group to come to power through elections. A
major consequence of this is that as of the mid-1970s the
requirements for obtaining a position on the municipal council have
come to match much more closely the requirements for effectively
performing the functions of the position which should be contrasted
by the reversal of this condition in the 1950s and 1960s.

AGRICULTURAL CO-OPERATIVES

The purpose of looking at agricultural co-operatives is to
provide an example of another kind of outside institution
introduced into the local society. From this additional example,
one may be able to draw out more general trends about the ability
of a society to accept new institutions as it changes, and about
the role of the government in the process.

The basic program for agricultural co-operatives was set up in
1952 by the Jordanian Co-operative Organization (JCO), an agency of
the central government. The local branches are jointly controlled
by the membership and the central organization. The members elect
a governing committee which, in turn, chooses its own president,
secretary and treasurer. The JCO gives advice, and has the right
to exercise control over the branch's finances when it considers
this to be necessary. The funds are derived from four sources:
shares purchased by the members, members' savings, interest paid on
loans, and the JCO's resources. The individual co-operatives lend
money to their members for various purposes, e.g. irrigation
projects, curing sick animals, land clearing and improvement, and
the purchase of seeds and fertilizer. Because there were numerous
cases of individuals borrowing money and then using it for bride
prices and weddings, the JCO demands that money be lent only for
specifically-defined projects, and it carries out periodical
inspections to ensure that the funds are being employed properly.
The local branches may also carry out joint programs or projects,
such as co-operatives buying of seeds, fertilizers, and
agricultural implements, or amalgamating small, inefficient

landholdings and making them productive -- the subject of a case
study traced below.

Both at the village and district levels, the tribal leaders,
who were also often the usurers, resisted the formation of the cooperatives, for they feared, and with reason, the loss of political
control as well as financial benefit. As each new branch was
established, they attempted, often successfully, to gain control
over it. The local administration of the JCO located in Al-Karak
town has, however, been partially able to educate the members of
the local branches with regard to the desired functions and
purposes of the co-operatives and they, in many cases, have
eventually wrested control for themselves. Similarly, these same
tribal leaders continually put pressure on the central government
to curtail the co-operative program in Al-Karak, and, as a result,
the local office of the JCO was seriously understaffed in the 1950s
and 1960s. But the two Karakis who ran the office were both
energetic and highly dedicated and the extent of the co-operative
program's success is due to their efforts and that of the
participating villagers.

The mid-1970s witnessed a marked change in the JCO and its
brief from the central government. The latter, in its desire to
start bringing more benefits to the rural areas and to increase the
production of grain in the country, put renewed emphasis behind the
co-operative program. This was manifested by the provision of
considerably enhanced financing for the JCO so that it could
provide greater credits to the local branches and the appointment
of a new director-general who had high qualifications for the
position as well as influence in the decision-making circles in
Amman.

This renewed emphasis has resulted in the improvement of
ordinary activities of the local co-operatives, but it was not
sufficient to realize success in an experimental program. The
following case study will once again indicate the critical
importance of the central government in effecting the
success/failure of a new institution in the Al-Karak context.
Also, it will demonstrate the partial flexibility of the local
society as well as the crucial role of a district leader in the
arena of the capital's politics.

In the early 1970s, an international organization (IO) in cooperation with the Ministry of Agriculture decided to launch an
innovative agricultural experiment in a Jordanian village. The
basic concept, briefly, was to join together all of the village's
productive land, contour this land and set up bunds for water flow
control, and then have the farmers, under technical supervision,
farm it in a semi-collective fashion. By thus putting the land in
essentially one operating piece, ploughing, seeding, fertilizing
and weediciding in common would become necessary. The result, if
successful, would be significantly increased grain production using
dry-land farming techniques.

The original intention of the IO was to conduct the experiment in a district to the north of Al-Karak where average rainfall was higher, the society less "traditional," as the IO put it, and the likelihood of success supposedly greater. However, one of the leaders of the Majaly (termed Muhammad here) who has considerable power and authority in Al-Karak district and a high position in the capital, was able to have the project moved to Al-Karak district and, more specifically, to a Majaly village (termed here Qarya). Such influence is not unknown in developing countries (or developed countries), but it does often skew development efforts and creates suspicions in the minds of those who are the subject of development programs.

The venture was initiated in Qarya. The organizational base from the village's standpoint was the embryonic agricultural co-operative, but in actuality the village as a whole was involved because of the scope of the project. A series of co-operative/village meetings were held on the subject. At the early ones, only IO and Ministry of Agriculture personnel were present from the outside.

Initially, the general reaction in the village to the scheme was negative. The reasons, as expressed by the villagers, were: (1) a lack of understanding of the scheme; (2) fear of domination of their affairs by the government, especially with respect to land which was their sole source of income; (3) a dislike of the methods of the IO and Ministry of Agriculture officials whom they often considered to be insensitive and not respectful of local norms and concerns (e.g. the visibility of land demarcation, measuring land without permission of the owner); (4) on the part of some of the poorer families and other families which were in conflict with leading village families, there was fear that they would be further dominated or lose their land; (5) some felt that the village would not be able to sustain the co-operation necessary to carry on the scheme successfully.

At one point, these concerns caused the preparation of the scheme to come to a virtual halt. However, Muhammad came to the village and held a general council to further explain the scheme and allay fears. He also sent the message to the IO and Ministry of Agriculture officials to pay greater attention to local sensitivities. Largely due to his efforts in persuading the villagers and influencing the IO and Ministry of Agriculture, the project did go ahead with the co-operation of all relevant land holders except one. (Only 30% of village land came under the scheme. The balance of the land was inappropriate topographically.)

Consequently, the IO did contour the land and build bunds. Under the technical supervision of the Ministry of Agriculture and IO but solely funded by the IO, the land was prepared, seeded and fertilized in common. Harvesting was executed by each landholder.

For one year, the project was quite successful, grain production
was enhanced dramatically. However, by the second year, the IO had
pulled out its funding and personnel, leaving the expense of
technical management to the Ministry. The timing and amount of
fertilizer application was crucial to the complete success of the
project, but the Ministry did not provide the necessary technical
expertise leaving the villagers to decide for themselves. For lack
of expertise, they were unable to apply the fertilizer properly, so
the benefit from the exercise diminished radically. Slightly
increased production as compared to pre-project years did result
from the additional moisture due to the contouring and bunds. And
these, it is feared, will fall into disrepair without advice from
outside.

As may be noticed, the villagers with patient explication were
able to join together in the innovative project, based
institutionally on the co-operative. Crucial to this acceptance
was the role of a major tribal leader who had a position both in
the capital and the district. But also crucial for success/failure
was the sustained input on the part of the central government.
When it was available, given the other factors, success was at
hand; without it, failure was the result. As with the history of
Al-Karak town's municipality, a long-term effort is necessary
before a new institution or a new agricultural arrangement based on
a new institution can realize its potential.

SUMMARY

In each of the above examples related to the introduction of a
new institution into a "traditional" setting, one can draw out a
series of crucial variables which reflect on the potential
success/failure of the institution. First, social processes and
structures often do not automatically accommodate the introduction
of a new institution. Second, conversely, an alien institution's
norms introduced into a given set of relationships are not easily
accepted. The relationship and processes of a community may
dominate the institution to the preclusion of the alien
institution's formal rules. With respect to both parties, however,
the "traditional" community's and the alien institution's forms
both tend to alter, each somewhat accommodating to the other. This
process may, though, so distort the institution that it no longer
adequately performs its defined functions. Third, all of the
examples indicate the importance of the role of the introducer, in
these cases the central government and the IO. If the introducer
does not persist in its efforts at helping the institution take
root in the society and does not take into consideration the norms
of the society, the likelihood of failure is enhanced. Equally,
during the process of introduction, mediocrity of institutional
performance must be expected for a period until the society
develops to the point where the institution may be able to operate
effectively. Fourth, the latter brings us to the last point. In
some cases, the society may evolve in a manner so that the intended
functions of an alien institution may be properly executed. This

evolution may result from changes in educational levels and economic structure which are in turn reflected, over time, in socio-political changes.

Viewing the foregoing from another standpoint, throughout the paper it appears that there is sort of a stylistic dilemma: the presence of too little and too much government. On the one hand, in every city example, the role of government was crucial. It injected itself into each situation, largely in the sense of providing control. On the other hand, it equally appears that the role of the central government was usually not strong enough or sufficiently sustained to have the impact it seemingly desired. As the development process accelerates, this dilemma should change to read: the presence of enough and too much government. Thus, with the growth of government capacity and in the attempt to implement development plans, it is expected that the central government will have a greater and more sustained presence in the rural areas. On the other hand, though, despite the creation of local institutions for hypothetical local control, ultimate control and the planning function (which will direct local decision-making) will rest with the center. And because the development emphasis of the central government will presumably affect more aspects of the people's lives, its control and planning functions will form constraints on local authority which will be, and will be perceived as being, more limiting than in the past.

NOTES

1. The data on which this paper is based was gathered for the most part by the author in Al-Karak, Jordan during the year 1968 and, for the lesser part, while in residence in Amman, Jordan in 1976-77. Part of the material was published in my Politics and Change in Al-Karak, Jordan, London, Oxford University Press, 1973.

2. For a description of the educated middle stratum, see Politics and Change, op. cit. pp. 130-5, 174-7 and passim.

3. Al-Ray (Jordanian daily newspaper) November 19, 1976, p. 12.

4. See footnote number 2.

8
Local-Level Politics and Development in Lebanon: The View from Borj Hammoud

Suad Joseph

INTRODUCTION

The people of Borj Hammoud, Lebanon -- settling there as refugees from regional and international wars, economic dislocation and social discontent -- constructed strategies for survival in the early 1970s through family, patron-client and ethnic-sect associations. Having little sense of identification with either the municipality or the country, they lacked a sense of belonging to a social body coterminous with local or national political bodies. Development, for these people, meant the advancement of family, patron-client or ethnic-sect groupings.

In this paper I argue that these local-level development strategies emerged as a response to international, national and local systems of distributing resources. Some groups received international and national aid in settling in Borj Hammoud. The aid -- offered on the basis of "national" or ethnic-sect affiliations -- reinforced the form of political affiliation in the emerging Lebanese state. Formally sectarian, the Lebanese state allocated representation in government offices and distributed public resources on the basis of a legally defined distribution of religious sects in the country. An informal system of distributing public resources through patron-client relationships underpinned the formal structure. However, the informal system similarly channeled resources through intra-sectarian relationships -- although these relationship often were simultaneously familial. Local-level distribution reflected international and national systems. The consequence of these systems of distribution was to reinforce family, patron-client and ethnic-sect commitments and to undermine local or national civic commitments.

I will use Borj Hammoud to demonstrate the local-level development implications of systems of resource distribution. In the first part of the paper I will outline a theoretical framework for analyzing local-level development strategies. A summary of Borj Hammoud history will be followed by details of the development strategies of its residents and their responses to international,

142

national and local systems of resource distribution. The paper concludes by raising the theoretical implications for local development of the allocation of resources along family, patronage and sectarian lines.

THEORETICAL FRAMEWORK

Balanced development of a municipality requires that those who control public resources acknowledge joint membership in a socio-political body, encourage community-wide participation in public institutions and commit themselves to the advancement of the community as a whole. Such requirements for balanced development -- often not met in "developed" countries -- are even less in view in developing countries. Kin, tribal, patron-client, ethnic and sectarian affiliations in these countries compete effectively with local and national governments for the loyalties of citizenry. Rivalries undermining civic commitments among such indigenous groups often have been exacerbated or instigated by external powers. In the 19th and 20th centuries, for example, European powers used the Ottoman millet system to recruit clients -- thereby further politicizing ethnic-sect identities.[1] The superimposition by European powers of state structures over these primordial groups in the 20th century did little to evoke civic sentiment as the political systems formally or informally incorporated primordial organizations -- particularly ethnic-sects -- into national governance.[2] Lebanon -- with seventeen different religious sects legally recognized and formally incorporated into government -- is the most extreme expression in the Middle East of a sectarian state (Joseph 1978b).

While scholars have disagreed about the impact of primordial affiliations on Lebanon's development, they have concurred on their centrality. Edward Shils, for example, asserted that even though Lebanon was prosperous, primordial loyalties deterred its development as a civil society (1966). Elie Salem, on the other hand, insisted that Lebanon modernized precisely because of its pluralism (1973).[3] Despite the apparent conflict in their positions, these two -- as well as most authors on Lebanon -- shared the presumption that the Lebanese had a priori commitments to their families, patrons and ethnic-sects superceding civic loyalties. This view of Lebanon has been part of a long-standing scholarly orientation toward the Middle East and other non-Western regions.

Observers of these countries -- impressed with the apparent historical depth of such primordial groups -- often have explained their continuity and the related "underdevelopment" of civic commitments in terms of the strength of the moral and emotional bonds among their members. Political and economic organization, in that framework, becomes a consequence of social organization. However, I suggest that -- while the contribution of normative and affective aspects of these ties must be recognized -- the long-term reproduction of primordial groups requires reinforcement in political and economic arenas. The arena of such development is the historical conjuncture of international, national, and local conditions. The theoretical framework proposed in this paper for analyzing local-level development strategies stresses the interdependence of international, national and local systems and the interlocking of social organization and political economy. The framework is premised on the motion that people will tend to organize themselves in forms consistent with systems of resource distribution. From this premise, several predictions will be suggested in the remainder of this section concerning the impact of international, national and local conditions on development in Borj Hammoud.

International Conditions

Most Borj Hammoud residents had settled there following international and regional wars and economic and social turbulence. Those who immigrated following international or regional wars usually entered Borj Hammoud rapidly, in large numbers at once, lost access to their villages of origin, received international and national aid in resettling and, for a time, were offered Lebanese citizenship -- if they were not already citizens. Those who moved in as a result of economic or social discontent entered gradually, in smaller numbers at a time, retained access to their villages of origin, did not receive international aid and were not offered Lebanese citizenship. Within the suggested theoretical framework, two predictions can be offered concerning local development strategies in Borj Hammoud: Those unable to return to their villages and who receive international or national aid in resettling are likely to be more highly organized than those able to return home and not receiving aid. International and national aid, distributed on the basis of affiliations at the time of entry, will reinforce those affiliations to the detriment of civic commitments.

National Conditions

Borj Hammoud was taking shape as a municipality during the emergence of the modern Lebanese state. The means by which the Lebanese ruling class distributed resources channeled the manner in which Borj Hammoud residents organized themselves. The ruling class constituted the formal channels of state structure on a sectarian basis. Participation in the political system formally required membership in ethnic-sects. Informally, they distributed resources and services through patron-client relationships. Clients, however, were recruited from family groups within the ethnic-sect of the patron -- the informal system, consequently, upheld the formal. The prediction for local development in Borj Hammoud, therefore, is: The more that the ruling class, formally and informally, channel resources through family, patron-client and ethnic-sect relationships, the more those affiliations will be strengthened and civic commitments undermined.

Local Conditions

Once the immigrants settled, additional local variables affected their development -- their proportion of the local population, percentage of voters registered in the municipality, neighborhood concentration and representation on the municipal board. Their organizational development, however, was the most critical local variable. Organizational development is affected by the presence, character, complexity and degree of centralization of organizing agencies. Earlier, I suggested that those groups receiving aid would achieve a relatively high level of organizational development. Several predictions can be added in relation to the local conditions affecting strategies of development in Borj Hammoud: While all groups will attempt to organize in manners consistent with the systems of resource distribution, those which are formally organized will be more successful in obtaining access to resources than those lacking formal organization. In order to gain dominance over local resources, a group will have to produce a higher level of organization than those currently in control. The more complex and centralized the organizations, the greater will be the success in gaining access to resources. Since the predominate local systems of resource distribution will reflect the international and national systems, then the local system will similarly reinforce family, patronage and ethnic-sect forms of organizing. Those groups most efficiently mobilizing all three forms of organization will dominate locally. The above aspects of organizational development will manifest themselves in the level and nature of local power, group consciousness, social relationships and socialization, values, civic commitment and planning.

The implication of these predictions is that, as international, national and local agencies channel resources through primordial relationships or organizations recruiting through primordial affiliations, they subsidize the reproduction of the values, identities, commitments and institutions associated with such relationships -- in effect, subsidizing family, patronage and ethnic-sects. Given that some groups are likely to be more successful than others in obtaining resources, the consequent uneven development will reinforce a socio-political hierarchy based on family, patronage and ethnic-sects. Borj Hammoud was an example of just such a development.

BORJ HAMMOUD IN THE EARLY 1970s

Borj Hammoud occupies two square kilometers of land on the Mediterranean coast, five kilometers northeast of Beirut. From a population of a few thousand at the turn of the century -- 20,000 in the early 1940s -- it grew to claim about 200,000 residents by 1973 -- almost seven percent of Lebanon's three million.[4] In the early 1970s, Borj Hammoud was one of the most heterogeneous municipalities in Lebanon, housing Lebanese and Syrian Armenians (thirty-five to forty percent of the population), Lebanese Shi'a (thirty-five to forty percent) and other Lebanese, Syrians and Palestinians (twenty to thirty percent). The ethnic-sect diversity was enormous. The Armenians were divided among Armenian Orthodox (eighty to eighty-five percent of the Armenians), Armenian Catholic (ten to fifteen percent) and Armenian Evangelicals (five percent). Among the Lebanese there were Shi'a, Maronites, Greek Orthodox, Roman Catholic, Druze, Sunnis and other sects. The Syrians, while primarily Sunni included Syrian Orthodox, Maronites, 'Alawites and Kurds. The Palestinians were predominately Sunni, Greek Orthodox or Catholic.

The residents of Borj Hammoud were mainly working class, earning between four to six hundred Lebanese pounds a month. Most worked in Borj Hammoud or the nearby industrial areas. As a craft-production center, Borj Hammoud offered many jobs: leather works -- shoes, purses, belts, jackets; furniture, rug and tapestry factories; photographic works; a slaughter house; auto repair shops; cement, brick and clothing factories, bakeries and various other services. While most work places employed five or less people, three factories employed one to two hundred.

By standards of developing countries, Borj Hammoud offered many amenities. It was the only municipality in Lebanon to have built low-income housing; a stadium second in size only to the national stadium; and, by the late 1960s, street lights and public sewers. Daily, the municipality collected garbage and cleaned the streets, while municipal police and nightwatchmen patrolled the neighborhoods. The municipality maintained a full-time doctor, an ambulance service and free annual cholera and polio vaccinations. In 1969 forty-one doctors, twenty-four dentists, fifteen nurses, four midwives, one hospital, nine clinics, and thirteen pharmacies were registered with the municipality. There were three government schools and ten Armenian and thirty-eight Lebanese private schools. The municipality was well-connected by public transportation services to all parts of Lebanon, Syria and Jordan.

LOCAL-LEVEL DEVELOPMENT STRATEGIES IN BORJ HAMMOUD, 1970s

In the early 1970s, Borj Hammoud was a prime example of uneven development. Development strategies of the various residents ranged from the highly organized, institutionally elaborated and centrally controlled Armenians to the fragmented, disenfranchised and socially and politically isolated Syrians. In this section, I will give a brief description of the circumstances of each of the major groups at the time I did my research in 1971-1973.

During this period, Borj Hammoud was known as the Armenian municipality of Greater Beirut. The identification of Borj Hammoud with the Armenians was based on past Armenian numerical dominance and continued political control. Their continued control -- despite the change in population distribution -- was possible because of the highly organized nature of Armenian development strategies in Borj Hammoud.

Armenian development was characterized by a proliferation of complex ethnic-sect agencies controlled through a few central organizations. The Armenians boasted ten schools (all owned and run by churches, political parties and benevolent associations), six churches (four Orthodox, one Catholic, one Evangelical), four Armenian Red Cross neighborhood clinics, one large multi-service clinic, forty regional/village associations, seven Akhkadakhnam (church-related charity associations), two low-income housing complexes, an old peoples' home, a school for the blind and mentally retarded and numerous social centers, benevolent associations, and youth, cultural and sports groups. These were among the more than eighty-five Armenian service agencies in Lebanon. They also claimed nine of the fourteen municipal board positions, seventy-five percent of the voters registered in Borj Hammoud and twenty-eight doctors and eighteen dentists registered with the municipality.

These agencies were almost all controlled through the combined forces of political parties and churches. The Armenians were organized into three political parties -- Dashnag, Hunchag, Remgavar -- and three religious sects -- Armenian Orthodox, Armenian Catholic, Armenian Evangelicals. The Dashnag was the most powerful Armenian party in Lebanon and in Borj Hammoud. They controlled the Armenian Orthodox Church and most other Armenian organizations. While the two other religious sects and political parties operated their own schools, clinics, churches and the like, they submitted to Dashnag control of Armenian life in Borj Hammoud.

The other groups living in Borj Hammoud in the early 1970s contrasted sharply with the Armenians in their development strategies. With the exception of the Palestinians, most relied more on family and patronage rather than formal political parties or other ethnic-sect organizations to obtain services and political protection.

The Shi'a, although equal in numbers to the Armenians, had far fewer formal organizations. There were only three small clinics and one mosque for the 70-80,000 Shi'a in Borj Hammoud. All of their schools -- over twenty -- were owned and run privately by individuals for profit. Most of these schools were vastly overcrowded. The three local public schools which the Shi'a attended -- no Armenians and few Lebanese Christians attended these schools -- also were crowded and understaffed. Despite their large numbers only five percent of the Shi'a were registered to vote in Borj Hammoud. They had only one member on the municipal board and six doctors and two dentists registered with the municipality. There were no formal political parties among them. They relied on family-based patron-client relationships for political leadership and service. Because their leaders came from their villages, most Shi'a turned there or to village-based networks for brokerage, voting and job-hunting. They also returned there for spouse selection and marriage ceremonies as well as other social activities.

The Maronites, while relying heavily on family and patronage, built more of an institutional base in Borj Hammoud than did the Shi'a. One complex --extensively expanded in 1973 -- housed a rather large church, school and social activities center. There were several church-related and non-church related charity and social service agencies. Claiming twenty percent of the registered voters and four of the municipal board members, the Maronites were probably overrepresented in the municipality. Maronites from South Lebanon, Mount Lebanon and other regions tended to retain their voter registration in their villages of origin where their extended families and political leaders were based. Numerous political leaders competed among the Maronites for followers. Only one party -- the Kata'ib -- was well organized. In the early 1970s, the Kata'ib was actively mobilizing support in Borj Hammoud. Because of the political dominance of the Maronites in Lebanon, the Maronites of Borj Hammoud benefitted from the extensive Maronite organizational development in surrounding districts. Access to these agencies was primarily through family and patron-client ties.

Other Christian groups varied in their development strategies -- both building ethnic-sect institutions and mobilizing family and patron-client ties. The Lebanese Roman Catholics had built a rather large and well-reputed school-church complex with subsidiary services at the edge of Borj Hammoud. The Lebanese Greek Orthodox had a church, a clinic, and a charity organization. Syrian and Palestinian Christians -- lacking their own organizations in Borj Hammoud -- often made use of Lebanese Christian institutions. Most of the Lebanese Christians who had moved to Borj Hammoud after World War II maintained voter registration in their villages of origin and were oriented toward neighborhood Christian districts for services. Like the Maronites and Shi'a, their access to these agencies was primarily through family and patron-client ties.

The Palestinians had few organizations within Borj Hammoud other than the UNRWA school. However, in the adjacent Tell el Zaatar Camp, many formal organizations served them -- unions, clinics, youth groups, militias, and so forth. Since their primary political leadership was located in Beirut, most of the Palestinians were affiliated with one of the many guerrilla organizations and looked to those organizations for protection and services.

The Syrians, like the Palestinians were not Lebanese citizens. However, unlike the Palestinians, they had no unifying organizations. Their national identity did not overcome familial, regional and sectarian differences. They had no legitimate claims on public resources and no social service agencies were designed specifically for them. The Syrian Orthodox had their own church outside of Borj Hammoud; generally, however, Syrians used the institutions of their Lebanese co-religionists or friends. The Syrians often complained that they political leadership in Syria did not protect them or offer them services in Lebanon, despite the fact that there were half a million Syrians in Lebanon in the early 1970s. They took care of themselves as individuals and families by constructing extensive networks with kin, fellow villagers, co-religionists and neighbors who could give them access to Lebanese patrons and institutions. They were the most vulnerable of all the groups in Borj Hammoud.

The circumstances of the various groups in Borj Hammoud in the early 1970s was the outcome of the conjuncture of international, national and local conditions. The unevenness of the development was the predictable consequence of the manner in which the systems of resource distribution channeled development strategies.

INTERNATIONAL CONTEXT OF LOCAL-LEVEL DEVELOPMENT STRATEGIES

Foreign governments, international agencies, world transformations and regional changes directly affected the strategies and contributed to the uneven development of the people of Borj Hammoud. Foreign governments contributed to Borj Hammoud development not only through the channeling of resources but also in the movement of peoples -- at times through direct intervention. Until 1920, the area -- not yet incorporated into a municipality -- was the home of Maronite farmers. After World War I, following the Turkish massacres, the world powers resettled large numbers of Armenians in Lebanon -- many in Borj Hammoud. By the 1940s, Borj Hammoud had become overwhelmingly Armenian. With the creation of the state of Israel by the Western powers in 1948, many Palestinians and Southern Lebanese refugees moved northward to Borj Hammoud. More moved there in the 1960s, as south Lebanon became a war zone between Israel and the Arabs. Regional economic and social turmoil in the 1960s and 1970s additionally pushed many Christian and Muslim Lebanese and Syrians to the Greater Beirut area looking for jobs. Many also found themselves in Borj Hammoud.

International forces affected each group of Borj Hammoud immigrants differently. The Armenians were settled in Lebanon directly by world powers. Through the intercession of the French mandatory powers, they immediately were given Lebanese citizenship. With the help of international and national agencies, they moved into Borj Hammoud systematically, in large numbers and in a short period of time. Foreign monies and personnel helped them organize. Swiss, German, French, American, and English agencies helped them found the old peoples' home, the school for the blind and mentally retarded, social centers, clinics, schools, youth clubs, sports and benevolent associations, and many other agencies in other parts of Lebanon designed specifically for Armenians. With this assistance the Armenians organized regional/village associations, bought plots of land and built schools, churches and homes in each Borj Hammoud neighborhood.

Armenians from all over the world joined this effort to organize their countrymen in Lebanon. They participated in and affected strategy decisions made by parties, churches and other agencies in Borj Hammoud. Armenian organizations in Borj Hammoud became local arms of international organizations. Borj Hammoud became a world center for Armenian culture and social life -- often becoming a way-station for Armenians from Eastern countries heading for Europe or the Americas. Very quickly, Armenian life in Borj Hammoud took on a highly organized character and an international orientation.

Financial aid, jobs and social services were distributed to Armenians on the basis of their ethnic and sectarian affiliations. This international aid was channeled primarily through agencies controlled by churches and parties. Control of these resources strengthened the churches and parties, enhanced their organizational development and reinforced the ethnic-sect identities of the Armenians.

The Palestinians also felt the direct impact of foreign governments and international agencies. They too left their homes because of an international war and a redefinition of political boundaries by the world powers. However, unlike the Armenian case, regional and world powers led the Palestinians to believe they would return to their homes shortly. Most of the aid offered was to make temporary adjustments -- thirty years later, they are still considered temporary residents. Furthermore, when the Lebanese state offered them citizenship, national and regional leaders encouraged them to refuse. Most did -- it has not been offered again.

Arab and world powers have constantly intervened in the development of the Palestinians in Lebanon. Palestinians have been able to survive and maintain their cause as a people, in part, because of the flow of funds from external powers. However, much of those monies were for military development. Several Arab governments, for example, have used their resources to establish their own Palestinian guerrilla groups. Although the Palestinians were able to achieve a certain degree of organizational centralization through the PLO (Palestine Liberation Organization), the impact of competitive funding from foreign governments was to stimulate fragmentation. The consequent proliferation of competing organizations made it necessary for Palestinians to have patronage and political affiliation to gain access to resources.

International conditions affected the Shi'a quite differently from the Armenians and Palestinians. The Southern Shi'a had left their villages because the Arab-Israeli war destabilized the economy of the South. However, they, like Shi'a from other regions, were not considered war refugees by regional or world powers. Living in their own country, they had access to their villages of origin. They moved into Borj Hammoud gradually, as individuals or families and without the benefit of international or national aid. Organizations were not established to help them resettle and they themselves established few. Although many eventually purchased buildings -- especially in the Shi'a dominated neighborhood of Nab'a -- they continued to identify their villages as home. Maintaining patron-client relationships with their village-based zu'ama', political leaders, they obtained access to resources through personalistic ties based on family and patronage.

Like the Shi'a, the Lebanese Christians -- Maronite, Greek Orthodox, Catholic and others -- had Lebanese citizenship, were moving within their own country, could return to their villages of origin and retained primary loyalties to those villages. While the Christians had church-related organizations to serve them, none had a unifying party like the Armenians or an overarching political framework like the Palestinians.

The Syrians also came to Borj Hammoud gradually, as individuals or families and could return to their villages where they retained their primary loyalties. Like the Palestinians they did not have Lebanese citizenship; but, unlike the Palestinians, they had no international, regional or national organizations to protect them. However, they were very much affected be regional developments. As regional economies and market conditions fluctuated they were pushed and pulled between Lebanon and their homeland. Furthermore, since political relationships between Syria and Lebanon frequently deteriorated, the Syrians in Borj Hammoud periodically were harassed by Lebanese police.

Most of the residents of Borj Hammoud had moved there in the past half century under the duress of tumultuous international conditions. While most moved to Borj Hammoud in response to international turbulence only two groups received international aid. Consistent with the predictions made earlier in the paper, the impact of the international aid on the Armenians and Palestinians was to stimulate organizational development and to reinforce the affiliations and identities they bore at their entry to Borj Hammoud. By the early 1970s, the Armenians and Palestinians had the most developed group organizations and group consciousness of any of those in Borj Hammoud. While international conditions directly and indirectly affected all the peoples in Borj Hammoud, the impact was mediated by the merging Lebanese state.

NATIONAL CONTEXT OF LOCAL-LEVEL DEVELOPMENT STRATEGIES

The character of the Lebanese state significantly constrained the strategies available to individuals in Borj Hammoud. The ruling class -- with critical assistance from the French during the mandate period -- constituted citizenship on membership in one of the seventeen officially-recognized ethnic-sects. They allocated representation in government and distributed public resources on the basis of a legal definition of the proportions of the ethnic-sects in the population -- a population distribution never officially reassessed after the 1932 census, when the Maronites were held to be the largest single group, followed by the Sunnis, Shi'a and Greek Orthodox. Legitimizing themselves in terms of the state structure they erected, the political leader in the ruling class represented themselves in government as negotiators on behalf of their sects, rather than on behalf of a national citizenry. Underpinning the sectarian formal state structure, the ruling class leadership constructed an informal system of resource distribution mediated through personalistic patron-client relationships. These relationships -- built upon family ties within the ethnic-sect of the patron -- reinforced the sectarianism of the formal structure.

The Lebanese government became, in the words of Malcolm H. Kerr, a "broker" distributing "guarantees to the recognized factions coexisting in the country of the means to defend their minimal interests" (1966:188). The zu'ama' -- political leaders -- preferred to subsidize development programs through non-governmental, rather than governmental, agencies. Government monies were channeled into private agencies -- sectarian in personnel and clientele and controlled, directly or indirectly, by the zu'ama'. The state was deterred from initiating programs. National development planning was non-existent or ineffectual. The Lebanese state-managed in this manner by the ruling class -- could "carry out isolated individual acts, but no coherent program" (Kerr 1966:188).

The vacuum at the state level and the channeling of public resources through patron-client relationships and sectarian non-governmental agencies controlled by the zu'ama', reinforced the primordial affiliations rooted in family, patronage and ethnic-sects. There was a state, but no nation in Lebanon. The emergence of national loyalties was continually obstructed by an archaic ruling class attempting to reproduce the basis of its own existence. In the process, they reinforced social and political fragmentation and undermined the development of civic commitments.

In Borj Hammoud the government provided only three small public schools for the population of 200,000. There were no government hospitals, clinics, welfare agencies, libraries, employment agencies, and the like. Rather the government subsidized these same functions in the private sphere. That is, the tuition of students in private schools was paid, in part, by the government. Private hospitals, clinics, social service agencies, clubs, youth groups could and did obtain government subsidies for social service activities.

In order to obtain these government monies, individuals and groups usually had to have the patronage of a political leader within their own sect. Their strategy was to create organizations which would qualify for government monies, establish patron-client relationships with a leader in their own sect, and promise political support in return for the services granted by the patron. This method of channeling public development funds strengthened the position of individual political leaders, intensified the family and sect ties that led to patronage and undermined the development of national loyalties.

The local impact of this national system of resource distribution was to further the uneven development of Borj Hammoud. The Armenians, with their well-developed organizational structure designed along ethnic-sect lines, were well-situated to take advantage of the system. The subsidization on a ethnic-sectarian basis by the Lebanese state further reinforced the Armenian organizational development and reinforced their dominance -- and Dashnag control -- in Borj Hammoud. The Dashnag aligned themselves with right wing Christian parties -- the kata'ib in particular -- and received much support in return. The state, for example, supported the Dashnag take-over of Armenian institutions in Borj Hammoud by turning their backs on illegal Dashnag actions.

The Dashnag Party made its bid for Armenian leadership in the 1940s and 1950s. In a struggle with the Hunchags and Remgavars -- waged in many countries -- they began, in Borj Hammoud, by taking over the local Armenian Orthodox school boards. At times falsifying election rolls, threatening opposition voters and creating hoax miracles they were able -- with the silent backing of the Lebanese state -- to take over all the Orthodox schools and churches in Borj Hammoud (Joseph 1974). In the mid-1950s -- again with the silent support of the Lebanese government -- the Dashnag manipulated a spectacular take-over of the Armenian Orthodox Catholicossate (Kouymigian 1961).

Building on this organizational impetus, the Party elaborated its own organization -- party cells coincident with neighborhood organizations, youth groups, militias, and the like. In the early 1950s, they took advantage of the local superiority of their organizational development and successfully lobbied with the Lebanese government for the establishment of Borj Hammoud as a separate municipality. By the 1960s, they had consolidated their control over the municipal board.

The Shi'a, unlike the Armenians, did not have extensive sectarian agencies. Their ties to the state were through family-based patron-client relationships established through their villages. They gained access to resources through these relationships. This system reinforced the Shi'a connections to their villages, families, and patrons and undermined the impetus to become more politically organized in Borj Hammoud.

Like the Shi'a, the Lebanese Christians were connected to the state primarily through village and family-based patron-client ties. However, the sectarian organizations -- particularly those directly generated from churches -- were channeled through patron-client relationships primarily, but through sectarian agencies as well.

The minimal public services in Borj Hammoud forced the Palestinians to depend heavily on Palestinian agencies. They had the additional disadvantage of being considered a threat both by the state and the local municipality. Therefore they could not rely on national or local policy to protect them -- turning instead to their militias.

The Syrians were even more vulnerable than the Palestinians. Their existence was not recognized by the state or local government. Their strategy was to align themselves individually or as families with neighbors, friends or anyone who could offer them wasta, brokerage.

The consequences of the formal and informal national systems of resource distribution was many-fold. In terms of the predictions suggested earlier, the channeling of resources through primordial family, patronage and ethnic-sect affiliations reinforced identification with those relationships at the cost of civic commitments -- to either the municipality or the state. Additionally, these distribution systems encouraged competition among ethnic-sects for development monies, undermining national development planning. Furthermore, the political vacuum at the state level facilitated the concentration of local control in the hands of leaders committed primarily to their own ethnic-sect clientele, rather than to the community as a whole. In Borj Hammoud, these effects translated into an uneven development -- bolstering the development of the Armenians and the control of the Dashnags to the detriment of the development and power of other groups. The impact of the national system of resource distribution, however, like the international, was conditioned by local circumstances.

LOCAL CONTEXT OF LOCAL-LEVEL DEVELOPMENT STRATEGIES

The local conditions affecting the development strategies of the people of Borj Hammoud included the proportion of each in the population, their percentage of the registered voters, neighborhood concentration, and representation on the municipal board. Organization development -- presence, character, complexity and degree of centralization of the organizing agencies of each sector of the population -- was, however, the most critical of the local variables. The following sections discuss the manner in which organizational development influenced local power, legitimacy, group consciousness, social relations and socialization, values, civic commitment and planning among each group in Borj Hammoud. The uneven development -- of which organizational development was a reflection -- was a consequence of the conjuncture of international, national, and local systems of resource distribution. That conjuncture received expression in the evolution of a social ecology which significantly affected development strategies available to the different groups as they moved into Borj Hammoud.

Social Ecology and Local Development Strategies

The strategies adopted by those moving to Borj Hammoud was influenced by those already living there. A social-ecological succession had transpired -- each entering set of people carving a niche, shaped in part by the niches carved by others.

When the Armenians moved into Borj Hammoud after World War I, the local Maronites had a peasant social organization rooted in extended family relationships. The Armenians could have assimilated, accommodated at an organizational level like that of the Maronites or dominated by producing more advanced organizational forms. Assimilation was preempted by the combination of the heightened group consciousness among the Armenians following the Turkish massacres, the impact of the international aid distributed to them on an Armenian basis and the Lebanese state structure which incorporated them into governance on an ethnic-sect basis. Accommodation at a peasant-family based social organization was unlikely both because so many Armenian families were dispersed or destroyed in the massacres and subsequent migrations and because international agencies stimulated the development of complex ethnic-sect organizations. Given these conditions, the power of numbers and the legitimacy of their newly acquired Lebanese citizenship, the Armenians soon took control in Borj Hammoud by producing more complex and centralized organizational forms than either they or the Maronites had had at the point of their first contact. By the time other groups entered Borj Hammoud, the Armenians -- unified under the Dashnags -- had achieved such local dominance that none was able to challenge them successfully. For example, in the 1950s and again the 1960s, the Dashnags used their control of the municipal board to build low-income housing for Armenians with municipal monies. The Shi'a protested this discriminatory use of public funds. While the Shi'a were challenging -- through government channels -- the allocation of apartments in the second project, the Dashnags engineered a spectacular midnight take-over of the buildings -- presenting the protestors with de facto occupation.

The Palestinians also organized as Palestinians, but could not challenge the Armenian hegemony in Borj Hammoud. They were too few in number, lacking the legitimacy of citizenship, and were more concerned with the camps and return to Palestine. The presence of two strong Palestinian camps adjacent to Borj Hammoud repeatedly juxtaposed the Armenians -- aligned with the right-wing Lebanese Christians -- and the Palestinians. However, Palestinian intervention in Borj Hammoud was prevented by the tight control the Armenians had achieved long before the Palestinians arrived.

The Shi'a -- equal in numbers to the Armenians in Borj Hammoud -- had taken over other Greater Beirut suburbs. While they were, in some sense, the most likely challengers to the Armenians in the early 1970s, they were precluded from making that challenge. They did not have an organizational development capable of challenging the centralized and disciplined Armenians nor did they receive the assistance in Borj Hammoud which would help them produce more complex organizations. Their orientation toward their families and patrons in the villages additionally precluded effective mobilization in Borj Hammoud.

The Lebanese Christians arriving in the 1960s and 1970s had merged in some respects with the older Christian population. Perceiving the Palestinians and the Shi'a as a threat, their political leaders had aligned with the Armenians to establish a "Christian" force in the region. Newer Maronites gained some advantages because of the long-term residency in Borj Hammoud of other Maronites. However, the power of the Christians in Borj Hammoud had more to do with the power of Christians outside the municipality than their organization within.

The Syrians had the least options of all. The political system was overloaded by the time of their entry. Any attempt to organize as Syrians would have been regarded as a threat by the Armenians, Lebanese and Palestinians alike. They therefore adapted by remaining organized along family and village lines.

The Armenians -- moving in early, in large numbers, with citizenship and international assistance -- had achieved the most complex and centralized organizational development. Subsequent groups had to accommodate to Armenian local power. The historical social ecology therefore conditioned the organizational development and power of each group.

Power and Local Development Strategies

Organization means power. In Borj Hammoud, power was in Armenian hands -- more specifically, Dashnag. The highly organized character of Armenian life had simplified the Dashnag centralization and enhanced their power. Dashnag control of Armenian life involved control of schools, churches, voluntary association, and the like. Decisions made by the party affected practically every aspect of Armenian life. Their ideology was taught in the schools, party calls, and youth groups. Their social conceptions penetrated the churches, voluntary organizations and family life. Their development philosophy was implemented by the municipality and charitable agencies.

The power of the Dashnag was reinforced by their relatively disciplined militia. Young men were recruited and trained on a regular basis. In addition the party hired "enforcers" for special jobs. With the combined forces of the milita, enforcers, and the broad range of institutions under their control, the Dashnag exercised a high degree of implementation power.

In the early 1970s, no group in Borj Hammoud matched the organization, centralization and power of the Armenians. The Palestinians and Lebanese Christians established organizations, including militias. Neither, however, at that time, had consolidated under a single leadership. Their different agencies often struggled over conflicting notions of communal development.

Those with compatible ideas did not have enough power to carry out their programs.

Family, patronage and village-based organization characterized all the groups in Borj Hammoud. Among the Shi'a and Syrians, however, these forms of organization existed almost to the exclusion of others. Consistent with these organizational forms, development among them was fragmentary, informal and familistic.

The organizational development of the Armenians facilitated the centralization of control under the Dashnag. Given this control, particularly of the Church, the Dashnag acted as a legitimating force behind Armenian development strategies.

Legitimacy and Local Development Strategies

For development strategies to gain popular support, they require the sanction of legitimating institutions. The Dashnag -- through their control of the Armenian Orthodox Church, the church-run schools, the municipality and other agencies -- achieved a legitimacy unparalleled by other groups. Mobilizing the lobbying function of the institutions they controlled, they could gain popular acceptance, among Armenians, of practically any program they advanced.

Other groups in Borj Hammoud had greater difficulty in legitimating their programs. The Kata'ib worked with the Maronite church but neither, in the early 1970s, had attained popular support comparable to that of the Dashnag and the Armenian Orthodox Church. The PLO, although popular, was too faction-ridden to achieve uncritical public legitimacy among the Palestinians. No organization even approximated such popular legitimacy among the Syrians or Muslim Lebanese.

The organization and legitimacy of the Dashnag was based on and allowed the reproduction of a social coherence that other groups in Borj Hammoud did not experience. This coherence expressed itself in the emergence of a group consciousness.

Group Consciousness and Local Development Strategies

For historical reasons connected to their minority status, the Christians more than the Muslims in Lebanon, established formal organizations geared toward the production of group consciousness (Joseph 1978a). Among the Christians in Borj Hammoud, the Armenians, in particular, expressed a heightened degree of group consciousness. Their political parties and churches for almost a century had campaigned for the establishment of an Armenian state. Armenian schools for generations taught children they were Armenians first and foremost. Their loyalties were to Armenia and Armenians. Centralized Dashnag control, therefore, built on a pre-existing group consciousness and intensified it.

158

The Maronites in Borj Hammoud, while not as aware of themselves as the Armenians, shared a Maronite consciousness that was the by product of Maronite dominance in Lebanon. Additionally the Kata'ib Party and Maronite Church were actively organizing among the Maronites to intensify the Maronite identity.

The Palestinians in Borj Hammoud had a notion of themselves as Palestinians. Numerous organizations worked among them to develop national consciousness. However, their identification as Arabs complicated the development of Palestinian identity. Furthermore, the struggle over organizational centralization among them deferred the production of a coherent self-conception.

Given their position in the local and national social hierarchy and the discriminatory popular stereotypes, the Shi'a struggle to create positive group self-definitions was difficult. Imam Musa Sadr's Association for the Deprived was working toward this end. It had had little impact, by the early 1970s, in Borj Hammoud.

The Syrians in Borj Hammoud similarly did not manifest positive group conceptions. They could not develop strategies for themselves as a group because they did not exist positively for themselves as a group. They existed for themselves only negatively -- by their shared alienness in Lebanon.

Power and legitimacy had enhanced group consciousness among the Armenians. The Palestinians and Maronites were moving in that direction. The Shi'a and the Syrians, while not unaware of the issues, had a difficult struggle to achieve positive group definitions. The question of group consciousness was centrally connected to social relationship and the socialization process.

Social Relationship, Socialization and Local Development Strategies

Consciousness is usually an expression of the social relationships to which people are committed. To change consciousness, one must change the set of relationships that produce and reinforce people's conceptions (Gramsci 1971). The institutions which control socialization -- by shaping individuals' relationships and conceptions -- are critical to social development. As a consequence, change agents -- churches, parties, states -- often struggle to dominate these institutions.

Among all the groups in Borj Hammoud, family was a strong vehicle of socialization. It was powerful, in part, because it represented vital social relationships. It mediated critical social, economic and political needs and shored up the moral content of personal life. The family not only controlled socialization, but also continued to affirm the individual's sense of identity throughout his or her life (Joseph 1982).

Only among the Armenians in Borj Hammoud did the family have a strong competitor as an agent of socialization. The Dashnag Party so systematically controlled the schools, churches, youth clubs and cultural associations that they effectively participated in the socialization of the young. The Dashnag also worked directly with families to reinforce their conception of the Armenian community.

The churches were important in socializing the Lebanese Christians but did not parallel the combined power of the Dashnag and the Armenian Orthodox church. Palestinian political groups were important socialization agents in the camps, but less so in Borj Hammoud. Lebanese, Palestinian and Syrian Muslim religious organizations were involved in the socialization process, but not as systematically as the Armenian. Among all these groups, family was the prime agent of socialization.

Social relationships and the socialization process in Borj Hammoud reinforced family identification, above all else. Organizations which either penetrated family structure or recruited from family relationships, in effect, mobilized the moral idioms of family relationships to legitimate other relationship. The Dashnag had succeeded in penetrating Armenian families. Lebanese Muslim and Christian churches and political leaders recruited their clientele through family relationships. In the process the parties, political leaders and churches capitalized on and helped to reproduce the values embedded in those familistic relationships.

Values and Local Development Strategies

Development is often defined in terms of the emergence of universalistic values. Values, however, are an expression of the social relationships in which they are embedded. Individuals in Borj Hammoud were evaluated by who they were and who they knew. If particularistic values predominated in Borj Hammoud, it was because those values expressed vital family and family-like relationships. While the Armenians had made inroads into the family, they -- like all other groups in Borj Hammoud -- built on family morality to inculcate other values. The centrality of family morality and values constructed from family-like relationships significantly influenced the development of civic commitments in Borj Hammoud.

Civic Commitment and Local Development Strategies

Local development strategies are influenced by a sense of belonging and commitment. Commitment to a place is usually an expression of commitment to social relationships in that place. For individuals to have a sense of commitment to where they live, they have to feel they can participate in shaping its future and that their actions on behalf of their city will improve their own lives and the lives of those significant to them. They need to see themselves as connected to power and to each other as part of a social whole.

This was impossible in Borj Hammoud. The conditions of social and political existence did not elicit identification with the municipality. There was little sense of pride in Borj Hammoud. Primary loyalties were elsewhere. The social body was fragmented. Despite the existence of the municipality as a political body, there were no effective public forums for community-wide participation. Political participation was channeled through the same avenues as public resources -- family, patronage and ethnic-sects. The low civic commitment was exaggerated by the large numbers of people who were refugees, did not have citizenship or for other reasons considered Borj Hammoud a temporary residence. The social fragmentation and the lack of commitment to Borj Hammoud manifested itself in unbalanced development planning.

Planning and Local Development Strategies

Planning requires a sense of clientele or community. Borj Hammoud, though, did not exist as a social body for local decision-makers. To whatever extent planning was implemented, it was for the decision-makers' own families, political clients or ethnic-sects.

The Armenians were the only group whose leaders self-consciously planned for group advancement. The Dashnag coordinated planning with the churches, schools, voluntary organizations and several international agencies which continued to work among the Armenians. They based their development plans on a relatively coherent policy aimed at maintaining Armenian cultural distinctiveness, improving the Armenian standard of living and providing Armenians with intellectual and technical skills for geographic and social mobility.

To achieve these development objectives, Armenian institutions stressed Armenian history, culture, and language at the expense of Lebanese or Arab history culture, and language. They emphasized English and French above Arabic. They established agencies to help Armenians emigrate and find jobs abroad. They built low-income housing to extract Armenians from Arab neighborhoods and to improve their standards of living. Armenian agencies, additionally, cooperated with each to deliver medical, social, cultural, and other services.

Only the Palestinians approximated the Armenians in long-range planning. However, that planning was aimed at the camps and only secondarily affected Palestinians in Borj Hammoud. Political and religious groups planned for the Maronites, with some degree of cooperation. Planning for other Christian groups was also mainly through religious institutions. The agencies working with the Shi'a worked on a first-aid basis. No organization planned for the Syrians.

The power, public legitimacy, and group consciousness among the Armenians had made long-term planning for them possible. Other groups manifested only minimal approximations of planned development. Consistent with the predictions made earlier in the paper, the Armenians -- more formally organized, having more complex and centralized organizations, and producing a higher organizational level than other residents at their point of entry into Borj Hammoud -- were more successful in gaining access to local resources than other sectors of the Borj Hammoud population. Other groups gained access to resources as well -- by organizing themselves in manners consistent with the systems by which resources were distributed to them. The Armenians, however, mobilizing family, patronage and ethnic-sect organizations in a more efficient fashion -- through complex and centrally controlled political and social organizations -- had achieved a near monopoly on local resources. The uneven development resulting from the conjuncture of international, national and local conditions affected local power, group consciousness, social relationships and socialization, values, civic commitment, and planning in Borj Hammoud.

While the Armenians successfully planned for themselves and other gained access to resources by various means, no one planned for Borj Hammoud as a social whole. Like the Lebanese state, Borj Hammoud did not exist for its population as a social whole. Like so many municipalities in both "developing" and "developed" countries, it was bound together more by political geography rather than social commitment. It is not that development did not occur in Borj Hammoud. Rather, the question is, development for whom and for what.

CONCLUSIONS: LOCAL-LEVEL DEVELOPMENT STRATEGIES -- FOR WHOM, FOR WHAT

Local-level development strategies must be evaluated in terms of whom they benefit and their impact on the social body. Borj Hammoud had many of the accoutrements of development. There were many service agencies, low-income housing, clinics, schools and the like. The residents, however, benefited quite unequally from these projects. The clientele of the municipality was clearly the Armenians. The strategy of the Armenian leadership was to improve the standard of living of their own people and isolate them from the remainder of the population. In this context other residents had to fend for themselves through their families, patrons, and ethnic-sects. The development strategies of each group was a predictable and rational response to international, national and local systems of distributing resources over the past century.

The theoretical framework I have proposed in this paper argues that the reproduction and political relevance of forms of social organization is tied to systems of resource distribution. Formal or informal incorporation of primordial groups into governance gives them access to public resources. In so far as international, national and local decision-makers channel resources through primordial groups, they subsidize their reproduction. Conversely, in order to maintain or expand themselves in state societies,

primordial groups must gain access to resources. To the degree
that they are successful, their members will experience development
through primordial affiliations -- primordial loyalties will be
heightened, civic commitments undermined. Given that some groups
are likely to be more successful than others in obtaining
resources, development will be unbalanced.

While Borj Hammoud was an exaggerated case in some respects,
in others it manifested the general problems of uneven development
in Lebanon. It is not that Lebanon did not develop or that the
Lebanese were uncommitted to development. On the contrary, Lebanon
was highly developed by world standards and the Lebanese highly
committed to development. However, the means by which they could
participate in their own development were channeled by systems of
resource distribution which had evolved through the interplay of
centuries of local, regional and world conditions. The resultant
socio-political fragmentation produced a political vacuum at the
state level and an illusion of local-level control.

Lebanon was caught in a paradox. On the one hand, balanced
development requires the emergence of sense of a shared socio-
political life, active participation in the polity on a community-
wide basis and commitment to the advancement of the community as a
whole. On the other hand, these phenomenon are the consequence of
balanced development. Like other paradoxes, it seems as though one
has to have balanced development in order to develop in a balanced
manner.

Lebanon, ironically, may have had the historic possibility of
living out the paradox. It was a prosperous country with a highly
educated citizenry -- all sectors of the population had benefitted
in some respects from its rapid growth after World War II.
However, it was burdened with an archaic ruling class invested in a
system of resource distribution no longer suited to its urbanized
and cosmopolitan population. The ruling class, in attempting to
reproduce the conditions of its own existence, reproduced and
reinforced the social fragmentation. Additionally, Lebanon was
burdened with an historical role at the nexus of regional and
international political struggles which also contributed to the
internal socio-political fragmentation.

The Lebanese state now only barely exists. Ethnic-sect
hostilities are far greater than they have been ever since the
formation of the modern state. People are even more dependent on
family and patronage than they were before 1975-76 civil war. And,
not surprisingly, the old zu'ama' are still in power.

While the intensification of family, patron-client and ethnic-
sect loyalties is a consequence of the current war; it is, at once,
the evolving consequence of international, national and local
history -- a history in which systems of resource distribution have
helped to reproduce and reinforce primordial affiliations to the
detriment of civic commitments. The people of Lebanon actively

participated in the construction of their own lives; however, they did not share a sense of joint citizenry or commitment to a common socio-political body. The evolution of such civic commitments continually had been preempted. In the end, the price for this fragmentation was paid not only by the people of Borj Hammoud, but by all those who lived in Lebanon.

NOTES

1.   The millet system was the Ottoman system of governance. In this system taxes were levied on the basis of ethnic-sect affiliation. Matters of personal status -- marriage, divorce, inheritance -- were legally delegated to religious courts. In this manner ethnic-sect groups were incorporated into government.

I use the term "ethnic-sect" to reflect the ethnic as well as religious sectarian divisions in Lebanon. While sectors of the population -- such as the Armenians -- considered themselves national groups, in the context of Borj Hammoud they acted primarily as ethnic-sects. The Palestinians -- partly because of their lack of Lebanese citizenship -- presented different problems, some of which will be addressed in this paper.

2.   While the Middle East has had a long history of indigenous state formation, the current state structures are as much a consequence of European intervention as of local history.

3.   For other works examining sectarianism in Lebanon, see Binder (1966), Smock and Smock (1975), Harik (1968), Suleiman (1967), Joseph (1978b).

4.   It was impossible to obtain accurate figures on population distribution in Borj Hammoud. The main reason was that ethnic-sect affiliation was a critical basis for allocating public resources. The Armenians controlled the municipality, even though they no longer were the majority. A new census might have fueled the discontent of the Shi'a who -- although about equal to the Armenians in Borj Hammoud -- received little of the municipal resources. Borj Hammoud reflected the national situation in which, by the 1970s, the Shi'a had become the largest single sector of the population but, legally, were ranked third.

164

REFERENCES CITED

Binder, Leonard, ed.
    1966   *Politics in Lebanon*. New York: John Wiley and Sons.

Gramsci, Antonio
    1971   *Selections from Prison Notebooks*. New York: International Press.

Harik, Iliya F.
    1968   *Politics and Change in a Traditional Society, Lebanon 1711-1845*. Princeton, N.J.: Princeton University Press.

Kerr, Malcolm
    1966   "Political Decision-Making in a Confessional Democracy." In: Leonard Binder, ed. *Politics in Lebanon*. new York: John Wiley and Sons.

Kouymjian, Dikran
    1961   "The Recent Crisis in the Armenian Church." MA Thesis. American University in Beirut.

Joseph, Suad
    1974   "The Politicization of Religion in the Emergence of the Lebanese State: A Study of the Armenian Schools in Borj Hammoud." Middle East Studies Association Meetings. Boston.

    1978a   "Muslin-Christian Conflicts: A Theoretical Perspective." In: Suad Joseph and Barbara L.K. Pillsbury, eds. *Muslin-Christian Conflicts: Economic, Political and Social Origins*. Boulder, Colo.: Westview Press.

    1978b   "Muslim-Christian Conflict in Lebanon: A Perspective on the Evolution of Sectarianism." In: Suad Joseph and Barbara L.K. Pillsbury, eds. *Muslim-Christian Conflicts: Economic, Political and Social Origins*. Boulder, Colo.: Westview Press.

    1982   "Family as Security and Bondage: A Political Strategy of the Lebanese Urban Working Class." In: Helen Safa, ed. *Urbanization in Developing Areas*. New Delhi: Oxford University Press.

Salem, Elie Adib
    1973   *Modernization Without Revolution. Lebanon's Experience*. Bloomington: Indiana University Press.

Shils, Edward
    1966   "The Prospects for Lebanese Civilty." In: Leonard
                Binder, ed. Politics in Lebanon. New York: John
                Wiley and Sons.

Smock, David R. and Audrey C. Smock
    1975   The Politics of Pluralism, A Comparative Study of
                Lebanon and Ghana. New York: Elsevier.

Suleiman, Michael
    1967   Political Parties in Lebanon, the Challenge of a
                Fragmented Political Culture. Ithaca, N.Y.: Cornell
                University Press.

9

Ta awun Mahwit: A Case Study of a Local Development Association in Highland Yemen

Richard Tutwiler

"The aeroplane descended and regarded Iknaf Square, and from it Al Ayni addressed the populace. Then the aeroplane descended and regarded al Dubr, and from it Al Ayni tumbled to the terrace."

This children's verse records a nearly disastrous visit in July 1974 made to the remote provincial capital of Al Mahwit by the Yemeni Prime Minister Muhsin Al Ayni and other dignitaries. Fortunately no one in the Government helicopter was killed when a sudden gust of wind overturned the machine and threw it to the ground, but the crash and rescue severely dampened the festive mood of the occasion. The trip had been made, in part, to officially open the first vehicular road connecting the town with the main San a - Al Hudayda highway. Although the ceremonies were indefinitely postponed, the significance of the road was ably demonstrated when the shaken and wounded officials were evacuated by automobile to a San a hospital.

The fifty-six kilometer track, called the Jabal Turba road, has had a tremendous impact on the people who live on the steep mountain slopes of Jabal Al Mahwit and its surrounding areas. In the words of one leader whose village is directly served by the road, the coming of the road "taught the meaning of life" to the people and "changed the world one hundred per cent." In permitting automobiles and trucks to carry people and goods into the highlands, the road has irrevocably changed the region's social and economic character. Ease of transport has resulted in the increased movement of people and has stimulated a boom in local construction and merchandizing activities.

Partially as a result of the introduction of outside

The author wishes to acknowledge the partial support provided by the Southwest Asia and North Africa Studies Program of the State University of New York at Binghamton for fieldwork in the Yemen Arab Republic.

commodities (both Yemeni and foreign produced), the expansion of economic opportunities, and the improved access to the outside, the townsmen and rural tribesmen of the province have begun to seek employment and business opportunities in Yemen's cities or abroad. Similarly, the road has encouraged closer communication between local government officials and their ministries in San a. The most frequent travellers on the road are migrants leaving the area and returning with great bundles of gifts and consumer goods purchased with their wages. Less frequent, but no less noteworthy, are Government civil servants and messengers travelling to San a, Al Hudayda, or destinations within the province. Finally, the road facilitates social interaction among the localities. This is important to families whose members are often scattered over large distances of difficult mountainous terrain.

These economic and social changes became apparent after the road was completed and regular vehicular traffic was established. However, other significant changes occurred in local social organization and public life long before the visit of the Prime Minister. These changes were the result of a handful of Mahwiti citizens who worked to articulate local priorities and organize the major implementation effort needed to marshal the resources needed to construct the road. While the Prime Minister's visit publicly proclaimed the road's importance in linking Al Mahwit to the rest of Yemen, the visit also acknowledged the accomplishments of the local organization which had overseen the project's completion. This newly formed institution, which had initiated the road project, mobilized popular and governmental support and taken responsibility for construction was the Qada Mahwit Development Cooperative.

The Qada Mahwit Cooperative was a new element in the existing social structure, a public institution with the expressed purpose of using local resources to undertake greatly needed development activities. After completion of the Jabal Turba road, the cooperative undertook a host of other projects. Following the visit of Muhsin Al Ayni, the Cooperatives' relationship with the people of Al Mahwit and with the Yemeni Government went through a series of changes, and the scope and nature of its activities correspondingly altered.

This essay describes the evolution of the Al Mahwit Development Cooperative (locally known as Ta awun Mahwit) from its origin in local public service organizations up to August 1978. The discussion explores the history of the cooperative movement and its role in the social organizations of Al Mahwit town and its surrounding region. Finally, the relationship of the Al Mahwit Cooperative to the central Government is examined in the context of national development goals. The discussion proceeds in three sections. The first describes the history of the institution and its activities. The second concentrates on the patterns of recent social and economic analyses the problems faced by the Cooperative and its future prospects.

THE HISTORY OF TA AWUN AL MAHWIT

Soon after the September 26th, 1962 overthrow of the Yemeni monarchy in San a, a number of prominent Mahwiti citizens resolved to petition the infant republican government for help in constructing a road between Al Mahwit and the newly completed asphalt highway between the port of Al Hudayada and the capital of San a. These men were landowners, merchants and administrative officials who represented a cross-section of local leadership.

Since the area possessed few financial resources and locally available qualified engineers or heavy construction equipment, the leaders hoped that the revolutionaries in San a would build the entire road using government resources and expertise. Not unexpectedly, the new regime was unable to give the Mahwiti proposal serious consideration. The new rulers in San a had displaced a feudal-style monarchy and inherited a governmental machinery without any significant civil administrative system or infrastructural base. The republican government had no Ministry of Public Works and no Highway Authority which could implement the road project.

The first representative of the new Yemen Arab Republic arrived in Al Mahwit in 1963 to help organize local government administration, but the continuing civil war against royalist forces kept San a's limited resources stretched, and communication lines to the provinces were frequently cut. A non-strategic road project was far beyond the capacity of a government that was never sure from day to day which territories it controlled and which were in Royalist hands. The government reply to the Mahwitis was that it supported their objective and that if Mahwit continue to show loyalty to the Republic then San a would implement the project when the political and financial situation allowed.

Undaunted by the lack of material support from San a, in 1968 the Mahwitis began to organize for local implementation of the project. Before the revolution the town of Al Mahwit and a number of villages in the area possessed informal welfare associations which collected monetary contributions from citizens and kept the money in common funds administered by local leaders. This resource was used in cases of emergencies to buy food for families whose crops failed, to provide medical treatment for sick or wounded villagers, and to assist in meeting blood money and court payments when appropriate. In 1968 the heads of the largest welfare associations in the qada of Al Mahwit[1] met and formed a loose confederation which would utilize the collective resources of the associations in the implementation of the road project.

This confederation formed in 1968 was in no sense a formal organization. It had no constitution, nor did it have an official name. The member associations were scattered throughout the five districts of the qada and the relations among them were tentative at best. Each association was represented in the confederation by its leader, who usually was the <u>shaykh</u> of a village, clan, or uzla (sub-district).[2]

Joint meetings were held infrequently and the confederation, like its constituent association, lacked a permanent administrative staff. The association leaders did, however, elect an overall president who was empowered to act as their representative in dealings with the central Government. The first president was a prominent member of a well established clan of landlords and religious experts (quda) in the town and district of Al Mahwit.

This confederation, called variously the Qada Mahwit Cooperative, the Qada Mahwit Association, or simply Al Sanadiq, "the treasuries," achieved little of a concrete nature in its five-year existence. Nevertheless, it served as a forum for the discussion of regional development priorities, provided further evidence to government authorities of Mahwiti concern over the importance of the road project, and demonstrated a willingness to commit local resources to development activities.

The confederation did manage to achieve a consensus over the eventual alignment of the road to Al Mahwit. It was decided that the road should leave the paved highway at a weekly marketplace called Khamis Bani Sa d, proceeding north along wadi Sari' to another market called Al Jum a. From here it would leave the populated areas and climb up to Al Mahwit town by the most direct route possible. This route ran up a long rocky ridge called Jabal Turba to the strategically placed village of Hijrat Unbir. From Unbir, the road would climb to Mahwit town, which sits high on the southern slopes of Jabal Al Mahwit. The road was to be fifty-six kilometers in length and would climb from an altitude of approximately 500 meters at Khamis Bani Sa d to 2100 meters at Al Mahwit town. The confederation's plan called for construction entirely by hand, using dynamite to blast away large boulders and rock faces where necessary.

Acceptance of this plan was the birth of the Jabal Turba road and marked the establishment of the Mahwit Cooperative as a significant local institution. Once the plan was accepted by local leaders, work began to the easier section of the road running through the wadi floor. This construction efforts, overseen by the confederation, proceeded slowly from 1970 until 1973 when a series of events significantly altered the nature of the development movement in Al Mahwit. In 1973 the qada's of Al Mahwit and Al Tawila were separated from the province of San a and were joined together in the new province of Al Mahwit with the town of Al Mahwit as its administrative center. Once Mahwit was recognized by the government as an independent province, the town and region became eligible for substantial ministerial services and government funds. In the same year, the first governor of Al Mahwit was appointed and arrived from San a to serve as the top administrative authority and central government representative in the province.

This year also marked the beginning of close cooperation between the central government and the numerous local development associations which had been formed during the previous decade throughout the country. In March of 1973, representatives of ten local associations met in San a under the auspices of the Ministry of Youth, Labor, and Social Affairs and agreed to coordinate their efforts and follow general policies to mutual advantage.[3] This goal of forming some kind of national organization was favourably received by both the government and by other local associations. On June 25th, 1973, delegates from twenty-six local associations held the first general assembly of the Confederation of Yemeni Development Associations, or CYDA. This general assembly's first act was to elect the emerging national politician and a prominent member of the San a Development Association, Ibrahim Al-Hamdi, as its first president. Under Hamdi's leadership, CYDA approved a constitution, established formal political and financial ties to the government, and actively sought assistance from foreign donor agencies.[4]

After the establishment of CYDA and the opportunity of government financial support, the Qada Mahwit Association applied (with the new governor's support) for a membership in CYDA. CYDA and the Ministry of Social Affairs sent a team to Mahwit to supervise the election and establishment of an administrative committee for a re-organized Qada Mahwit Cooperation Development Association, which would qualify for both CYDA membership and government funds.

By the end of 1973, the new Qada Mahwit Cooperative was established and functioning, working closely with CYDA, the Ministry of Social Affairs, and the governor of Al Mahwit Province.[5] Although the Cooperative now had a formal legal structure and institutional ties to the government, its membership and leaders were essentially the same as those who founded and led the original confederation of welfare associations. Moreover, the immediate goals of the cooperative remained the same, and work on the Jabal Turba road was intensified as the government, and, in particular, the governor, threw their weight behind the Cooperative's efforts. The completion of the road project in the spring of 1974 was the result of close coordination among the Qada Cooperative, the governor and the citizenry.

The system of communal labor contributions which has been used in the majority of Cooperative sponsored projects is called the ja ish system. In recruiting labor for the road, the cooperative first surveyed the uncompleted portions of the road with the help of local people and made estimates of the required labor. The Administrative Committee and local leaders then decided how many man-days of labor were needed, and divided this number by the number of adult men in the community to determine each man's contribution. Individuals not present, or unwilling or physically unable to contribute their own labor, were required to provide an alternative sum of money. Community leaders - a Cooperative member, Shaykh or Amin (village notary) - coordinated the local labor contributions, and the governor supervised the overall effort.

During the final push to complete the road, ja ish labor teams from the entire qada travelled to the work site and lived in makeshift camps by the road. Through CYDA and the governor's office, the Cooperative arranged to rent bulldozers from the Ministry of Public Works in San a. After the ja ish teams blasted away the rock faces and cleared the initial track, the bulldozers widened and smoothed the road surface until it was ready for vehicles.

Money to rent the bulldozers, buy diesel fuel, and pay the operators came from two sources, Cooperative central income (zakat taxes and municipality funds), and cash contributions from villages along the road. This system of raising funds, when central government sources were added, was to become the method for the financing of cooperative projects undertaken after the Jabal Turba road.

The social, economic, and political impact of the road on Al Mahwit has been indicated briefly above. This link to the rest of Yemen has enabled Mahwitis to establish and maintain frequent contacts outside the region, particularly in the cities of Al Hudayda and San a. These contacts have served to facilitate directly ties among culturally and economically diverse individuals and groups. The road has forever broken Mahwit's isolation, and has done much to change Al Mahwit's reputation as the "forgotten province" of Yemen.

The Jabal Turba road and succeeding road projects inaugurated the "era of the Toyota truck" in Al Mahwit, and these rugged four-wheel drive vehicles have replaced donkeys and mules as the area's principal form of transportation. Since the road's completion, the entire range of commodities available in the larger cities can be either brought in to Al Mahwit, and the number of shops in the town has more than doubled since the Prime Minister's visit in 1974. Moreover, in the rural areas served by the road, villagers have begun to open road-side shops to serve both travellers and nearby communities. Once weekly market places are becoming small towns with permanent shops open daily to serve customers who travel along the road.

In political and administrative terms, the road link firmly established Al Mahwit as a viable provincial capital. Regional rivalries among the various districts were temporarily overcome in the efforts made by the governor and Cooperative to bring the road to the provincial capital. Following the road's completion the San a government established in Al Mahwit numerous offices representing ministries, and national agencies. The Saudi Arabian projects office in San a contracted to build a modern school in the town, and the Kuwaitis granted funds for a hospital. As part of the plan to modernize Al Mahwit, the governor and the Cooperative began taking steps to electrify the town and nearby hamlets.

The successful completion of the Jabal Turba road marked the establishment of the Mahwit cooperative as a viable local institution which commanded significant local resources (zakat taxes and political support) and had working relations with national institutions (the governor, CYDA, and various ministries). The Cooperative's role in the social organization of the region had changed from that of an informal forum for the presentation of the ideas of local notables to a legal entity with a constitution, administrative structure, yearly income and clear responsibilities to the people of Al Mahwit and the government in San a . Through the mechanism of the Cooperative, public works projects meant to benefit the population at large had been moved from the arena of the national government into the local political arena.

Before the re-organization of the Cooperative in 1973, such infrastructural projects as roads, water systems or schools were undertaken in two different fashions. At the village or hamlet level, wealthy notables often constructed public facilities such as cisterns or mosques in order to gain influence, prestige or religious merit. Larger projects such as roads were initiated by government authorities in order to extend their influence in rural areas. The Cooperative did not replace these two functions, nor did it incorporate them directly, but it provided a mechanism whereby communities could plan local projects and be reasonably assured of receiving help in implementation beyond strictly local capacities. As the activities of the Cooperative became more important at the town and village level, the position of local representatives in the General Assembly became increasingly influential and emerged as a new political role beside those of Shaykh and amin.

The Cooperative's entrance into the areas of public politics put new strains on its organizational structure and resources. The administrative committee found itself swamped with petitions to undertake projects throughout the qada . In particular, the people in the districts of Hufash, Khabt, and Milhan resented the fact that they had contributed substantially to the building of the Jabal Turba road which ran through Bani Sa d and al Mahwit, but there were no plans for similar qada-wide efforts in their own areas. Similarly, many of the communities in Al Mahwit district itself argued that they labored on the road, but had received no direct benefit from it since it did not serve their areas. Once these people realized the benefits that a road could bring, petitions for other road projects began to flood the cooperative's office at Al Mahwit. On the political side, the representatives from the more remote areas accused the members from Al Mahwit of being unfair in setting Cooperative priorities and allocating funds. During the year between the completion of the Jabal Turba road and the summer of 1975, the Cooperative found that regional dissatisfaction and the centralization of development activities in Al Mahwit town were making it increasingly difficult to implement the original three-year plan drawn up in 1973.

During the same period, the relationship between CYDA and the central government was changing. CYDA's president, Ibrahim Al Hamdi, had also become Chairman of the Command Council which headed the republic government. Hamdi's regime was in the process of instituting a program of wide-ranging reforms which, he hoped, would de-centralize decision making and, at the same time, give local leaders more responsibility in managing local affairs. As part of this program, called the 13th June Corrective Movement, the government and CYDA devised a new administrative structure for local Cooperative Development Associations which, in effect, made each district in the country responsible for its own development activities.[6]

These developments in San a were timely for the represen-tatives of the dissatisfied districts in the Qada Mahwit Cooperative. They proposed that the Qada Cooperative be disbanded in favor of the establishment of independent nawahi cooperatives which would have control over the allocation of resources originating in their own areas.[7] After much discussion, in-cluding consultation with the governor of Mahwit, the administrative committee sent the re-organization proposal to CYDA, asking for permission and help in setting up five new and independent cooperatives in place of the Qada Cooperative. CYDA and the central government readily agreed to this proposal and sent a team to the province to supervise the elections for and organization of the new cooperatives in Al Mahwit, Bani Sa d, Khabt, Hurash, and Milhan. By the end of 1975, these cooperatives were organized and beginning to plan and implement their own development projects, each with a revised list of priorities.

Each new Cooperative had an administrative structure similar to that of the old Qada Cooperative. The basic membership consisted of a General Assembly elected on the basis of uzla representation and the division of the population into constituencies containing a maximum of five hundred adult men. For example, the General Assembly of Al Muhwit Cooperative contained forty-one representatives with each uzla in the district electing one to three men, depending on how many adult men lived in the uzla. Elected from the General Assembly and responsible for the day-to-day affairs of the cooperative was an Administrative Committee of seven men. The officers of this committee were minimally, the President of the Association, the General Secretary, and a Treasurer/Accountant.

The majority of the new cooperatives continued to be run by the same personalities who had been involved in the Qada Cooperative. These men generally came from prominent landowning families within their respective districts, but the primary qualification was previous involvement in self-help activities at the district level and a commitment to the local population (no matter how informal) to get on with the task of implementing the projects which the people sought.

The one exception to this rule of past leadership was in the Al Mahwit Cooperative. The leading personality in the Qada Cooperative movement did not enter the elections for the new president. Instead, he was nominated to represent all five new cooperatives in San a as a member of CYDA's national adminis- trative committee. In his place, a farmer from an uzla neighboring Al Mahwit town was elected president of Ta awun Mahwit. AFter five months in office, however, this man died in a car accident while visiting the neighboring province of Hajja. A new election was held, and a young man from the town of Al Mahwit became the new president.

After the demise of the Qada Cooperative and the elections to the new district cooperatives, each administrative committee was faced with the task of drawing up a new three-year plan for approval by CYDA and the central government.[8] Sectoral sub- committees were formed from members of the cooperative general assembly, and they then visited each uzla in the district. Priorities and project needs for each sector (roads, water, education, and health) were determined on these visits, and the final plan was prepared from the sub-committee reports. These plans, of course, varied from cooperative to cooperative. In most areas, roads were first priority. In Al Mahwit, however, proportionately more attention was given to cooperative support of the town's hospital, school and electrification project.

As Ta awun Mahwit began to implement its new three-year plan, certain inadequacies in planning and organizational strength became apparent. Many of the originally elected members of the general assembly left Al Mahwit either to work in Saudi Arabia or to study or take employment in San a and Al Hudayda. Thus they were not available to help in the implementation of projects planned for their communities. Another problem was that many communities were dissatisfied with the projects slated for their areas under the plan. In particular, a number of villages to the west of the Jabal Turba alignment wanted to construct an alternate route to Al Mahwit which would directly serve them. Their argument carried considerable weight for, though the new alignment would be five kilometers longer and involve considerable expenditure of money and labor, it would serve a much greater population and would link up with new roads under construction by the Hufash and Khabt cooperatives.

The new leadership of Ta awun Mahwit agreed to proceed with this proposed project, called the Jabal Taraf road, although its implementation presented a number of serious problems. In part, these problems were technical and financial. Because of the split into district cooperatives, the Al Mahwit Cooperative had considerably fewer financial resources to command in 1976 than the

Qada Cooperative had in 1974. Also, the Jabal Taraf road clearly needed to be planned by a qualified road engineer who could evaluate the practicality of the alignment which the different villages were proposing. Apart from these issues, there were political complications threatening the Jabal Taraf road project. The road had become a point of contention in a local power struggle between one faction representing young men who had returned from Saudi Arabia and who wanted to open the way for commercial activities and another faction representing a family with large landholdings who felt threatened by both the loss of their influence and the appropriation of some of their valuable qat-producing land for the road's right of way. Finally, the Ta awun Mahwit realized that it would be necessary to get material help from a number of the other cooperatives in building the road.

Acceptance of the Jabal Taraf road project was the biggest challenge yet faced by any cooperative organization in Al Mahwit province, and it put the ideology behind the concept of a "development cooperative" up against the reality of environmental and social conditions in the region. Due to the commitments of a number of men in the Cooperative and a number of fortunate events the Jabal Taraf road was built during 1976 and 1977 and has now replaced the Jabal Turba road as the principal artery in the western half of the province.

Ta awun Mahwit first met with the leadership of the Bani Sa d, Hufash and Khabt cooperatives to discuss ways in which the four associations could join forces in building a new principal route to Al Mahwit town. This meeting took place in early 1976 at a marketplace called Suq Al Quta situated on the border of the four districts. During the Quta meeting, the representatives from Al Mahwit managed to forge an agreement in which all four cooperatives would coordinate their road projects and would act together in requesting support and material help from CYDA and the central government. Through a campaign of letterwriting and official visit to San a, this alliance of cooperatives was able to obtain the services of two Irish volunteer road engineers and their CYDA counterparts who toured the area for a month and planned roads in the four districts (and in Milhan). Among the roads planned was the Jabal Taraf road. The districts of Bani Sa d, Hufash, and Khabt agreed to take responsibility for constructing the road section between Khamis Bani Sa d and Al Quta . From there, the Al Mahwit Cooperative would build the road to Al Mahwit. Also from Al Quta, Hufash and Khabt undertook to construct roads to their respective government centers. With the realization on of these projects, the province capital of Al Mahwit would be tied by road to the administrative sub-centers of Hufash and Khabt. Following the report to CYDA made by the Irish engineers, the Al Hamdi regime presented to the cooperatives of the province a heavy caterpillar bulldozer as a gift to be used in road construction. After discussion and consultation with the governor, it was decided that the bulldozer should be used first on the Jabal Taraf road

project.   The other cooperatives would wait their turn to use   the
bulldozer in their districts.[10]

Once   actual   construction   work   got   underway,   the   local
political   and   economic issues over the road became public.   The
landlord   faction   so   strongly   opposed the road that   they   were
prepared   to   use violence to block its passage through   the   areas
they   controlled and in a number of armed confrontations along   the
completed   sections of the road a few people were shot and   several
cars   destroyed. Apart from the issue of the road's alignment, the
faction   supporting   the road felt economically threatened by   the
landlords.   These young men were returned migrants who hoped   to
invest   their savings in the transport business by buying   vehicles
which   could deliver freight to their own and nearby villages.   On
their   side,   the landlords recognized the increasing influence   of
these   young   men   and   saw   them as not only   an   economic but   a
political   threat in the villages which they controlled. As if   to
substantiate   these   fears, the returnees had entered a   successful
candidate in   the   recent   Ta awun Mahwit elections,   and   their
representative   had been a member of the official delegation   which
went   to San a to request help for the road project from CYDA   and
President Al Hamdi.

The   administrative   committee of the Al   Mahwit Cooperative
reacted to   the violence over the Jabal Taraf road by turning   the
matter   over to the governor and the provincial security force   for
arbitration.

When the landlord faction took the measure of arresting people
involved in the incidents, the governor issued an order   arresting
the   leaders   of both factions, summoning them to Al Mahwit   for   a
trial,   and   releasing   the   men arrested by the landlords.   The
central   government, at the governor's request, sent a committee to
investigate   the   entire situation, and after a series of meetings
this committee sent a report to San a.

During this time, the governor was himself transferred to
another   post outside the province. Action on the case was delayed
by   the   two succeeding   governors,   but because of the   prompt
government   intervention, there was no longer any serious local
opposition to the project's implementation.

The road was opened in the summer of 1977 and has all but
replaced the Jabal Turba road as Al Mahwit's link to the cities and
the   principal   factor   in   the region's economic growth.   The
leadership of Ta awun Mahwit clearly views this road as   its
greatest accomplishment to date. Government support for the
cooperative's activities has proved to be a stimulus for other
communities   of   the   district   to   actively   seek   cooperative
sponsorship of their own projects.

During the period of the Jabal Taraf project, an institution
was   organized by CYDA and the local cooperatives which was to   act

as a mediator between the individual cooperatives and the government. This institution was called the Coordinating Council fo Local Development Associations (Majlis Al Tansiq). The Tansiq was essentially a committee composed of the presidents from each cooperative in the province. From among these members a General Secretary and an Assistant General Secretary were elected. The governor of the province served as the President and chief executive officer of the Council. Unlike the cooperative themselves, the Council was allocated funds by CYDA for the hiring of a permanent, professional staff which, along with the elected members, were responsible for collecting and officially publishing the five year plans of each cooperative. These plans were incorporated in a single province-wide development program, and the Council was empowered to seek funding and logistical support for the cooperatives as a group and as individuals. Thus when the bulldozer was given to the province, the Tansiq became responsible for assigning it to specific projects and arranging for its care and maintenance by individual cooperatives. As part of its liaison role, the Council takes an active part in securing the Zakat taxes and other government monies for its member cooperatives.

The Coordinating Council also acts as a court of appeals and as a mediator between cooperative officials and the citizens who take an active part in local development projects. Specifically, the Council receives complaints concerning the arbitrary or inappropriate expenditures raised in communities for local projects. This common problem, which is not unlike the issue which split the original Qada Cooperative, has been recognized by CYDA at the national level, and Council officials spend a great deal of time working towards the formation of responsible uzla or village cooperative committees which will work with the district cooperatives and also manage money raised in local contributions.

Finally, the Council has been active in giving logistical support to member cooperatives. Council employees are especially active in giving cooperative officials on-the-job training in managing account books and the proper handling of official communications. In at least one instance the Council provided organizational support in the establishment of a new district cooperative in the province.[11]

Taken as whole, the cooperatives of Al Mahwit have achieved significant accomplishments since 1975, particularly in road construction. Although no cooperative has attempted to asphalt a road, the regional road network has been extended far beyond the immediate areas served by the original Jabal Turba road. All the major population or administrative centers in the districts of Al Mahwit, Bani Sa d, Hufash and Khabt are now accessible by four-wheel drive vehicles. While the cooperatives others than Ta awun Mahwit continue to regard roads as their first priority, the Al Mahwit Cooperative has made significant investments of its limited resources in other areas. Their largest non-road expenditures have been in the field of education, where they cooperate closely with the Ministry of Education office in Al Mahwit. The Cooperative contributes one-third of the cost of each elementary school built in the district.[12] In addition, through an agreement with the Ministry of Education, the cooperative provides salary supplements and living allowances to all non-Mahwiti teachers employed in the district.

Another significant cooperative-sponsored project is the electrification of Al Mahwit town and nearby hamlets. The cooperative contributed a significant amount of the initial capital required to organize the Al Mahwit Local Electrical Company and purchase its first generator. A member of the administrative committee travelled at his own expense to London to arrange the purchase of the generator. The company is now partially staffed by returned migrants to Saudi Arabia, who take an active part in other cooperative projects.

Finally, the cooperative is involved in the support of local health services and water systems. The cooperative has an arrangement with the Ministry of Health similar to that with the Ministry of Education with regard to locally employed hospital personnel. Water supply projects have been mostly the repair or construction of village cisterns which provide water for animals and washing.

These construction and institutional support activities are clearly within the preview of a local development association, but Ta awun Mahwit also provides informal social services and serves as an arena for conflict resolution. The offices and officials of the Cooperative serve as a public forum for the mediation of marriage disputes among the towns people and villages.[13] In repayment for this service, the Cooperative collects five hundred riyals from the bridewealth in each case it successfully solves. The Cooperative continues to engage in many of the activities characteristic of the local welfare societies from which it originates. The Cooperative, when it feels appropriate, arbitrates in cases of blood money disputes brought to its office.

It also makes contributions towards alleviating the condition of injured or sick individuals. Finally, the Cooperative is active in mosque restoration and in supporting the organization and programs of sports and culture clubs.

While the Cooperative remains intimately involved in local social organization through the implementation of projects and the mediation of social conflicts, it also acts as the principal spokesman for central government policies at the local level. Cooperative officials establish and maintain close ties with the government offices and with provincial ministerial officials. Policy and programming are closely modeled upon the guidelines which are received from CYDA and the experiences gained working with government officials in San a. Indeed, to many villagers, the Cooperative is the most accessible representative of the central

government.   Particularly   through   the   activities   of   the
Coordinating Council members of the cooperatives spread information
about   and   give   explanations   of government   policies,   laws   and
development plans to the village and hamlet level.

Despite these   strong   links to the central   government,   the
Cooperative   remains   an autonomous institution.   Its   members   are
leadership are local citizens who are chosen by their neighbors and
relatives to represent them in front of other communities and the
government in San a.   Above all, the Cooperative is an organization
which uses   local   resources   in an   attempt   to   fulfill   locally
perceived needs in a program of locally planned, implemented, and
maintained development projects.

SOCIAL AND ECONOMIC DEVELOPMENT IN AL MAHWIT

The history of Ta awun Mahwit is, in large part, a reflection
of the general patterns of social change since the 1962 revolution.
Economically, the most significant trend is the growth of the
commercial sector and the displacement of the household-based
subsistance sector.[14]   Occupationally, the number of full-time
cultivators has decreased relative to the number of residents and
migrants involved in wage labor, government employment and merchant
activities.   The exchange of goods and services has become almost
exclusively based upon money transactions. In the marketplace
itself, locally produced goods and services face a competitive
disadvantage when compared with less expensive imported items.[15]
The flow of migrant remittances into the rural areas and the town
combined with the increasing dependence on imported food and
manufactured items, has fueled an inflationary spiral which has
reached rates of over 100 per cent per annum for labor and some
commodity prices.[16]

Partly as a result of the monetization of the economy, social
relations previously derived form the division of labor, have been
greatly altered.   Prior to the Revolution, rural Yemeni social
structure displayed a reasonably well-defined status hierarchy
based upon social relations among endogamous occupational
groups.[17]   Aspects of this hierarchy continue to exist in Al
Mahwit today, but new patterns in the ideology and practice of
social relations are emerging which reflect the changing economic
realities.   Ideologically, the younger generation of Mahwitis are
expressing values which stress the importance of the individual
over class and kinship associations. These post-Revolution views
are most often expressed in the idiom of Yemeni tribal customs and
practices.   Particularly among the younger men of the landlord-
educated-administrative elite, there has appeared the phenomenon of
a kind of "revolutionary tribalism" which stresses the equality and
independence of all citizens and, in particular, the common
aspirations which override familial and class divisions.[18]   This
ideology of tribalism is counter to the traditional hierarchy of
ascribed, ranked groups and is perhaps a result of the upheavals of
the civil war and the spread of national feeling. Certainly, the

new ideology opposes the privileged positions once enjoyed by the large landowners, the sada religious aristocracy, and hereditary judges.[19]

The introduction of the money economy and the subsequent breakdown of many patron-client relationships (in the market, in education, in security) have encouraged social mobility based on personal achievements. Significantly, most of this mobility is downward in the traditional system of ranking. The sons of landlords and the religious elite are choosing to become merchants in the suq, a decision which would have been abhorred twenty-five years ago. The social structure of the town and countryside is becoming more fluid, and the old boundaries separating kinship and occupational groups are more ambiguously defined than they were a generation ago. As part of this general process of change, new social categories are emerging and their members attaining a sense of common identity through the recognition of common aspirations and interests. As the economic and social structures alter, new strategies for pursuing individual and group interests have emerged.

Money is becoming an increasingly critical resource. A man who commands money resources can gain important social and political influence in his community. Apart from this desire to gain prestige, many household heads are discovering that they must have a money income simply to support the life styles they want. Reliance on the predominantly subsistence agricultural sector, whether as a producer or rent receiver, is no longer sufficient to establish and maintain an independent household, and the majority of domestic economies are, of necessity, mixed. In the rural areas, the men are leaving the land and either migrating or opening small shops. Subsistence farming is left to the women who grow sorghum to feed the household's animals and supplements supplies of purchased grain.[20]

One response to this insecurity in the agricultural sector and the increasing mobility in social relations has been temporary migration by young men who go to Saudi Arabia and work as unskilled or semi-skilled laborers. Although there is no doubt that recent economic conditions in rural Yemen have served to "push" this labor off the land, the oil-financed economic boom in Saudi Arabia and the Gulf States has also "pulled" Yemeni farmers from their fields. Wages in Saudi Arabia may be twice as high as wages for similar work in rural Yemen, and even though inflation and labor shortages have dramatically raised wages in Yemen itself, migrants continue to claim that they can make and save much more money in Saudi Arabia than in their home villages or in Yemen's cities.

Although their purpose in leaving is clearly to make money, few migrants seem to have a definite idea of how they will invest their money when they return. Many simply seek a sufficient income to feed and house their families while they are away. Others work until they have saved enough money to return, many, build a house and establish an independent household. Finally, there are those who work to learn a skill or save enough capital to open a small business in their native village or town. It is clear that the best investment opportunities are in commerce, transport or small manufactures, and not in agriculture.[21] The one notable exception in agriculture is the cultivation and sale of qat. In areas ecologically suited to qat growing, cultivators (owners and tenants) are far less inclined to migrate. Market conditions are such that their incomes more than keep pace with inflation.

A second strategy for upward mobility is education. People who invest their own to their childrens' time and labor power in studies are usually members of the more economically secure families. In the case of Al Mahwit, to earn a secondary school certificate the student must live in either San a or Al Hudayda, as there are no secondary schools in the province. These "migrants" are the least likely to return to the town or village, for employment opportunities are limited. However, a number of townsmen have returned from secondary school (or, in a number of cases, preparatory school) to take important positions in governorate offices.[22] The most visible and most influential new group present in Mahwit is the new "middle class" of small businessmen and construction contractors. These men, many of whom are former migrants, own and operate small stores, mechanized workshops (e.g. blacksmiths, carpenters, welders, window makers), or public places such as restaurants and hotels. The contractors are skilled workmen who negotiate construction jobs and then arrange for the materials and workmen necessary. Given the increasing scarcity of labor, these contractors have in recent years been able to earn considerable sums of money. Finally, there are the wealthy merchants and wholesalers who finance most of the new commercial construction.

Small farmers and tenants, where constrained from cash cropping by the environment, market, or access to land, look first to the opportunities offered by migration, then to merchandising. The workers and craftsmen, while seeking to keep the price of labor high, are being forced to compete with foreign-manufactured consumer goods and, to some extent, labor-saving machinery. Above all, these men wish to remain independent and retain their bargaining position in the market. To this end, members of a few occupations have formed associations which serve as informal pressure groups.[23] The merchants and small shopkeepers wish to improve the transport facilities between Al Mahwit and Yemen's major cities and from Al Mahwit to nearby markets and villages. Like the workers and artisans, these men cherish their independence of action. Although there is no Mahwit Chamber of Commerce, the merchants maintain close personal relations with government officials and the Development Cooperative. Indeed some merchants serve as government employees or elected members of the Cooperative. Finally, the landlords and traditional educated elite seek to retain their position by pursuing both formal education and commerce. These men are particularly active in wholesaling, and some have agencies outside Al Mahwit. As in commerce, this group appears to seek brokering positions within the social organization. These families are the most likely to have members in government positions and to arrange strategic marriages between lineages.

The clearest goal for a young man is to establish an independent household of which he is the head. This is certainly not a new or introduced desire, but in recent years it has become more easily obtainable for young men, particularly those who decide to spend their migrant earnings in this fashion. A second traditional, but very common ambition is to achieve a brokering and mediating position in the community. This requires not only the command of financial and political resources, but also the ability to maintain a neutral position between conflicting parties. This third party mediator position is the essence of the political role of the shaykh in rural Yemen, and many of the younger leaders in the town carefully follow the substance of the role while denying its more historical connotations.

Young men who are relatively free of family responsibilities are the most likely to pursue new and innovative activities such as migrating to a city or foreign country. They are also the most likely to disregard or deny what they perceive as the un-natural restrictions imposed by the rules and the norms of the pre-Revolution social structure. The personal networks of these young men include a wide variety of people and criss-cross many of the traditional social boundaries. A man's network of kinship, economic, political and friendship relations will of course be partially a result of his social origins, but these men seeking alternative roles in the social organization are less likely than their forefathers to recognize the traditionally accepted guidelines for building social networks. In fact, the pattern of change in Al Mahwit indicates that many of these guidelines have lost their validity and practical importance.

Perhaps the most telling factor underlying the actions of the young men is the search for economic security. Individual financial situations and prospects for improvement or deterioration often serve as the most relevant constraints and incentives determining immediate and short-term choices of action. As in other societies, young men faced with important life-choices look to the examples of their peers.

Studies of the nature of Yemeni social structure have stressed its vertical divisions and the lack of horizontal integration. Despite the continuing debate over hierarchically ranked status groups, most students of Yemeni society have agreed upon the overriding significance of patriarchal family groups and the reliance upon extremely personalized patron-client ties in social, economic and political relations. Juxtaposed on these vertical relations is the tri-partite division separating tribal agriculturists, non-tribal market people and the educated landlord and administrative elite.24

Even if this interpretation of the formal social structure is accepted, there is evidence that a number of mechanisms exist which provide in varying degrees what might be termed horizontal integration. These may be seen in the form of migrant networks, trades associations, youth clubs and the boycott of certain laws or individuals by groups with common interests.

Perhaps the most notable manifestation of horizontal integration is the growing gap between the generations. In Al Mahwit, the distinction is commonly made between the shabab (youth) and the shaybat (oldmen). These two roles are seen as sitting at opposite ends of a continuum of local cultural ideals. The shaybat are seen as traditionalists and arch-conservatives. The shabat, in contrast, seek new ways of doing things and consider themselves progressives and children of the Revolution. In general, it is the shabab who pursue the new-found social mobility and extol the virtues of social equality. By these criteria, any action may be labelled as being the act of a shayba or that of the shabab. Interestingly, those who consider themselves shabab never employ the singular form of the noun but always refer to an individual as "one of the shabab." The opposite is true of references to old men or their values. They are always referred to in the singular.

Perhaps the most self-consciously integrative of all Mahwiti institutions is the Development Cooperative. The Cooperative, as conceived by the government and CYDA, is a reformist organization which acts as an expression of the popular will and circumvents the pre-existing local hierarchical structures if these cannot, or will not, act in the best interests of the citizens. The Cooperative is designed to return the agricultural taxes to the people who pay them in the form of development projects which should benefit the broadest spectrum of people, and not just traditional elites.

The ideology of the Cooperative is a mixture of republicanism and popular democracy. Its leadership consists of publicly elected "volunteers" who carry out their duties as a "human service." Where government reform or development policies are unable to penetrate through local self-interest power groups, the Cooperative is expected to provide an alternative governing structure more responsive to popular needs and aspirations. As one governor of Mahwit replied to a question about local administration - "there is no government here except the ta awun." Although this statement is far from the literal truth, it does reflect the role which the Cooperative has come to play in the social organization of Al Mahwit.

It is a fact that the projects undertaken by the Cooperative have differentially affected the people of Al Mahwit, and certain groups have clearly benefitted more directly than others form the road, electricity, water and school projects. For the most part it is the shabab, the change-minded young men, who have become actively involved in the cooperative movement and who have been the

first to take advantage of the opportunities offered by Ta awun
projects. It has been the shabab who have been Cooperative
officials, who have implemented projects against the resistance of
traditional leaders, who gave financial contributions to projects,
and who invested their money in enterprises made possible by the
Cooperative's activities.

THE FUTURE OF TA AWUN MAHWIT

The 1976-78 five year plan of Ta awun Mahwit has been
officially incorporated into the government's First Five Year Plan
for the Yemen Arab Republic. In this major planning effort, the
government has relied heavily upon Local Development Cooperatives
for the implementation and administration of a broad range of local
projects.[25] This final section of our discussion of Ta awun
Mahwit examines the problems faced by the cooperative in realizing
its goals.

In its efforts to respond to popular demands for projects, the
Ta awun must operate within the limits of its legal authority. By
law, the Cooperative may not use coercive force in its activities.
Therefore, it must seek the tacit or active support of either
government officials or local leaders. This situation has led to a
continuing debate among Cooperative members about the best course
to follow when faced with the obstruction of a project's
implementation. Should local shaykhs be appealed to, or should the
Ta awun attempt to involve the government directly? Past
experience indicates that only the particular circumstances of each
situation, and not a fixed policy, determine how the Cooperative
will react. If both the government and the local leaders oppose a
project supported by the Cooperative and citizens, then it appears
that the project has little chance of implementation.

Although the Cooperative has no legal mandate to act as an
independent arbitor of local conflicts, its leadership has played a
successful mediating role in the past. The Cooperative has become
an alternative forum which citizens may use in submitting petitions
against various authorities or for publicly airing complaints
against local conditions. However, it should be remembered that
the Cooperative is a socially heterogeneous body, and many
petitions brought to its offices have resulted in splits within the
membership. Nevertheless, it is clear from observing the daily
activities of the Ta awun leaders that the mediation of conflict
and the careful balancing of local and national pressures is one of
the most critical and time-consuming of their activities.

The execution of this middleman role between government
administration and local pressures for development actions tends to
foster a kind of identity crisis among Cooperative members. This
is perhaps most directly expressed by members in terms of the
division of responsibilities between "elected officials" and
"employees" of the Cooperative. In the eyes of those active in Ta

awun Mahwit, these two roles have very different sets of rewards, liabilities, and standards of evaluation.

Elected officials, though they may be either volunteers or recipients of nominal salaries, are responsible to both local leaders and ordinary citizens. Their role is as much a matter of local politics as it is a function of administrative performance. An elected official, in the Mahwiti view of the Ta awun, is responsible for his actions; he will ultimately reap any political benefits or suffer any ill consequences of a Cooperative project. His decisions are scrutinized and evaluated by the community.

Employees operate under a different set of conditions. Their responsibilities are determined by the terms of their employment agreements, and their performance is evaluated according to written achievement forms completed yearly by the Cooperative's president. Unlike an elected official, an employee has no fear that a "problem may come to rest on his head" for he is not considered personally responsible for the Cooperative's actions. Similarly, the employee has little to gain from involvement in problem-solving. Unlike the elected official, he is a political outsider.

This situation has caused severe recruitment problems for the Cooperative. Its salaries budget is extremely limited, and few qualified professionals are willing to work under the difficult conditions in Al Mahwit. At the same time, the responsibilities of elected officials provide little incentive to become fully committed to Ta awun work. Elected officials seldom take strong actions on their own initiative, without having first secured a sound political position outside the Cooperative. (Locally, this position is called "a base of support among the tribesmen.") The result is that elected officials often have divided loyalties and rarely commit themselves full-time to Cooperative work. (Such men are termed "dispersed" in Al Mahwit.)

The problem of identity manifests itself in the very real danger that the Ta awun may become absorbed into the local authority structure. This would negate the Cooperative's purpose as envisioned by CYDA and the central government. Absorption into local structures would mean an end to the Ta awun's function as an independent agent in decision-making and resource allocation.

The degree to which this danger exists, however, is dependent upon a number of factors. First, the existing social organization and the characters of the men involved in the Ta awun is a crucial variable. In the areas where the Cooperative has been most effective, the local members are usually shabab -- young men who have seen the directions of change and been able to use available resources in innovative ways. Another factor underlying the Ta awun's independence from traditional authorities is its capacity to raise its own funds -- either from citizen's contributions or from central government grants. In part this has been done by publicizing the cooperative ideology and showing its practical applications. Finally, the success of the Cooperative depends upon the ability of its leadership to operate within the two systems: local social organizations and central government administrative structures.

The young men who, for the most part, from the Cooperative's leadership fulfill ambiguous roles. In purely social situations and among friends, they behave as "one of the shabab." There is no clear protocol to indicate status and hierarchical relationships among those present. In gatherings whose purpose is Ta awun business there may be government officials, CYDA representatives, local shaykhs and common citizens present. In such mixed company, the Ta awun officials choose between two very well-defined role models. Depending on the people present and the exact nature of the business at hand, an official may act as a traditional shaykh or as a modernist civil servant. In either case, they consciously or unconsciously place themselves in the role most advantageous for persuading their audience to follow a particular course of action. Although every member of the community is able to present a variety of roles in social interaction, Ta awun leaders have the broadest range. They have both roots in the local system and legitimate positions in the wider, national society.

This role manipulation is usually related to specific problems of project implementation, but occasionally the officials mediate disputes entirely unrelated to Ta awun business. Fulfilling an ambiguous role may result in becoming over-committed. Ta awun officials often complain of too much work, much of it unrelated to their specific responsibilities. Moreover, they feel that people are judging them by two, sometimes contradictory, standards of evaluation, depending on their observer's system of values. The Ta awun president has repeatedly remarked that the uneducated villagers do not understand the official procedures, and at the same time that San a officials do not understand the local economic and political situation.

Apart from these constraints related to the social system, there are two constraints originating from the formal structure and resources of the Ta awun itself. The first of these is the Cooperative's financial base. It has become clear in the past year that the zakat taxes will not provide sufficient funding for Ta awun Mahwit's five year plan. The Cooperative can often afford only token support for village projects. This situation tends to undermine the Cooperative's support in rural areas and its credibility in general. Ta awun members have reacted to criticism of unfilled promises by publicly stating the Ta awun's financial situation, but they are often forced into a position of defending themselves personally while criticizing the Cooperative as an institution.

The second immediate problem faced by the Cooperative is that it is unable to adequately administer its projects. Largely due to its financial weakness, the Ta awun has only a small office staff and no technical personnel. The elected officials who work on a volunteer basis are too few and are under qualified to supervise all Ta awun activities. These elected officials are becoming increasingly demoralized by continuing public pressure and the inability to pay additional employees to lighten work loads and lessen responsibilities.

Many people, knowing these problems, are reluctant to enter elections or become active Ta awun members. Their personal aspirations may be better realized by labor migration, academic study, or establishment of a business. The current dilemma of the Cooperative members has been brought to a critical point by CYDA's recent announcement that general elections to all Cooperative General Assemblies and Administrative Committees will be held in October 1978. None of the members of the present Ta awun Mahwit Administrative Committee intended to run for re-election and, as of August 1978, no one else had announced his intention to enter the elections.

Just one month before the new elections, the Ta awun found itself in an over-extended financial situation with a demoralized leadership and no announced candidates for office. This negative assessment was offset by a noticeable increase in central government support of the cooperative movement at the national level and indications that CYDA was preparing to provide financial assistance over and above zakat funds. At the village level, local Ta awun members and citizens were initiating large numbers of small projects, most of which were being implemented with the help of the administrative committee. In practical terms, the Ta awun had established itself as an institution and had gained broad popular support, but at the same time had over-extended its limited resources.

In the minds of the present leadership, the upcoming elections will give the people a chance to re-affirm their support of the Cooperative movement. Although they appear to no longer wish to serve as elected officials, these men are actively seeking ways in which they may continue to be involved in Ta awun activities. The best way of doing this, in their view, is to become regular employees of the Ta awun.

What does the future hold for Ta awun Mahwit? The only certain answer is that there will be new elections. There seems to be no question that the Ta awun will remain as a feature of the Al Mahwit community for some time to come. Indeed its achievements -- from the completion of the Jabal Turba road to the construction of uzla schools -- have established it as an important, and for the present a necessary institution. The historical interaction between local initiative and government policies laid a firm groundwork for a viable and effective institution responsive to the aspirations of Al Mahwit's people and the changing nature of their community. Determination of the direction for future Ta awun Mahwit programs must await the resolution of its financial and personnel problems.

NOTES

1.   In 1968, the Yemen Arab Republic was divided into eight
provinces.   These   provinces   were   further   divided   into
administrative units called qada . Each qada was composed of a
number of districts called nawahi (sing. nahiyya). A nahiyya was
divided into sub-districts called uzlas, and   uzlas were made up
of a number of villages and hamlets. The original qada   of Al
Mahwit contained five nawahi: Al Mahwit, Khabt, Hufash, Milhan,
and Bani Sa d.   In 1968, qada Al Mahwit had an approximate
population of 90,000 people.

2.   Political leadership in the Al Mahwit area revolves around
various authority roles to which people give the generic term
"shaykh".   There are several kinds of shaykhs, and they operate at
different levels in the political hierarchy, depending on the size
and scope of their followings. A shaykh may simply be a lineage or
clan head, or he may be the officially recognized representative of
a village or an uzla.

3.   See "Agreement of Establishment," General Union of Yemen
Development Commissions, Preparatory Committee, March 1973, mimeo.

4.   CYDA's constitution set forth a common political and
administrative structure to be followed by all member associations,
henceforth to be called Local Development Associations or, more
popularly,   cooperatives.   Through   CYDA's   efforts,   these
cooperatives were eligible by law to receive twenty-five per cent
of the net zakat agricultural taxes collected in their areas, after
the costs of collection and administration were deducted. Between
the years 1973 and 1977 this percentage was increased to sixty-
eight per cent of the total zakat plus shares in various other
government   revenues, such as municipality funds and customs
receipts. Through CYDA, cooperatives were also eligible to receive
foreign donor assistance, which became increasingly available in
the mid-seventies, particularly from oil-rich Arab states.   For
more information, se "Development of the Cooperative Movement in
Yemen," CYDA, San a, mimeo, and "Al Ta awun," Dar al-Hina lil-taba
a, San a, 1977.

5.   The structure of the Qada Mahwit Cooperative contained
two administrative bodies. The first was a fifteen member General
Assembly which contained three representatives from each district
in the qada.   These men were chosen locally from the previous
confederation before the CYDA team arrived to supervise the
election of the seven man Administrative Committee which was chosen
from among the General Assembly. The Administrative Committee's
primary responsibilities were to draw up development project plans
(e.g., roads, schools, and water projects) for the entire qada   ,
and to oversee their implementation. The members of the General
Assembly submitted the requirements for their respective areas, and
the Administrative Committee set the over-all priorities.   The
first plan contained project objectives for the next three years

and was approved by the General Assembly, CYDA, and the central government.

6. During its first few years of operation, CYDA negotiated a series of arrangements with the central government for the funding of various kinds of projects at the local level. Roads were classified by their length. Roads between one and twenty kilometers long were entirely financed by local citizen contributions and cooperative funds. For lengths between twenty and thirty kilometers, the formula was that citizens and the cooperative paid seventy-five per cent with the state paying the remaining twenty-five per cent of the budget. Roads over thirty kilometers long were split fifty-fifty between the state and the citizens and cooperative. The formula for village water projects was set at fifty per cent from the villagers themselves, twenty-five per cent from the cooperative and twenty-five per cent from the central government. Village and 'uzla school buildings were to be paid for by an equal division among the citizens, the cooperative and the Ministry of Education.

7. Because of the diverse ecology of qada Al Mahwit, agricultural regimes vary strikingly from one district to another. Since the central incomes of cooperatives are based to a large extent on the zakat agricultural yield taxes, the level of revenues varies greatly among the districts. For example Hufash and Milhan districts produce great quantities of qat, a mild stimulant chewed by most Yemenis. The value of the zakat levied on a field of qat far and away exceeds the value of the zakat returned on a similar field planted in sorghum or vegetables. Thus the annual zakat tax collected in Hufash or Milhan is, in most years, almost four times the amount collected in, say, Al Mahwit district, which produces mostly sorghum.

Another factor affecting regional cooperative budgets is money supply in each area and the willingness (and ability) of citizens to contribute to local development projects. To a large extent, this is a function of the level of labor migration. Khabt district, for example, has an extremely high level of labor migration (indeed, one of the highest in all Yemen). These migrants are willing and have the cash to contribute substantial sums to cooperative projects but, of course, they want to see the money spent for projects which directly benefit their own communities.

8. These three year plans for 1976-1978 were altered to meet central government planning strategies in 1977. The plans, with suitable modifications, were incorporated into the national Five-Year Development Plan for 1976-1981.

9. The cooperative of Hufash also had an economic incentive for building these roads, for their leadership was under considerable popular pressure to build a road by which the Hufash

qat crop could be easily delivered to markets within and outside the province.

10.   As it happened, Hufash (because of its high qat income), Khabt (because of contributions from migrants), and Bani Sa d (because it expended no funds on other activities) all bought or rented bulldozers for their own road projects before the Jabal Taraf road was completed.   Al Mahwit, having to rely almost exclusively on zakat returns from sorghum production, has of this writing (August 1978) been unable to accumulate sufficient funds to purchase a bulldozer of its own.

11.   The district of Al Rajum was created in 1976 from parts of Al Tawila district.   The Al Rajum Cooperative Development Association was founded, with Council and Ta awun Mahwit help, in 1977.   This fledgling cooperative has begun an ambitious program of road construction which will link settlements through branch roads to the newly opened Al Rajum - Al Mahwit road.   Al Rahum and Al Mahwit have been sharing the province's bulldozer in this effort.

12.   The 1976-1981 five year plan of Ta awun Mahwit lists the building and staffing of a modern elementary school in each uzla of the district as a major priority.   Construction on these twenty-one schools was officially begun on 26 September 1977, the fifteenth anniversary of the Revolution.

13.   The arrangement and maintenance of marriage contracts became an important social issue in Yemen during the 1970's due to a phenomenal rise in the money component of bride wealth.   In an attempt to remedy this situation through legislation, the Al Hamdi regime set upper limits on the amount of money transferred or spent in contracts and weddings.   In support of these efforts, CYDA directed its member cooperatives to "implement the laws for the facilitation of marriage, including the restrictions applying to divorce."   (See "Al-Hashru a lil lijnat al-ta awuni," CYDA, 1977 mimeo.)

14.   According to an occupation survey taken by the author in September 1977, the active workforce in Al Mahwit town numbered 930 persons out of a total population of 3,742.   This figure does not include 174 residents who were students either in Al Mahwit or elsewhere.   Of these 930, 83 were labor migrants 202 were merchants and vendors, 209 were farmers (i.e. landlords, tenants and women), 195 were workers (i.e. agricultural and non-agricultural wage workers), 97 were government employees, and 144 were in other categories (e.g. artisans, personal service, professional, etc.). Not including migrants twenty-five per cent of the workforce was dependent on agriculture, twenty-four per cent on market activities, twenty-three per cent on wages, and eleven per cent on government employment.

15. It is indeed surprising that in the midst of an agricultural area, locally grown sorghum is a rare commodity in the Al Mahwit market and, when it can be found, it is priced above the cost of imported Ethiopian or East African grown sorghum. In a similar fashion, locally forged agricultural tools average six to eight times the price of the same types of tools imported from China, Japan, or Germany.

16. The daily wage for an unskilled laborer in either agriculture or construction rose from thirty riyals in May 1977, to sixty riyals in May 1978. Moreover, even at this price it is difficult without a long-term arrangement to find such an unskilled laborer who is also above the age of 15.

17. See Tomas Gerholm's recent discussion of "traditional stratification" in chapter four of his Market, Mosque and Mafraj (Stockholm, 1977).

18. Among the young men aged twenty to thirty-five in Al Mahwit town, the notion of the "tribe" (qabila) as an ideal model of social organization serves as a common reference point in social interaction. Reference to the "tribe" is never specific and fellow tribesmen in this context are never thought of as members of any particular tribe. Rather this new form of popular tribalism recognizes no intra- or inter-tribal relationships, only that the tribe ascribes equality of status and rank to all citizens.

19. Large landowners often maintain privileged social positions similar to those of a feudal nobility. During the Revolution the peasants and tenants of the area were able to arm themselves, and on several occasions groups of them confronted and sought concessions from members of landlord families. These armed groups in Al Mahwit called themselves tribal militias.

During the reigns of Yemen's kings, rights to education were restricted by the government. Common citizens (or tribesmen) studied in locally organized Koranic schools which often only taught the rudiments of literacy and mathematics. One of the most important achievements of the Revolution, from the Mahwiti point of view, was freedom of education and the willingness of the republic to help in the construction and staffing of modern schools.

20. It is significant that the only full-time occupation held by women and recognized by both sexes in Al Mahwit as a legitimate vocation for women is agriculture (see note number 14 above).

21. This statement is generally true for the areas under discussion. In others parts of Yemen, such as the coastal and highland plains, irrigated cash crops raised for the domestic urban and foreign markets have proved remarkably profitable. Much of this land was brought under irrigation through the investment of migrants' earnings.

22.   Certificates of formal education are required for government employment above the level of servant, guard, or driver. Returned "educational" migrants include the current president of Ta awun Mahwit, the Deputy Director of the Education Office, the town school headmaster, and the Director of the Governor's Office of Technical Services.   No native Mahwiti has yet received a university degree, although a number are currently studying for their Bachelor's Degree. These men have no plans to return to Al Mahwit after graduation.

10
National Seeds in Local Soil: Will Development Grow?

Barbara K. Larson

INTRODUCTION AND BACKGROUND

Development plans must ultimately be judged in terms of their effectiveness at the local level. When Tunisia embarked on a course of development following independence in 1956, it did so in two separate phases. The first put primary emphasis on developing Tunisia's human resources through education and social services. The second, beginning in 1961-62, put primary emphasis on developing Tunisia's economic resources through an extensive system of state-run agricultural and commercial cooperatives. Both programs, but particularly the latter, were predicated on a policy of mobilizing the populace behind the government's programs and involved extensive government penetration into the local communities.

The success of these programs and policies has varied (the cooperatives were scuttled abruptly in the fall of 1969), and their achievements and failures have been analyzed from a number of points of view, but I would like to analyze and evaluate them from a somewhat different perspective. namely, that of their appropriateness and effectiveness at the local level. In particular, I want to focus on the specific factors which led to the relative success or failure of three national development policies -- cooperativization, political mobilization, and improvements in the status of women -- in the Tunisian village of el-Qarya (a pseudonym) where I carried out field research in 1969-70. I then will go on to consider the implications of my analysis for future development planning.

The main thesis of the paper is that the success or failure of any government policy or program on the local level will depend on two broad factors: 1) how well the policies and programs are designed, organized, and managed from a technical and organizational point of view; and 2) the degree to which they are compatible with or take account of the needs, social structure and values of the local community for which they are developed. If either of these factors is lacking or inadequate, then the program or policy is likely to run into difficulty. A program that is in concert with the needs, values and social structures of the village may fail because it is poorly managed. Conversely, a program that is well designed and managed from a purely technical point of view is unlikely to succeed if it fails to take account of local values and structures and work with them as much as possible. This means being aware not only of broad organizational features and value orientations of North African society generally, but of specific local variations as well. It is particularly in this context that an anthropological analysis of local socio-cultural conditions becomes relevant, indeed essential, to effective development planning as a whole. Let me then examine this thesis by looking at the outcome of three specific development programs and policies in the Tunisian village of al-Qarya.

Al-Qarya is a medium-sized village of about 1500 people, located midway between two provincial capitals in western Tunisia, not far from the Algerian border. It is a village with a mixed economy, based partly on agriculture, and partly on income from other sources. The original base of the local economy was subsistence agriculture, with a primary reliance on dry-farmed cereal crops (predominantly wheat and barley), supplemented with small livestock (sheep and goats) and fruits and vegetables grown on land irrigated by the village spring. The land was worked by animal team and traditional Arab plow, but since the 1950's, mechanized agriculture has become common. Land was for the most part individually owned and managed, except for isolated cases where brothers continued to work their patrimonies jointly after the death of their father. The size of landholdings varies,[1] but in general ownership has been rather fluid over time. Those without sufficient land or labor engage in various kinds of sharecropping arrangements to get the necessary land or labor, and used to engage in reciprocal exchanges of labor (called ma una) or equipment if their shortages were only temporary or slight. But today such reciprocal exchanges have largely been replaced by wages or rent, though sharecropping continues to exist.

While land provided the base of the original economy, other sources of income -- notably from mining, commerce, wage labor, and professional and white collar jobs -- have become increasingly important in the twentieth century, until today they effectively dominate the local economy. Thus today, despite the fact that almost half of the village households possess some orchards or cereal land, only 6% of the men list their primary occupation as agriculture, and most households derive their income from more than one source. Substantial variations in wealth do exist in the village, but no one is so wealthy that he does not personally work for a living, and wealth differences are fluid and graduated rather than rigid and sharp.

The basic social unit in the village is the household, which may be either nuclear or extended. It constitutes the primary unit of production, distribution, and consumption, and is the primary locus of affective ties. Beyond the household there are no indigenous corporate groups (leaving aside the formal organizations of national government, most of which have been only recently implanted in the village), but personalized kin networks and neighborhoods serve as a basis of social relations in their stead.

Sunni Islam is important in the village as a focus of cultural identity and of ceremonial and ritual life, but it has little significance outside the personal and familial domain. There are no sectional divisions in the village on the basis of religious differences or affiliations, and membership in religious brotherhoods has all but disappeared except in some of the outlying hamlets. Religious expression is largely confined to observing Muslim rites of passage, visiting the mosque and cemetery on Islamic holidays, and fasting during Ramadan. While religion and religious learning is respected, it is still only a minor factor in establishing an individual's prestige, and even its role in shaping values has been diminished in competition with the more secular values that have pervaded the village. Thus, in general, villagers wear their religion lightly, and have relegated it primarily to the personal and cultural domain.

Politically, the village has been the headquarters of an administrative district since 1968. It articulates with the district, provincial, and national levels of Tunisia's centralized political structure through a mayor and a local branch of Tunisia's single party, the Neo-Destour. While the village is located in the provinces, the villagers themselves are not unsophisticated in the ways of the world: They pride themselves on being modern and progressive; they have personal familiarity with Tunis, the capital, and with other cities of the east coast. Furthermore, most of the men, at least, are relatively well-informed about national and international developments through radio, television, and personal contacts in the cities.

Prestige in the village is measured in terms of a blend of 'traditional' and 'modern' values, and attaches primarily to the individual and his immediate household, rather than to a larger circle of kin. It is primarily achieved rather than inherited, or if inherited, must at least be maintained by acting in appropriate ways. There are a number of separate indicators of prestige, which may work together or separately to establish a man's status. (A woman's status is affected by her conduct, but is in general derived from that of her husband or father.) These are economic success, proper moral character and social virtues, the conduct of one's women, and religious piety and learning.

Of these, the first three indicators are the most important. Economic success involves not only wealth, but the ability to manage one's assets wisely and well. As a result, a moderately wealthy man who is self-made is more respected than a man who has inherited his wealth and is not particularly astute in managing or increasing it. Proper moral character and social virtues means that a man must be 'serious,' that is, hard-working and not given to frivolities, vanity, or overindulgence in wine or women. A man should be cordial to all and familiar with none, and a certain amount of aloofness in public is deemed desirable. A man must also have a good sense of what actions are or are not appropriate in a particular situation, for propriety is often situation-specific.

The conduct of one's women refers back to traditional notions of honor and shame, which remain strong in the village, despite the inroads of education and a government-sponsored women's organization in the village, and despite the villagers' strong desire to be thought of as progressive. These traditional notions of honor and shame insist that a family's honor is inextricably bound up with the chastity, modesty, and sexual fidelity of its women, and even the appearance of wrongdoing on the part of the latter is enough to tarnish the family with shame. In the context of the village, this concern expresses itself in the near absence of women from public places, and a sharp division between the women's and men's domains.

Though the village is in many ways a typical village, sharing many broad features of North African social organization and cultural values, there are also specific features of el-Qarya's historical development which have predisposed it to be particularly entrepreneurial, pragmatic, and outward oriented, and these factors are, I think, relevant to its general receptivity to change. These factors are essentially two: economic, and political.

The economic history of the village was somewhat unusual, in that although the original economy was based on subsistence agriculture, other sources of income were available to the village from the early twentieth century on. The most important of these was the reopening of local lead, zinc, and iron mines by the French in 1911. This was important not only because it provided jobs, but because it offered an alternative to land as a source of wealth and a channel of upward mobility. Unskilled workers could, if capable, enter the mines and work their way up to skilled positions sufficiently lucrative to enable them to invest their earnings in more traditional sources of wealth, such as land (and later commerce). This had two major consequences for the village: 1) It contributed to a continuous circulation of elites in the village thus keeping village social structure fluid and making it difficult for any single group to establish itself as a permanent, hereditary elite. 2) It put a premium on individual, entrepreneurial activity, thus reinforcing individualistic behavior and values, and making it possible for wealth rather than land to become the most important basis of village prestige. Both of these consequences in turn had the further effect of undercutting the strength of corporate groups in the village, for corporate groups tend not to develop in the absence of a corporate estate to manage and protect (defend).[2]

These trends were further intensified by the availability of new sources of income and mobility into the village from the 1940's on: the expansion of village commerce in the 1940's (made possible by improvements in transportation), construction opportunities on a nearby dam in the 1950's, white collar and professional jobs as Tunisians replaced the French in the 1960's. All of these sources of employment worked not only to foster pragmatism, entrepreneurial ability, and an individualistic outlook, but they also broadened villagers' exposure to and contact with the world outside. However, certain political factors were also responsible for increasing villagers' exposure to outside influences and developments. Two political factors are particularly important: One is the French occupation as it affected the village; the other is the village's early participation in the Neo-Destour. Though the French were never stationed in el-Qarya itself, many villagers worked for the French either in agriculture or in the mines. On the one hand, villagers admired their efficiency. On the other hand, they resented their arrogance, especially as exhibited by the French soldiers stationed at a neighboring village or by French officials in Le Kef. In addition, villagers retained bitter memories of the arrival of the French in 1881, when they strode into the village and summarily shot three village leaders. Thus, when Habib Bourguiba began to organize a more militant nationalist party (the Neo-Destour) in 1934, villagers were receptive, and responded by organizing one of the earliest party branches in the region in 1936. Thus twenty years before independence, the villagers' were already actively participating in national political developments (mainly to gather money and support). This had two consequences for future government efforts at political mobilization. One is that by the time the government was actively trying to encourage local political activity in the 1950's and 60's, el-Qarya already had a national orientation and a history of active political participation. The other is that because villagers already had a strong positive identification with Bourguiba and the party, they were by-and-large predisposed to offer general support for his general policies and development goals, unless they had specific reason to object to them. In other words, they were in the years following independence willing to give the government and government policy the benefit of the doubt.

With this basic description of the village in mind, let us now turn to look at the success and failure of three development programs -- the cooperative, political mobilization, and improvements in the status of women -- in the village of al-Qarya.

THE AGRICULTURAL COOPERATIVE

In 1961-62 the national government embarked on a sweeping program of economic and social development which aimed to bring virtually all of the nation's agriculture and commerce into state cooperatives by 1969. The primary purpose of the agricultural cooperatives was to increase production through the pooling of small holdings into larger, more efficient production units which could benefit from better management, more sophisticated technology, and the economies of scale. To this end small holdings were brought into the cooperatives first. Large holdings, which were presumably more efficient already, were to be incorporated somewhat later.

Each cooperative had a locally-elected administrative council to oversee general policy for that cooperative, and a salaried local director to supervise day-to-day operations. Beyond that, a Local Union of the Cooperative, made up of prominent local agriculturalists, advised the district administrator (the "delegue) on the local cooperatives in his district (delegation). But effective decision-making authority over the cooperative lay outside the local level in the hands of 1) the delegue, who had effective authority for all that went on in his district, and 2) the national cooperative structure, represented at the district level by a district-level director and agricultural engineer. All three of these officials were outsiders; salaried, appointed, and recruited through national channels.

Only a limited number of landholders were to be employed by the cooperative to work the land at a fixed wage, depending on the labor needs of the cooperative; these individuals were known as direct cooperateurs. Other individuals with land in the cooperative were simply to receive a share of the profits proportional to their investment of land or capital equipment; these were known as indirect cooperateurs. At no time was there any intention of redistributing either land or wealth.

A state agricultural cooperative of this type was not established in el-Qarya until 1967, though others had been established elsewhere in the region as early as 1962. The support of both the party structure and the mass media was enlisted to help pave the way for the introduction of the cooperative -- indeed, one of the members of the local party cell attended a two-month training session near Tunis to prepare him for his task -- and el-Qarya was made the headquarters of a new administrative district to allow for closer government supervision of the cooperative effort.

Village reaction to the government cooperative was initially cool, for villagers were reluctant to put their lands under collective, government-dominated control. However, in the fact of government pressure, the villagers passively acquiesced, and adopted a wait-and-see attitude.

The cooperativization of agriculture in al-Qarya proceeded in two phases. In the initial phase, beginning in 1967, only cereal land was brought under cooperative control. In the second phase, beginning in April of 1969, the village orchards and vegetable gardens were cooperativized as well. By the time I arrived in the village in the summer of 1969, approximately 70% of the village's most fertile land (in the plain) had already entered the cooperative, and the rest of the land (including the holdings of the four largest landowners with over 100 hectares each) was scheduled to be incorporated by the end of the year.

However, that final stage of cooperativization never came into being, primarily for two reasons: First of all, because national opposition to and problems with the cooperatives which surfaced at this time caused the government to reverse its policy and make participation in the agricultural cooperatives voluntary rather than compulsory. (See Ashford 1973, Simmons 1970 and 1971, Stone 1971 for a discussion of the pressures and problems that led to that decision on the national level.) Secondly, because local experience with the village cooperative persuaded the villagers that it was not in their interest to remain in the cooperative, despite the fact that al-Qarya's cooperative (unlike many others in the area) managed to break even financially.

From a narrowly economic point of view, the first phase of the cooperative was a success, for the cooperative managed to break even at the end of the year. In this respect, its track record was better than average, for only 5 out of 204 cooperatives in the region of Le Kef were really producing well. However, in terms of the broader economic goals of the cooperative program, and the needs of the participants, it was not a success. For the increase in productivity was not sufficient to offset the higher administrative and technical costs involved in running the cooperative, particularly when 40% of each year's profits were set aside by fiat for reinvestment and social needs rather than being redistributed to the participants. (10% of the profits were set aside for capital reserve; 10% for social and cultural needs, 20% for seed and supplies.) As a result, individual participants got less of a return on their land than they had gotten under private management.

That productivity was not higher is attributable to a number of factors. In part, the cooperative suffered from many of the same problems which plagued cooperatives nationally (See Ashford 1973; Dutton 1976, Purvis 1976; Simmons 1970-1971; Stone 1971). Equipment was not properly maintained; fertilizers and machinery failed to arrive on time, drop advances and distribution of profits were minimal and often delayed. (One informant said that in the two years of the cooperative he had received only 2 canters[3] of wheat per hectare, whereas prior to the cooperative he regularly got 5 cantars. When the cooperative was disbanded in 1969, each participant got only 30 kg. of wheat per hectare.)

First of all, although the lines of authority over the cooperative were in principle divided between local supervisory councils and government officials along the lines mentioned above, control in fact was concentrated in the hands of the government, specifically those of the delegue (the district administrator). In part, this was because the delegue was ambitious, and wanted to maintain control. In part, it was because the local director, who had been chosen by the delegue rather than elected by the cooperateurs, was humble and deferential to authority, and so offered no resistance to the delegue's control. Against this combination, the cooperative council had little clout, and in conflicts between the council and the director, the latter regularly prevailed. (Once, this resulted in the disbanding of the council for a limited period of time. Later, when the challenge to the director was taken up by the party cell, it resulted in a vote of confidence for the director and a public scolding for the party cell.)

Thus, decision-making for the cooperative generally rested outside of local control. While this may not in and of itself have interfered with the economic success of the cooperative, it certainly lessened villagers' feelings of commitment and responsibility to it. However, in the case of al-Qarya, concentration of power in the hands of the delegue had another negative consequence as well. The delegue allowed his political ambitions to overcome his good judgement when, in the spring of 1969, he decided to bring the orchards into the cooperative. By rushing to implement this phase of cooperativization, he hoped to enhance his political image vis-a-vis his immediate superiors. The problem was that he did so hastily and without adequate preparation, and the consequent drop in yields and income was sufficient to turn villagers' skepticism of the cooperative into rejection once and for all. To give some idea of the magnitude of the losses, one man's tress yielded only 125 dinars worth of fruit under cooperative management in contrast to the usual 300 to 400 dinars worth under private management. For another the drop was from 25 dinars to 1 1/2; for a third, from 30 dinars to 9 1/2.

The reasons for the drop in yields and income were several. Many of the trees did not receive the cultivation and fertilizers necessary to produce a high yield: in part because cooperativization occurred right in the middle of the cultivating season, and individuals, hearing their trees were going to be cooperativized, dragged their heels in doing the necessary work, in part because the cooperative could not pick up the slack. In addition, there were several instances of mismanagement within the cooperative itself. Irrigation water was not evenly allocated among the various gardens and orchards, with the result that some cooperateurs suffered substantial losses in yields. (This rankled all the more because the cooperative had decided for the first year to give each cooperateur a share of the profits only on his trees, which meant that the losses were not shared equally by all cooperateurs.) Villagers reported seeing rotting fruit lying on the ground, suggesting that harvesting was poorly timed. Profits were so low that rumors ran rampant that workers were selling the harvest on the open market and pocketing the proceeds on the sly.

The blame for much of this was laid at the director's door, and resulted in attempts by the party cell to remove him. But there is ample evidence to suggest that the real problem lay not with the managerial competence of the director per se, but with the fact that the orchards were cooperativized so hastily that adequate preparation had not (and could not have) been made. If this was indeed so, it means that the delegue rather than the director deserves the lion's share of the blame.

It seems clear at this point that technical, organizational, and political errors did the cooperative in, and that villagers' rejection of the cooperative when given a choice was entirely reasonable in light of their experience with the cooperative's declining profits and yields. But were technical and organizational factors solely to blame, or would prevailing values and social structures have prejudiced the success of the cooperative from the outset?

In the case of al-Qarya, I think there was nothing about the cooperatives that was inherently incompatible with village values, social structure, or needs, despite villagers' initial skepticism. Indeed, one could even go further and argue that certain village values and attitudes might even have predisposed the population favorably to the idea of accepting a cooperative, provided only that they had some evidence that it would be an economic success. My qualified optimism is based on two kinds of evidence: One is the villagers' attitude to land and other economic resources; the other is their potential for cooperation in the attainment of individual goals.

As I have mentioned earlier, al-Qarya's general outlook and orientation in economic matters is exceptionally entrepreneurial and pragmatic, for some of the historical reasons I have already outlined above. This is evidence both in their attitudes toward land, and toward various sources and strategies of employment. Land is seen as a good investment or a source of subsistence and/or security, but does not in and of itself confer higher status than other non-agricultural forms of livelihood. Instead, prestige and status rest on a combination of wealth, demonstrated entrepreneurial ability, and proper conduct. Hence wealth more than land is the basis of social prestige. In addition, even landowning households do not live primarily off agriculture, but rather depend on several varied sources of income. Thus if someone else were to manage their agricultural holdings efficiently and produce a profit, it would free them to pursue alternative sources of income more effectively. While it is true that individuals do not like to give up managerial control of their assets, I think it likely that they might be willing to give up some control if the financial incentives were enough. For these reasons, then, I think that if the cooperatives had been more efficient, profit-producing, and somewhat less subject to central government control, many villagers would have had strong positive incentives to accept them.

Secondly, while many authors have suggested that traditional peasant social structure and values are inimical to collective forms of cooperation (see Banfield, 1958, on "amoral familism," and Foster, 1965, on the "image of limited good"), this is only partially true for al-Qarya. For while there is little precedent for enduring community organizations in the village or for that matter in North African culture generally, thee is ample evidence of cooperative, reciprocal, or collective actions on an intermittent basis and in accordance with need. In al-Qarya, this is best evidenced in the commitment to the service cooperative Amal, which the villagers set up in 1960 to rent out mechanized agricultural equipment at reasonable rates. Though set up with government aid, it was locally run and directed and was more efficiently managed than the state agricultural cooperative which later absorbed and replaced it. It set its own rates, decided whose field would be plowed in what order, and kept its equipment in good repair. Anyone in the village could use its services, but members of the cooperative paid a reduced rate.

The reason that it succeeded is that it was well-managed and met a perceived need. Prior to the establishment of Amal, villagers had perceived the benefits of mechanized plowing and harvesting, but few were in a position to take advantage of it, since the tractor and harvester owners (who came from outside the village) were unwilling to go to the trouble of coming to al-Qarya unless the amount of land to be plowed was substantial and the tracts continuous, which was rarely the case for any given landowner. As a result, only the largest landowners had been able to take advantage of mechanization. But with the establishment of Amal, small landholders could also, for the first time, take advantage of the benefits of mechanization. Thus villagers were not only receptive to the idea of a limited cooperative of this sort, but proved amply able to organize effectively and cooperatively when they perceived it in their interest to do so.

Thus in the case of al-Qarya, I would argue that there was nothing about village values, structures, and needs that was inherently inimical to the success of the cooperative. Rather the cooperative failed to win acceptance because it was poorly managed and run.

POLITICAL MOBILIZATION

The second area I wish to discuss is political mobilization. The idea of political mobilization of the populace has always been an integral part of independent Tunisia's idea of national development, both as an end in itself and as a means of furthering economic and social development. Toward this end, the government has actively worked to promote a strong sense of national identity (as opposed to pan-Arab, pan Islamic, or parochial tribal and regional identities); bring about active (though controlled) participation in the national party and party organizations, and elicit strong support for national development goals, particularly in the era of cooperativization and Destourian socialism after 1961.

In the village of al-Qarya, these efforts have met with varying degrees of success. On the one hand, the government has generally been successful in promoting national identity and gathering general (though sometimes qualified) support for its policies and goals. The reasons for its success are several. First of all, the government must be credited with extensive and effective use of the mass media and the party organization to publicize and promote both of these goals. Secondly, the government, through its publicity efforts and the provision of services, built upon and added to the considerable stock of legitimacy which Bourguiba and the Neo-Destour party had already acquired as a result of their leading role in the struggle for independence. They were then able to extend this legitimacy to their policies and programs as well. On the village level, this meant that because villagers trusted in and believed in Bourguiba, they were often willing provisionally to go along with particular policies and programs they might initially have disapproved or been skeptical of, at least until their misgivings proved to be well-founded.

This was, I think, one of the things that enabled villagers initially to accept the cooperative, however skeptically and passively. It is also significant, in this context, that even after the failure of the cooperatives locally and nationally, villagers refused to allow Bourguiba to take any share of the blame. Instead they put the blame entirely on Ben Salah, who indeed had been the minister of planning and the chief architect of the cooperative plan, but who never could have implemented his program without the extensive knowledge and support (including being given control of several other ministries) of President Bourguiba. However, for other villagers, the failure of the cooperatives began for the first time to sow seeds of doubt about the continuing wisdom and capabilities of the President, no matter how illustrious his part.

At the same time, however, that the government must be given credit for the effectiveness of some of its strategies of mobilization, it must also be noted that villagers were already predisposed to move in these directions anyway, for reasons having to do with the specific economic and social history of the village. As we have seen earlier, the combined effect of al-Qarya's early settlement pattern and the availability of non-agricultural opportunities which promoted economic mobility had several consequences for village organization and attitudes: Village economic and social structure remained fluid; the strength of kin ties and lineage were undercut; individualistic rather than collectivist orientations were reinforced. In addition, villagers were early exposed to various kinds of outside influences, both commercial and political, through the economic and political activities of the French. These features of village life in turn facilitated the achievement of national political goals in two ways: First, by weakening any competing solidarities of kin group, tribe, or religious fraternity, they paved the way for the acceptance of a national rather than parochial identification. Second, by giving the villagers an orientation which was essentially progressive, entrepreneurial, and outward looking, they made them generally receptive to most aspects of development and social change.

Thus, in these areas, both government programs and underlying predispositions facilitated the implementation of political goals. However, when we come o the goal of fostering active and meaningful participation in national organizations, here features of national political structure and of local values and structures have rather different effects. Though people do participate in elections, political rallies, and political organizations (such as the local party cell and branch, and party-linked organizations such as the youth organization, the women's organization, and so on), such participation is generally lackluster and ritualistic, even cynical. People tend to participate just enough to keep up appearances, but not enough to expose themselves to any risk-taking activity which might tarnish their image with party or state. For example, people vote for Bourguiba in national elections because their absence might be noticed or their blank ballots found out, but few participate in local elections because they consider them essentially meaningless.

What, then, explains the failure to get active and meaningful political participation? Are there problems in the national political structure itself, or is there something about village organization and values that predisposes villagers not to take political action or organize effectively for political goals? It seems to me that the answer lies in a combination of both. On the one hand, it is true that villagers do not ordinarily organize collectively on a frequent or permanent basis: Even holidays, weddings and the like are family rather than community celebrations. Similarly, cooperative work arrangements traditionally occur among a small circle of neighbors and friends rather than on a wider community level. This is true not only in al-Qarya, but seems to be a general feature of North African society as well, where collective political action has by-and-large not been an on-going feature of social life, but rather has occurred on an intermittent basis and in response to need.

On the other hand, ample precedents for collective action also exist, both in North African society generally and in al-Qarya; and the option to organize is in fact exercised, but mainly when there is a felt need. In traditional North African (Arabo-Islamic) society, this is seen in such phenomena as the jemaa, the fusion mode of segmentary lineage systems, and in the potential for religious movements to forge powerful, if temporary, alliances.[4] In the village, the ability of the villagers to sustain collective action has been demonstrated both by the success and longevity of the clandestine Neo-Destour party organization in the village for twenty years prior to independence, and more recently by the ability of the villagers to organize effectively in operating the service cooperative Amal.

Hence, precedents for participation and for non-participation both exist. The relevant question is not, then: Can villagers organize? Rather it becomes: Under what kind of circumstances do villagers organize and respond positively to opportunities for political action? In al-Qarya, there appear to be two circumstances: one, when they perceive it in their interest to do so; and two, when real power and influence are involved.

Thus, if we review the history of al-Qarya's participation in party activities, we find that villagers participated most actively in the period prior to independence, when the party was decentralized and independence was the goal. They continued their active participation in the years immediately after independence, when the party cell was influential in recommending people for jobs and acting as liaison between the village and the state. During this period, some of the most prominent men of the village ran for office and were elected. Then, as the central government grew stronger and the party cell's importance and influence declined, in the 1960's, the prominent men of the village turned their attention to other things. During this period, party cell membership mainly consisted of young, educated men using party cell membership as a stepping stone to better jobs, while general public interest and participation declined.

Finally, the events of 1967-69 brought about yet another pattern of political participation.

On the one hand, there was an increase in participation: There were more meetings and more committees as a result of the cooperatives and al-Qarya's new status as the headquarters of an administrative district. Prominent men ran once again for election to the party cell, in the hope that it would now be able to assume real responsibility as overseer of many of these activities, though this seen proved to be a vain hope. On the other hand, as an indicator of active local participation in the political process, the increase in political participation was essentially meaningless, or ritualistic and token at best. The party cell spent much of its time in ritual rather than substantive activities (for example, sending congratulatory telegrams to higher authorities), and frequently found itself officially reprimanded when it did try to take an independent stand. People attended meetings and elections when they felt it politically wise to attend, but they voiced no opinions that ran counter to what they thought the government wanted to hear. The explanation for such behavior lies in villagers' awareness of two fundamental features of the political system at that time: 1) There was no effective decision-making power delegated to the local level; rather all power was concentrated at the top. 2) The government at that time controlled most of the resources on which villagers' livelihood and well-being depended. In such a climate of excessive and centralized control, not only of political structures but of most of the economy as well, it is not surprising that local initiative was stifled and villagers followed a pragmatic and somewhat cynical

course: They participated only when they had to or when it did
them personal good, doing just enough to curry favor with party and
administrative officials without incurring any risk.   But in
general they remained apathetic, preferring where possible to
remain aloof.

What all this means from the point of view of national
government policy is that if the government wants to get effective
local participation, it will be able to do so only as long as
national institutions meet real needs and allow the exercise of
some local power. But if they do not meet these conditions, then
participation will remain token and ritualistic at best.

THE STATUS OF WOMEN

The third major area I wish to discuss is government policy
concerning the status of women. From the beginning the government
has been actively involved in improving the status of women and
encouraging them to take a more active role in the country's
development.   To this end it has initiated social legislation
giving women the right to vote, divorce, consent to their
marriages, and so on; it has introduced compulsory primary
education for girls, and sought to educate and mobilize women
generally through the use of the mass media and creation of a
national women's organization (Union Nationale des Femmes
Tunisiennes, or the UNFT) with branches at the regional and local
levels.

Though many of these programs and policies have had an impact
on the village, and though villagers often boast of the progress
that has been made in this area, in fact villagers are rather more
conservative in this domain than they are in any other. While many
villagers profess to be in favor of improving the status of women
(in accord with their progressive self-image), they tend to see it
as a gradual process appropriate for the next generation rather
than their own. In the immediate context, they see such changes as
a threat to custom, status, and honor. As a result, though many
changes have been accepted, there is much resistance as well. For
example, most villagers now accept primary education for their
daughters, but are reluctant to let them go on to secondary school.
Though girls are no longer veiled or secluded at puberty, higher
status families still restrict the movements of their adolescent
daughters.   Similarly, once married or betrothed, all women of
child-bearing age don the sefsari (the Tunisian veil), curtail
their movements, and avoid public places when they do go out.
While women do go out to vote (in national, but not local,
elections), they do not work in the fields, do marketing, or fetch
water in al-Qarya, and hence have few opportunities to meet other
women aside from relatives and neighbors. (It is worth noting
however, that the completion of a public bath in the village in
1970 should change this pattern somewhat.) The government has
tried to establish a UNFT branch in the village and a woman's night
for television in the village meeting house, but these have met

with only limited success: The UNFT is the exclusive domain of teenage girls, women's night at the clubhouse has so far attracted only a few.

What, then, are the factors that account for the villagers' cautious attitudes to change in this domain? To a large extent, the answer lies in the traditional values of honor and shame, which are reinforced by economic and social factors. As is well known, women are and have been, through their chastity and modesty of behavior, the repository of familial status and honor in Arab society, and thus guarantors of the status and honor of men. Since men judge other men according to the conduct of their women, changes in the status of women are linked to changes in the prestige structure of men, and therefore will be slow to change unless alternative sources of prestige outweigh them. Economic success is one such source of prestige which theoretically could bring about change in the status of women in the village. In the cities, where jobs are more available and European norms are more widespread, women's earnings have become increasingly valued (see Durrani 1976), and the equation between the seclusion of women and a man's honor and status has begun to break down. But in the village, where even many men are underemployed and must rely on government help and irregular work in order to make ends meet, there is little likelihood that substantial employment opportunities will open up for women in the immediate future. Furthermore, it is unlikely that men would approve of such opportunities, for they would only serve to bring women into direct competition for jobs with men. As a result, the employment of women could be construed as a threat to the economic position of men, as well as to their status and prestige. In other words, here economic factors act to reinforce rather than challenge the traditional prestige structure in the village, and work against radical change in this domain.

Thus, from a local perspective, it is not that the government's policy on women has been poorly designed or implemented, or that the villagers are totally unreceptive to change. Rather, the status of women is slow to change primarily because local economic and social constraints continue to lock people into traditional patterns of behavior, even while attitudes in this area are beginning to change.

CONCLUSIONS

What, then, can we conclude from these specific analyses, and what are their implications for development? One conclusion that we can draw is that technical and organizational features of national government programs and policies are crucial in determining their probable success. In al-Qarya, they were primarily responsible for undermining the cooperative and stifling political participation. In particular, excessive centralization of power must be singled out as an especially damaging feature of government programs and policies, for not only did it inhibit the accurate flow of information and produce policy decisions insufficiently adapted to local conditions; but more importantly, it cut off the very kind of effective participation (of which villagers were capable) which was needed to put development goals across, and substituted self-serving ritual, cynicism, and apathy in its stead.

The second conclusion that we can draw is that national development plans and goals must take account as much as possible of local conditions, and be aware of underlying structural arrangements and value orientations that may facilitate or impede the acceptance and effective implementation of national development goals. This means looking not only at the general features of North African social structure and value orientations, but examining their concrete and historically specific manifestations in each particular community, in order better to adapt national goals and policies to the specific community. For North African culture is not monolithic in its general patterning and modes of organization, but rather represents a range of variations clustered around some basic organizing principles and themes: For example, the basis of personal identity and group loyalty tends to be relativistic and situation-specific rather than absolute, with kinship and religion being particularly but not invariably important for each. Segmentary lineage systems contain a potential for both fission and fusion; and there is a regular tension between centralized, hierarchic forms of political organization on the one hand, and the democratic, non-hierarchic character of segmentary lineage systems and the indigenous jama a on the other. As a result, local communities are not identical, but vary according to the particular historical circumstances which have pushed them in the direction of one organizational mode or variant rather than another. Thus, because local communities vary in terms of their organization and underlying orientations and predispositions, it is of utmost importance that national plans and goals be designed in such a way as to allow maximum flexibility of implementation at the local level to ensure that national development goals and programs are indeed suited or adapted to local conditions and needs.

The third point to be made is that change or development does not necessarily occur in an even and harmonious fashion. Often there is a disjunction or even a conflict between attitudes and behavior, or between the constraints of one part of the social and ideational systems and another, and different parts of the system may pull in different directions. Thus, for example, in al-Qarya, attitudes toward change in the status of women were cautiously favorable, in keeping with the villagers' own self-image as progressive, but changes in behavior lagged behind, because of social and economic constraints. In addition, there was a clash between value sets as well: On the one hand, a positive valence given to modernization and a recognition that a change in the status of women was one of the components of such modernization; on the other hand, continued adherence to traditional definitions and markers of prestige, which define a man's status and honor in terms of the conduct of his women. Similarly, in the area of the cooperatives, different sets of value orientations pulled in different ways: On the one hand, resentment of centralized decision-making and lack of local control gave villagers a negative predisposition toward coopertivization. On the other hand, their generally pragmatic and entrepreneurial orientation to land, technology, and strategies of resource management would, I think, ultimately have led them to accept the cooperatives, _provided_ that they proved to be profit producing.

Thus, while both ideational factors and structural factors are important and may in and of themselves facilitate or inhibit change, one must also be aware of how they work together and with what effect: Do structural factors reinforce or work at cross-purposes with prevailing or desired value orientations and attitudes? Are values and structural factors in one domain of social life compatible or incompatible with values and structure operating in another? In other words, only by looking at the total system and the way in which its different elements work in concert or at cross-purposes can we hope to get the kinds of information which is needed to design more effective programs for local development and social change.

FOOTNOTES

1. In 1969, 25% of the landowners had less than 2 h. of land; 33% had 2-19 h.; 33% had 20-49 h.; 9% had 50 h. or more.

2. The initial pattern of village settlement, in conjunction with these economic factors, also contributed to this effect. Because the village was originally established by several individuals of different familial, tribal, or regional origins within a fairly short period of time, no single kin group was ever able to establish a firm position of preeminence. In this the village is similar to the Sahelian village described by Moore (1963).

3. 1 cantar equals 53.9 kg.

4. The _jama a_ is a North African tribal council, made up of representatives from each tribal segment. Its organization is democratic and non-hierarchical, and it deliberates on matters of tribal concern. The fusion mode of segmentary lineage systems refers to the capacity of lineage segments to unity for common action automatically in response to an outside threat. The reference to religious movements refers to the capacity for religious brotherhoods to mobilize large numbers of people for a political goal, such as was the case when the Sanusi movement in Libya organized resistance to the Italian occupation (Evans-Pritchard, 1949).

210

REFERENCES

Ashford, Douglas
1973a   Organization of Cooperatives and the Structure of Power
         in Tunisia. In Man, State, and Society in the
         Contemporary Maghrib. I. William Zartman, ed. New
         York: Praeger. pp. 380-394.

1973b   Succession and social change in Tunisia. International
         Journal of Middle Eastern Studies 4(1):23-29.

Banfield, Edward C.
1958   The Moral Basis of a Backward Society. New York: Free
         Press.

Durrani, Lorna H.
1976   Employment of Women and Social Change. In Change in
         Tunisia. Russell Stone and John Simmons, eds. Albany,
         New York: State University of New York Press. pp.
         57-72.

Dutton, Roderic
1976   Farming in the Lower Medjerda Valley. In Change in
         Tunisia. Russell Stone and John Simmons, eds. Albany,
         New York: State University of New York Press. p. 3-
         24.

Duvignaud, Jean
1970   Change at Shebika. London: Allen Lane/Penguin.

Evans-Pritchard, E.E.
1949   The Sanusi of Cyrenaica. London: Oxford University
         Press.

Foster, George M.
1965   Peasant Society and the Image of Limited Good. American
         Anthropologist 67(2):293-315.

Geerta, Clifford
1975   On the Nature of Anthropological Understanding.
         American Scientist, January/February.

Purvis, Malcolm
1976   The Adoption of High-Yielding Wheats. In Change in
         Tunisia. Russell Stone and John Simmons, eds. Albany,
         New York: State University of New York Press. pp.
         25:38.

Moore, Clement H.
1963   Politics in a Tunisian Village. Middle East Journal
         17(5):527-540.

Rosen, Lawrence
    1972   Muslim-Jewish Relations in a Moroccan City.
                International Journal of Middle Eastern Studies
                3(4):435-49.

Simmons, John D.
    1970, 1971   Agricultural Cooperatives and Tunisian
                Development, Parts I and II. Middle East Journal
                24(4):455-465; 25(1):14-26.

Stone, Russell
    1971   Tunisian Cooperatives Failure of a Bold Experiment; the
            Social Consequences of Attempted Agricultural and
            Commercial Reform. Africa Report 16(3):19-22.

11
Development in Rural Turkey: Leadership or Patronage?

Mubeccel Kiray

INTRODUCTION

In the 1950s when the great majority of the rural communities in underdeveloped societies first faced the upheaval of basic social structural changes and when the tensions, frictions and search for new relations within the process of change became very conspicuous a world-wide effort for "community development" became a major concern. Though the notion has not been clearly defined and, usually, included everything from primary school education to agricultural extension and medical care, the underlying assumption, at its best, was that many of the problems in rural areas of the underdeveloped countries could be solved at the community level, with community resources, while outside intervention would be limited to major technical aid.

On the other hand the demand of the metropolitan countries and the decision of the centers of the developing countries for the extraction of more surplus from agriculture brought, for the first time, to the rural areas of the latter, a very different type of production with new techniques and social relations. The decision concerning the change of production in agriculture was a matter for urban and metropolitan centers and countries. But its penetration to villages and its acceptance and assimilation was something difficult to control from outside. For the first impact was of external technological economic, social and political factors. Consequently all the early simplistic community development approaches met with the expected difficulties and remained simply ineffective when great structural changes, new interaction patterns, new powers and dependencies swept away the characteristics of the old settlements (1). As changes went on and the communities became very different from the old ones in every aspect, once more local problems came to the foreground and had to be solved at the community level with the new resources of the community. A second phase of community development started in the 1970s emphasizing productive infrastructure such as road, water, machinery and new crops. Still, as all these aim at change in the productive forces, the control of the newly achieved surplus and

212

the resultant external power relations remain out of reach of all the projects.

It is interesting to note, for instance that in 1978 international agencies which pool all information from every source, academic, official and others, still report that one does not have much useful, definite knowledge about the subject of rural development.

USAID reports that their own much more sophisticated projects in the Middle East "... have limited effectiveness at best... and AID has done nothing to establish a professionally defined and job classified cadre of skilled rural development specialists" (2).

It has been observed that there has always been a reality gap between the environment in which the people live and work and which is in fast change, and the designs of the projects of national or international agencies. A similar gap is also observable between the aims and targets of plans and the organizations available for implementation and administration.

It seems that even at this second stage of rural community development efforts lack theoretical knowledge and encounter organizational difficulty.

At this level of our knowledge we know something about large evolutionary stages of change; but we know very little about actual micro-processes of change in various societies at various stages of development. By the 1970s enough had been said about the indivisibility of economic and social aspects in development. But social and political aims have never been articulated: such as whether the members of the community have become less dependent, or whether life opportunities have been maximized and equalized for the majority. Furthermore it has not been emphasized enough that the specific processes involved will be different at various communities with different levels of development. According to the configuration of the new structure of a society and the speed with which it is changing, there appear certain intermediary processes, relationships and institutions specific to that situation. At the next step they also enter into interaction and affect, positively or negatively, further change. This feedback may or may not change the direction of change, may or may not accelerate the speed of change. Lacking good knowledge on such processes it is no wonder that development strategies had failed.

What is known today is that no local community changes its basic structure simply by its inner dynamics. There is always effective interference from outside. These factors first of all change the relative position of the main channels of interaction between that community and other centers outside of it. In developing countries not only the local communities but the whole society is also changing. Consequently the local communities are always under the influence of changing factors for new types of transformations, and experience differential pressures from different sources for change and adjustment at different times. Particularly various inputs in the form of new technologies, crops, or transportation-communication facilities alter not only the possible surplus achieved in the community but directly affect the emergence of new surplus drainage channels and control mechanisms, which further influences the network of relations and the interaction patterns, leading to new social and political changes. Agrarian transformation alters the nature of the political and economic relationship between the local agrarian community on the one hand and the city and the state on the other. A key set of institutions are the financial, commercial and marketing networks that tie the rural economy more firmly to a national and international system. Any planned change for a specific period for a local community becomes obsolete in a short time simply because the forces pushing change in other directions arise from outside, from larger centers with which the local communities must interact. It seems that change in local communities is always dependent on the changes in large centers. If change there is slow it creates intermediary dependency relationships and institutions which may hinder further change. Fast change on only one aspect does not achieve much "development" either. On the contrary the fast change of all aspects even if limited in scope, transforms the whole community in a conspicuous way.

Thus planned strategies aiming at a limited sphere such as "campaign for one type of crop," campaign for "literacy," or "campaign for home economics" remain ineffective when the relative position of the community in relation to other dependency centers is stagnant. When this relationship is altered, not only does change from inside start, but also no matter how substantial the local, simple planned change was, it is abandoned.

THE QUESTION OF LEADERSHIP

At this stage of development when the basic social structure has mostly changed and new human relations are taking place the people have more complex, anonymous relationships. New socio-economic life has brought new organizational development. Also, in this new and much more complex society it is clear that "leadership" is not, and anyhow never was, a matter of personality characteristics, nor is a person a leader just because he holds a position or post. Leadership in fact is an attribute that emerges in the process of new group formations with the demands of that new "situation." Leadership implies a rather definite kind of relationship to other people. A leader by definition is the most influential member of a group. If a group is newly formed the leader's position is among the first to be stabilized in the process of group formation. In periods of flux whoever takes effective initiative and influences the activity of others becomes a leader. Each group, however, would have a different aim or task to perform. Thus for each situation the influential person would have different characteristics. Leader-follower traits are relative to a specific social situation. Leadership seems to be both a function of the social situation and a function of personality; better, a function of these two in interaction. The main difference between leadership in formal organizations and informally organized groups is the leaders' sources of power. Power in actual groups is usually related to larger power structures. As group members face new situations, as new goals or values emerge in interaction, leadership may change hands. Even if a leader emerges informally in group interaction, much of his power in the group may stem from his relationships with persons and resources outside the group.

In order to persuade and influence a group and break down its various defense mechanisms, communication has to be highly persuasive. A great deal of social psychological research and theorizing have delineated the basic factors in such persuasive communication and pointed out methods and techniques of increasing its effectiveness. In general four basic components stand out, namely source variables, communication content, target variables and context variables. The source of the persuasive communication should be credible, and for credibility, trustworthiness, expertness and attraction are important characteristics. Thus who is communicating is a key factor.

The content of the communication itself is also important. So are the characteristics of the target group-community. The level of their knowledge of the issue, whether they agree or disagree with the view advocated in the communication, how committed or ego-involved they are with their own views and how strongly they feel about them are all found to be determing factors for their persuadability (3). However one should add immediately that basic social structure and interactions are the most important determinants of acceptance. If people are not ready to accept the suggestion no matter how much the findings are implemented, the issue remains dysfunctional and not integrated. The local system of leadership which is synonymous with influence and power refutes the social psychological laboratory findings except in rare cases. And this can not be emphasized enough.

As in development, when new groups with new interaction patterns emerge in communities it seems that certain new forms of leadership also emerge. How much this would contribute to which type of change remains a function of the new social configuration there. What type of new dependencies and what type of control mechanisms appear directly influences the leadership. Still our knowledge from social change is obviously very limited.

Systematic research on the interdependence of socio-economic development, local community adjustment problems, and arising "situational" leaderships is still limited. In this paper with such a problem in mind I shall examine the socio-economic development and changing networks in relation to the problem of leadership and emerging dependency relations (patronage) during the last thirty years in a village in Western Turkey.

Rural communities in Turkey, particularly in western Anatolia have long ceased to be closed, self sufficient communities. There are no more peasants. The rural population today takes part in a well organized national and international market. Cash crops are the main products, cash income the main form of income; new non-agricultural enterprises, migration, new authority patterns are all its various aspects. In fact rural Western Anatolia at this stage is further evolving into integration with industrial complexes. One of the most striking features in this transformation is the changing occupational structure, leading to new organizational development and power relations. New adjustment mechanisms arise because people are not only earning money in new ways, achieving new standards of living, and new forms of political participation, but also establishing new social networks and following new leaders. Systematic observation on these aspects with the main aim of delineating models of strategies would be valuable for our knowledge and goal of local rural development. Taskopru, the village I wish to examine here, distinctly exposes the phases of change and the end result of the external and internal factors of change in a complicated interaction. It particularly displays the acceleration of change that comes with the cumulative effect of the increasing number of various dominant factors which one by one could not do much for the community.

The necessary observations have been made by numerous visits and indepth interviews with the source individuals in the community between January 1978 and June 1979. A probability sample survey was taken in the community during the last week of April 1978 in which specifically trained students from Istanbul Technical University acted as interviewers. One hundred forty-four completed questionnaires, seventy three percent of the original sample, constitute the other major source of data and information. This survey was administered to the heads of the households in the village.

THE VILLAGE AND TRADITIONAL LEADERSHIP

In 1950 when Turkey's rural areas and agriculture was for the first time opening up to cash cropping, the small Taskopru village on the narrow coastal plan bordering the Marmara Sea near Yalova had fifty households with a population of around two hundred fifty. It was 11 kilometers to Yalova, then a small settlement, rather unimportant as it was only a small market town. The road that connected the village with the town was a narrow macadam road. It was a typical immigrant-peasant village of a type which used to be numerous in Anatolia (4). It also had a rather widespread characteristic of social organization of Anatolian marginal rural settlements (5), in that an influential man dominated the community. He decided when and where a house could be built, a new field should be plowed, even what the name of a new born baby should be. Although he had only five hundred <u>donums</u> of land and used extra-family labor as farmhands (not wage <u>work</u>) he had power. He was the headman of the village and dominated the insecure peasants in a patron-client relationship. He solved their problems with outside circles. He gave them wheat at the end of the winter when their stock ran out. He acted as arbitrator in disputes as a true patron (6).

Taskopru was a concrete example in recent history where, in a rural context, leadership as influence lay solely in one powerful man who demanded respect and loyalty from the rest of the villagers. D. Bey, as said above, controlled every interaction with the outside, acted as arbiter in disputes and was responsible for the welfare of the peasants. In fact, here influence, power and leadership totally enveloped each other. The lord -<u>aga</u>- D. Bey symbolized also the general respect for authority and carried it further to loyalty to and respect for state. In fact he was a member also of the single party of the time as well. He had no children and he preferred to leave Taskopru when state authority gained a new character with the introduction of a multi-party parliamentary system to Turkey.

The elderly were also a source of influence and leadership. Among kin the relations of influence followed age line. The old used to be consulted and followed when the aga did not practice his authority. Thus the traditional leadership was very clearly delineated by the Aga's position in the village and elder members' authority in the family. Whatever change Taskopru experienced had direct impact both on D. Bey and on the role of the elders.

Thus in 1950, Taskopru was one of the typical settlements of relatively self-sufficient cereal growing villages with an <u>aga</u>. The aga family occupied the better adobe house with two stories and a tiled roof. Change and development came to Taskopru first as intensive vegetable cultivation followed by fruit growing. An agricultural practice several millenia old, based on the simple technology of ox and plow changed in fifteen years into various types of vegetable gardening. More enterprising men with larger landholdings turned to apple and peach growing. Orchards that had been started in late 1950s matured by the sixties and the village started to enjoy an increase of income. Marketing and transportation, which is sometimes an obstacle to full benefits, was not much of a problem, since the town and Istanbul were near and roads were developing. In 1965 the narrow road was made into a hard surfaced large highway which connected various nearby towns to each other and to Bursa, a larger center. At the same time Istanbul's contact with Bursa, whose metropolitan area was industrializing, increased the importance of the nearest town, Yalova. So Taskopru was not only gaining better accessibility to a town but to a town which was becoming an important center. Fruit growing in general was, at the same time, gaining importance and the apples and peaches were even marketed internationally. At this time not only orchards but cold storage establishments, transportation facilities and organizational aspects also grew fast in the area.

Meanwhile for those who did not have land in the village the chance to earn more money opened up. Western European countries had demanded unskilled labor (7). This certainly raised expectations in this village too. Between 1965 and 1971 ten families, men, women, children, went to Germany to work. One came back in 1968, two others in 1975. Also as the village is situated in the metropolitan growth area of Istanbul, two large artificial fiber and one cellulose factory were established in the area. They suddenly opened up chances for wage-labor in industry for the villagers. It also opened up the village for outsiders to settle. As if all those changes were not enough Yalova, the nearby town, found itself the breaking point of routes that developed in the metropolitan area of Istanbul. Yalova is the terminus for the ferry-boat service from Istanbul that carries the half of the transportation to the Aegean sea coast and the west-central Anatolia. Indeed Yalova today with its daily contact with Istanbul is just an adjoining sub-center for all Istanbul's metropolitan services. In fact, the whole sub-region uses Yalova for its banking, transportation and communication services.

The growth of Yalova led to expansion of its residential area towards Taskopru. The coastal strip became a desirable residential area for the urban development of Yalova and environs. All of this meant an unheard-of increase in land prices. Some agricultural fields became urban, in fact metropolitan land as building lots.

By the time metropolitan residential development had reached Taskopru, it also became obvious that three large industrial complexes had obtained the central government's permission to use all the underground water in the area and they had channeled all artesian wells at the depth of 10 m. to their reservoirs. Orchards, large or small, in the area are in need of water and they are fighting cases in the courts about the permission the plants obtained. What is further interesting is that even all the wells can not supply the plants with the necessary water and they have to have proper dams to collect the running streams in the area. If this could be provided before the orchards die, perhaps, both the plants and the agriculture would flourish otherwise both agriculture and industry will suffer.

Taskopru participated in land speculation by simply selling as well as by speculating which become one of the most effective factors of change. Thus Taskopru from 1950 to 1978, in less than one generation passed roughly from simple self sufficiency to intensive cash cropping on an international scale. Overlapping with the last stage there came heavy industry with new demands on the natural reserves of the region and new ways of employment and earning a living which means new dependencies and class formations. What could take place in another time and place in the world in three or four generations has been experienced here in less than two decades (8).

PORTRAITS FROM THE VILLAGE: B.BEY

As the community lived through from one stage to the other, each member had his share of change. Some stayed in cereal growing. Some passed from self sufficiency to factory wage work or to small trade. B.Bey and his family provide a dramatic picture of what development brought to Taskisla people at its maximum. In 1966 he was a man of 19 without land and without family. All he could do was to work for wages in agriculture. By 1955 the old fashioned irgatlik was over and he was employed as wage worker in the orchard of A.Bey, a strictly modern cash cropping large land owner as we shall see further down. When in 1961 it became possible to go to Germany as an industrial worker, he applied immediately, married one of the poorer girls who was a maid in the house of A.Bey. They went to Germany together and worked there up to 1968. In an industrialized country this could be the last stage of of his career. Or even if he migrated to Istanbul the result could be the same. But now they came back with some money they had saved. First he bought land to raise vegetables. He also attempted cattle raising for milk. The gardens succeeded. But cattle raising, for which he collaborated closely with the government extension service, failed sadly. After three years of hard work and the loss of considerable money he gave up cattle raising and turned to the land again. By 1972, however when he gave up cattle raising, land speculation and the metropolitan growth had reached new heights. He sold some of his garden and bought new land on the coast. He sold it immediately at a very high price. From then on, although he lived in the village, he shifted his sphere of activity to Yalova, opened up an office as a real estate broker.

However, he also kept his garden with an overseer and built cold storage capacity to rent out. Now he is considered one of the richest men in the whole area. His first attempt has been to build a new large concrete house in the village. He installed electricity and running water to the house, furnished it with modern sets of living, dining, and bedroom furniture, curtains and other household utilities such as a refrigerator and a washing machine and he bought a Mercedes car. He no longer goes regularly to the coffee shops in the village. He also entered, in addition to village contacts, into a new network of relations in the town. He is becoming a Yalova and Istanbul man. He entertains, in his home, the district officer (kaymakam) and the judge with their wives. Something like this is truly new for Taskopru. What really symbolizes the processes of change for the family and is a model for the village is the education of the daughter. She was born in 1961. She completed village primary school in 1971. As it is usually for rural Turkey they decided that this much education was sufficient for a daughter. But three years later in 1974 when family started to change their status and started to circulate in circles different from Taskopru, they changed their minds and decided that their daughter deserved better education. After a period of intensive private tutoring the daughter took the examinations as an external student and eventually graduated from the junior high-school. Then she attended the high-school (lycee) proper. In 1979 she graduated from there as well and took university entrance examinations. Obviously she is a talented person. But no capacity on her part could have made her parents reconsider, particularly after they had made her stop going to school, if they had not changed their socio-economic status and gained much power and influence.

The wife of B.Bey was the daughter of a poor peasant. She started to work as maid in A.Bey's house and was illiterate. She learned how to read and write in an adult literacy course for women, conducted by a voluntary association. She also learned the ways of life of an elite family with different, finer ways of cooking, dressing, and cleaning: in short a higher level of living. Such an intimate knowledge of upper middle class urban life together with the experience of Germany enables her to carry her family to higher status. She further showed infinite flexibility in transferring her role from the expectations of the villagers to the expectations of her husband's urban contacts. She had no difficulty in entertaining them with teas and cakes and dinners at home.

Her clothing, however is something controversial. The village women of her age group still cover their head with scarves and many of them wear baggy pantaloons. She wears usually normal dresses but when only with the village women she changes into long and large skirts. As for head covering, she says she does as her husband asks: If he says she should not cover her head today with such and such people she complies, if she is asked to cover another time she puts on her scarf. In the village when alone she goes around with a scarf. Her daughter dresses totally as her urban age group including blue-jeans and t-shirts. The son is still young, he goes to junior high school in Yalova. The father does not worry much about him, saying that he has earned enough money to last his son up to his death. It is intriguing to see now how the need for education had changed. For the girl it became a necessity and for the boy not so urgent a need.

B.Bey, extending his influence as an employer in his cold storage establishment and as somebody who lends money and sells the land of the villagers, has become a patron. He has also run for the headmanship to back up his influence with political authority as well.

A.BEY

The most pain giving slow change from self sufficiency, to intensive vegetable growing took place in early 1950s as the result of an external factor. The son of an upper class Istanbul family with a graduate degree in fruit growing from the United States decided to invest capital, given by the family, in farm land. He shopped for suitable land all around the fertile coast of the Marmara region and found Taskisla Aga D.Bey, then an old man, selling his land basically because of political changes in the country. He bought the land and equally important perhaps for the village he settled in the village with his wife. He was very much involved in successful farming but his interest in the village had nothing to do with the patron-client relationship of the old aga. He needed labor from the village and paid them the prevailing wages. The feelings of the villagers were ambivalent at the time as some of the middle aged people now acknowledge. They were accustomed to borrow wheat in time of need in winter and return it with some extra after the harvest. A.Bey also at the beginning before the vegetable gardens and orchards were grown raised wheat and gave all the wheat asked by the villagers. But he did not accept their payment in turn at the end of harvest. This, they say, made them realize that his work and relationship in the village were different. Accordingly they did not borrow wheat ever again, but worked for wages in his orchard. His practice of sheep and chicken raising and especially his apple growing became a model for the village. Men did not only work for wages in A.Bey's orchard but also learned how to water, to fight pests, to prune and pick, and other related activities. His installations and establishment formed a model. It seems he was always patient enough to show and teach whenever anybody asked questions about agriculture, but never accepted any role of a patron-client type which would lead to dependency.

The role his wife played, though, in the community was very different. She was also trained as an agriculturalist with the best elite education the country could give. With a very inquisitive mind she became involved with the women and children of the village. As far as the change of the style of the life in the houses are concerned a lot came from her. She took over the role of a patron to help the villagers with hospitals, schools. and certain government circles and it seems that only her contacts and behavior really made the family an integrated part of the community. A. Bey's wife, as she took an active interest in the village also tried to bring larger organized change to the life of the women and girls. With the cooperation of an international women's association she organized the women in a club or association for mutual help in home economics and various other activities. Some of their activities are rather interesting. To learn how to can fruit and vegetables was very attractive to the members. Many learned how and they are still practicing it. But village grocery stores are now full of commercially tinned fruit and vegetables. One may easily assume that the practice will die out. Another action was a literacy course for adult women. Government school teachers participated and the school facilities were used. It was successfully completed. But R. Hanim also admits that the following year in the elections none of the women signed their names but used their finger prints. However their daughters today are all graduates of primary school and if they are not going to secondary school, it is because there is not one in the vicinity.

However the social life of the family of A. Bey and the informal network in which they circulated was outside of the village. They kept all their relations with the city; they frequently entertained both the Istanbul and the national elite as well as international groups. So the village accepted the couple as one of themselves, but also surely very "different" from themselves.

In fact the villagers explicitly indicated that for instance R. Hanim could go around with a short sleeved dress and without covering her head as she was "different." Still there is no doubt the couple constituted a model for many things, from their agricultural practices, to the way they educated their children.

A.Bey's family who were involved with the political life of the country from the beginning took an active part in politics after 1973 and left the village in 1974 for national political activities. Their enterprise continues however with supervision from a distance and they occasionally visit the village. The role played by A.Bey in the development of the village is unexpected but also rather interesting, since he did influence the pattern of agricultural change into cash cropping without intending it and never acting as a leader. Still he trained his wage workers in the necessary skill and knowledge, and perhaps because he did not interfere with their activities in their gardens and fields, contrary to traditional aga, that was enough stimulation.

CHANGES IN WAYS OF EARNING A LIVING

After giving a picture of the development of Taskopru in its dramatic characteristics, we may now turn to a more detailed examination of the village. We shall first examine the change in the ways of earning a living, then changing consumption patterns, as they are closely related to one another. In these aspects we shall try to see the relative place of local strategies of development and the effect of national ones. Today intensive farming constitutes only the second largest field of activity (Table 11.1). The leading one is skilled labor which includes drivers of various cars and jobs in the factories and workshops. Unskilled work, particularly as agricultural wage work, is the third most frequent. One has to notice that traders and salaried people who do not normally belong in the self sufficient peasant village are here as well. In fact even those who say that they earn their living through cereal growing or sheep raising are a few old people who are helped by the younger generation for their main expenses. When today's activities are compared with that of the fathers' generation, the contrast stands out rather strikingly. While only a tiny fraction (3.1%) today is dealing with growing grain more than the half of the fathers were really living by it. In addition, another 11.8% of the fathers were landless tenant peasants. So the self sufficient basis of the village of thirty years ago can easily be pictured (Table 11.2).

TABLE 11.1 - Ways of Earning a Living

	Household Heads %	Fathers %
Grain grower	3.1	54.2
Orchard-Vegetable grower	26.0	6.2
Agricultural wage labor	6.2	---
Skilled industrial worker	34.0	4.2
Unskilled industrial worker	10.4	11.8
Trader	9.7	2.7
Artisan	2.8	4.8
Salaried employee	1.0	4.8
Unemployed	7.6	---
Not clear		11.1

N: 144

The small orchard or garden owners all have their wives, sons and daughters working on family property. Furthermore if the farm is very small, men are likely to work for wages in the larger orchards, and women are likely to work in the cold storage establishments that have appeared like mushrooms all around the area. Continuous or temporary wage work in agriculture, and in factories in the vicinity, is so widespread that except for the oldest everybody is gainfully employed. Households with more than one wage earner constituted 80 percent of the households (Table 11.2). Self sufficiency based on cereal growing gave way to orchard and garden farming and that gave way to either agricultural processing or proper industrial wage work. Industrial wage work certainly does not pay as high an income as a small to medium orchard. But it is definitely considered better than agricultural wage work because of its social security schemes and the possibilities for higher skill acquisition on the job.

TABLE 11.2 - Gainful Employment in the Households

	The Head	Wife	Son	Daughter
Grain Growing	5.1	--	--	--
Orchard-Vegetable growers	23.6	50.0	15.8	21.4
Trade	9.7	--	7.9	
Artisan	2.8	--	--	--
Skilled workers	34.0	12.5	32.2	50.0
Unskilled workers	10.4	37.5	39.5	28.6
Salaried Employee	6.9	--	2.6	
Unemployed	7.6			

N:144

Interestingly enough the respondent villagers of Taskopru with all the variety of possibilities of earning a living, are hesitant both in deciding whether they should change their way of earning a living or what type of job they would wish for their sons (Table 11.3-4).

TABLE 11.3 - What They Wish to do to Improve Their Condition

	%
Nothing	51.4
To start agriculture	6.9
Trade	9.0
Manufacture	4.2
To change crop	7.6
To change trade	2.1
To change manufacture	1.1
To save money	4.2
To educate children	2.1
Others	5.5
Not clear	5.5

N: 144

TABLE 11.4 - The Occupations They Wish for Their Son

	%
Educated good man	22.2
Professional (engineer, lawyer, doctor)	18.7
Highly skilled worker	16.0
White collar-salaried	10.4
Farmer-Orchard owner	3.5
Businessman	3.5
Religious man	1.1
Others	4.5
Not clear	15.3

N: 144

Still 16 percent of the fathers wish their sons to have vocational school training and to be skilled workers. The vague answer of "let him be educated" still constituted a 22.2 percent. Certainly to be a doctor and an engineer is also attractive (8.7%). But their indecision is conspicuous. One has to accept it as the consequence of fast changes and the variety of possibilities of earning a better living. As a result 15.3 percent left the question without an answer. Taskopru at the moment with clashing interests in agriculture, industry, and services just cannot make up its mind as a rule what to choose. Obviously, although they enjoy more income and diversity of resources, members of the community are caught in a strong current of change that is beyond their control. How they should avoid behavior that will be an adventure, they do not know. They are also aware that many types of "adventurous" behavior ended in more income and power. Still a great majority in this ambiguous situation do not want to change jobs (65.3%). Another 16 percent howevezr are ready to turn to trade, which requires the least skill of any job. The capital will come from selling land. At the moment for instance there are four families that own land but do not cultivate it. They are ready to sell. Among those who had land one fifth has already sold either all or a substantial part of their land.

The change in crop is very clear too. Only ten years ago among those who had land almost 60 percent were cultivating cereals. But already the other 27 percent had turned to vegetable gardening and 10 percent to fruit. Cereal was rarely sold as a cash crop. Today only one fifth of the villagers do grow cereals as a partial crop for home use. But the ratio of fruit growers increased to 62.3 percent while the vegetable gardening went down to 14.7 percent (Table 11.5).

TABLE 11.5 - Agricultural Crops (percent)

	Now	10 Years Ago
Cereal	21.3	58.2
Vegetable	14.7	26.9
Fruit	62.3	10.4
Others	1.6	4.5

N: 62
Do not cultivate   4
Do not have land   78

In turning from self sufficiency to cash cropping, marketing appears as the most devastating problem, both in terms of technology as well as human relations as it leads to dependency for the peasants. Taskopru, because it is close to large cities, found it easy to start in a small way. Ten years ago the vegetables which constituted the main crop was basically sold in the weekly open market of Yalova, the most primitive way of marketing. Today only one gardener is still doing so. The larger producers even ten years ago sold wholesale to the exporters. The next most important outlet is the wholesalers in Istanbul who are nearby and easy to contact. Such a way of marketing was practiced by only 17 percent ten years ago, while today it affects 40 percent. As the country as a whole demands more agricultural products both for local consumption as well as for export, the organizations developing in metropolitan areas also make an effort to find the crop in the orchards and to make arrangements to buy on a large scale. Now 14 percent of the growers sell their product to the representatives of the big city firms right on their gardens (Table 11.6).

TABLE 11.6 - Mode of Marketing

	Now %	Ten Years Ago %
Did not sell	16.4	28.4
Wholesale from the fields and orchards	22.9	10.4
Intermediaries in Istanbul; Wholesale	41.0	17.9
Occasional-Individual-Purchasers from the gardens	13.1	11.9
Local traditional open markets	1.6	29.9
State	4.9	1.6

N: 66

Today one may say that the market is coming to the small producer, but certainly on its own terms and prices. Moreover, there are always intermediary people on whom the villagers become dependent. One can ask if there is anyway it could be different. Marketing still constitutes a part of production that could be planned and organized with a different strategy.

Before marketing, however, one has first to learn how to cultivate a different crop. Although an extension service of the government has been in the areas since the 1930s, the interaction between the villagers and extension officers has remained a minimum. The demonstration effect of the larger producers definitely constitutes the main source of knowledge in agriculture (88.8 percent). The other sources for the younger generation are fathers and friends. And because many learned it in similar ways but are not articulate about it there were many vague answers and some stated that there was no need for a special skill in gardening (11 percent). Obviously, whether intended or not, those who came from the outside with knowledge and practiced successful agriculture did become leaders in changing the basic mode of earning a living. Furthermore the totality of the changes in the country, particularly in the metropolis and city, triggered the first change, and with a time lag the village followed suit.

At the moment non-agricultural work predominates. Skills that would be necessary in industry, or education and knowledge useful in white collar jobs or in trade are not taught in the village. A general primary school education, which started with difficulty at the end of 1950s. remains very short of the need. Here is another dilemma. Resistance to schools and literacy has turned into demand for higher and specialized education in the village. In a country where depeasantization attains 18 percent a year, to have such a school in the village certainly does not meet the needs. As far as Taskopru goes, our survey has shown that training courses on the job have been a source of skill. Twenty-seven percent of the respondents have stated that they learned their industrial skill in this way. It seems that by the time the campaign for literacy came to our village it was already in the demand for different specialized types of education.

Today rather extensive individualism prevails in the village. Villagers are hesitant about who could help and advise them about their problems. Change is fast. New situations arise daily, and the men are not sure whose interest lies where. Thus a significantly high amount of self reliance is evident. More than half of the villagers insisted that they ask advice from nobody and another 20 percent seeks only the advice of the family. Another 22 percent is vague about whether they will ask advice or not.

They are aware also that many questions they have today are beyond their experience. Those who have adjusted themselves to non-rural life, who work in the factories or other business places, are aware that the complex organizations of urban life such as trade unions, banks, government offices can help them (27.8 percent) (Table 11.7).

TABLE 11.7 - Borrowing Money (percent)

Nobody	29.9
Anonymous organizations	27.8
(Bank, Insurance Company etc.)	
Village influentials, friends	20.1
Relatives	13.2
Boss	4.2
Not clear	4.8
N	144

Financing the enterprise in different stages is another bottleneck for villagers who have now experimented with gardening and fruit growing. First of all the size of the enterprise determines whether anonymous complex organizations, such as banks, would be used or not. The small ones insist that they do not borrow money (34 percent). The only party they can ask for money is their close relatives (14 percent). However the larger the enterprise the more dominant the banks become. Credit given by banks is rarely enough to keep the business going. Thus a lot of borrowing is done, although they do not readily accept it, from wealthier members of the community. Wage workers, whether agricultural or factory, or other type of employees, claim that they do not borrow money. But they always buy their needs from the grocery stores on credit (Table 11.8).

TABLE 11.8 - Whom Do They Go For Assistance for Their Enterprise? (percent)

Nobody	30.5
Family	13.9
Influential Villagers	9.4
Complex organization	10.4
Employer	4.5
Not applicable	33.8

More has to be said about borrowing from wealthier fellow villagers. Such borrowing requires signed papers and repayment provisions at specific times in specific ways. Thus it is relatively formal. The transaction takes place, for instance, in coffee shops. But still a new type of dependency and patron-client relationship arises in the village. This opens new influence, power and leadership channels.

Taskopru is experiencing a fast change from self sufficiency to intensive cultivation within the metropolitan region. The best indice of its development is the expression of income in cash. Instead of saying that one has so many donums of land and so many heads of sheep, villagers talk about how many liras they spend per month and how many liras they earn in a given period. Nothing could show the transformation better. The average declared income in the village today is between 3000 to 5000 Turkish liras (40.3 percent). One fifth of the households earn between 2000 to 3000. Another 20 percent earns up to TL 10.000, and 6.9 percent earn more than TL 10.000 which is a relatively high income even on the scale of the larger urban centers (Table 11.9).

TABLE 11.9 - Approximate Monthly Income
of the Household Heads (percent)

None	3.5
Less that 1999 TL.	6.2
2000-2999	17.4
3000-4999	40.3
5000-7499	16.0
7500-9999	5.5
1:0.000 and more	6.9
Not clear	4.2

N: 144

To see the subjective evaluation of their earnings we asked them how much income one would need for a decent living in Taskopru. The mode of responses is very close to the average declared income in the village today. It concentrates around TL 5000 (Table 11.10). Roughly one third of the villagers actually earn this income. One fourth is earning more than this and the income of the rest is below it. This is rather unexpected. If one compares the great gap we had observed ten years ago in other cash cropping areas of Turkey, one realizes that here in an extremely short time income has risen so that expectations did not have time to go up at the same time (9). Subjectively the income is higher than they had anticipated. But it made them suspicious and insecure which was very clear in their attitude towards occupations and towards the research.

In previous similar research projects in areas with less increase in income but where people were more confident of their ability to predict the near future, the responses in the survey did not have such a high ratio of vague answers and participation was hundred percent. In Taskopru participation dropped to seventy-five percent.

TABLE 11.10 - Income per month required for
a decent life in village (percent)

Less that 1999 TL.	0.7
2000-2999	5.5
3000-3999	21.5
5000-7499	51.4
7500-9999	9.7
10.000 and more	9.0
Not clear	2.1

CONSUMPTION AND DEVELOPMENT

Since the immediate impact of agro-economic development and increasing income should be reflected in the standards of living of the people experiencing the changes, we shall now focus our attention on housing and consumption. Such an analysis will give us the micro level results of development. The consequences of income increase in the life of the people is, however, never limited to the rising standard of living.

The first impression of standards of living in this village could be obtained from the outside appearance of the houses and from housing conditions in general. The earlier houses (1960) in Taskopru seem to be very different from what one sees today. Only two of these older houses remain today and both are being used for storage. These houses were built of a frame of woven canes plastered with mud or, rarely, of adobe bricks. The mud floors were level with the street which made them damp. Windows were also rare or very small. Latrines were outside and so was the "barn" or "stable." Simple kerosene oil lamps, some vaporized oil lamps or hurricane lamps were used for light. Cooking was done in ovens burning wood and charcoal, and over open fires in fireplaces. Drinking water was obtained from primitively dug out wells and from brooklets and springs. These details indicate rather primitive housing facilities.

It seems that this house type lasted until 1965 and in 1970 electricity became available. Building new houses of brick and cement came in waves to Taskopru. Our survey shows that it started immediately with the change to cash cropping around 1967 and started to have a very special place after land started to be sold in early seventies (Table 11.11). Electricity became available in 1970. Today there are no more cane houses or thatched roofs. They are all of brick and cement. Eighty percent of them have separate kitchens, 90 percent a separate place a bath, in 60 percent of them the lavatory is in the house and 40 percent have running water. Outhouse latrines are also better equipped and village fountains are accessible to every household (Table 11.12). A great majority of the houses (62 percent) have 3 or 4 rooms. Average number of rooms per house is 3.2 and number of persons per room only 2.4 (Table 11.13).

TABLE 11.11 - The Period the House was Built (percent)

1977-76	15.5
1975-1974	13.8
1973-1970	25.9
1969-1965	16.4
1964-1959	11.2
1958-1953	6.9
Before 1953	10.4

N: 116

TABLE 11.12 - Utilities in the House (percent)

	Yes
Kitchen	80.5
Bath	89.6
Lavatory	56.9
Running water	39.6

N: 144

TABLE 11.13 - Number of Rooms (percent)

Single	2.1
2 Rooms	30.5
3-4 Rooms	61.9
5-6 Rooms	4.2
Not clear	1.4

N: 144

With better housing comes a higher quality of household goods and living. Television sets and refrigerators are not anymore novelties in the village. Their purchase follows the building of new houses by two or three years and is a good indicator of change in the style and quality of life in the village (Table 11.14).

TABLE 11.14 - Periods of buying household goods (percent)

	Bed-stead	Furni-ture	Carpet	Tele-vision	Refri-gerator
1977	8.4	21.3	15.3	34.9	24.0
1976-1975	14.5	34.0	27.1	42.2	33.3
1974-1973	12.2	21.3	18.6	15.7	26.7
1972-1970	10.7	8.5	11.9	3.6	2.6
1969-1967	16.0	10.6	8.5	1.2	10.7
Before 1966	38.2	4.2	18.6	---	---
N.	131	47	59	83	75

The change of agricultural structure is followed some five years later by construction of new houses, two years later that is followed by furnishing and buying household goods. Here the most persuasive agency seems to be mass communication media with its advertising.

Breakfast with tea, cheese, olives, and bread, which certainly is more balanced and pleasure-giving in comparison with the previous plain cereal soup and bread, has become a well established custom. As for lunch and dinner, protein rich food is still lacking but various vegetables and leguminous food with yogurt constitutes a better diet. One has to admit that canning learned through the activities of the women's association under R. Hanim's leadership has definitely brought possibilities for vegetable consumption in winter, too. But as indicated above observation in the village grocery stores also has shown that commercially canned fruit juices, stewed fruits, and vegetables are also bought. One may expect that if women's labor is shifted more intensively to wage work, canning at home will lose all its importance soon. There also seems to be a great tendency for expenditure on luxury items like tea, coffee, even chocolate and sugar, to increase with per capital income.

No matter what is the income, meat consumption is still limited. So are eggs, chicken, and fish. Yogurt is the only exception. What should be stressed in the noncereal based diet is the place of yogurt and sugar. In this village it seems there was hunger before. But today there seems to be no danger of hunger per se but perhaps of malnutrition. The rising income did not alter the quality of nutrition as dramatically as it did the housing. The reason lies in a very unexpected aspect of family life.

It is truism of course to say that the home is the women's domain. In this domain, women's important role of coordination and decision making shows itself in the consumption patterns of the family. At the stage of self sufficiency, when the limited resources had to be stretched from harvest to harvest in food and from cradle to tomb in other consumption items, not only women's producing and processing activities, but also and more importantly their decisions on consumption in general determined the level and style of living of the household unit.

The change of the income source, the amount of income, the new speed of earning money changes the consumption patterns as well as the values pertaining to consumption and wealth. When change affects such patterns, at least at certain stages of change, rather significant differences appear between the consumption of men and women.

Taskopru women who are responsible for the family almost without exception spend one day of the week (Saturday) in the nearby town in shopping. This is the day when traditional weekly open market is held in Yalova. Once upon a time it was the market where the women sold their tiny surplus of eggs and vegetables. Now these weekly markets are nationally organized mobile shopping places where every consumption item from salt to canned vegetables, from sheets and coats to farming implements is on sale. Now in this weekly market and on the main street shops the women of Taskopru spend the money income allocated to the family's consumption. As they have now attained the cash economy, and more than one person is gainfully employed, the income is pooled by the men of the house and the basic items of food, clothing, and furniture are bought, with the wife's planning and demand, by the men on a weekly, a seasonal, or yearly basis. Therefore, only small amount of cash are given to women for daily purchases from nearby stores, or from the weekly market.

The income of the family is divided into two parts: one for the family consumption at home and the other for the husbands' own consumption outside the family. Men spend rather large amounts on their own consumption as they eat out a lot, and do their own shopping for clothes. Spending for pleasure, for cigarettes, or for drinks may reach large amounts for their budgets (Table 11.15). It has also been observed that when they do not like the food prepared at home, the usual traditional simple dishes consumed by the wife and children, they leave home, and have more extravagant dishes, broiled meat and other delicacies in the restaurants. The increase of income, for many families where men spend more time alone outside the home:, leads to double standards of food consumption. The male population of the village has the habit of eating outside whenever they can. The restaurants in town serve men who after shopping or running an errand gather around a table here and eat and drink for long hours at night. As long as income was limited and was not changing, such outings of men were also rare. Now that the village is becoming a part of the town with relatively efficient transportation and incomes are raising beyond expectations this old custom is gaining a new dimension. Men are eating out more frequently and also much better than their families. A limited amount of the increased income is spent for the family as a whole. Important amounts of money are reserved for the man's own consumption and particularly for food consumption outside of the house.

TABLE 11.15 - Amount of Pocket Money Required for Men
(per month percent)

None	0.7
Less that 249 TL	6.2
250- 499 TL	11.1
500- 999	29.9
1000-1999	37.5
2000-3999	9.1
4000 and more	2.1
Not clear	3.5

CHANGING FAMILY AND LEADERSHIP RELATIONS

The subject of family carries significance for many aspects of the analysis of development and leadership. First of all in the traditional village it was the only social organization in which the members of the society established their relations with others. The family was a patriarchal closely knit kinship group. Then as mentioned before the elder members always had influence and authority on the others and they functioned as leaders for their families. Whatever change is taking place in the social networks signifies a change in the family relations as well. Thus the place of the elders, the relations of husbands and wives, the women's activities in general and the youth, all can be analyzed only in reference to the changes in the family.

Taskopru today consists of two hundred sixty households. Among them traditional patrilinial extended families are as low as 4.8 percent (Turkey's average for rural areas is 25.4 percent). The ratio of nuclear families, on the other hand, is as high as 75.1 percent (Turkey's average for rural areas is 55.4 percent). Families with one or the other parents of the husband living with the family is 15.3 percent (Table 11.16) (10). The transient extended families, as these are called, are partly those in the process of change from an extended to a nuclear structure, and partly a result of the changes of new family cycles. A typical pattern of change in the rural family appears to be the following. The newly married couple is patrilocal, living with the husband's parents for a while. This patriarchal extended structure then dissolves itself when the young couple move out to form their own separate household. Later, the aged parent(s) when they cannot look after themselves move in with the young couple, but the head of the house is now the young man.

TABLE 11.16 - Composition of the Households (percent)

Nuclear	75.1
Patrilineal extended	4.8
Transient Patrilineal extended	15.3
Mixed forms	8.8

N: 144

We do not count them as a traditional extended family because the head of the family is the son. For our purposes it is further significant that the leadership and authority now is with the younger generation when the family affairs are in question. In fact today 30 percent of the heads of the families seem to be less than thirty years of age and more than 50 percent below forty years of age. As for the average size of the households it is 4.56 (average for Turkey's rural areas 6.1, average for Turkey as a whole 5.4 - metropolis 4.1), (11) (Table 11.17). This figure also together with the nuclear structure of the families and age of their heads indicates the drastic changes the main social institution of the village has undergone. The average number of the children also is relatively low: 2.5 per household which also compares very favorably with the average of rural Turkey (4.1) (Table 11.18).

TABLE 11.17 - Size of the Households and Number of Children

Frequency	Number of Members %	Number of Children %
1-2	11.8	47.9
3-4	42.2	26.4
5-6	33.3	10.4
7-8	13.1	----
9 +	0.7	

Average size of Household: 4.56   N   Household 144
Children per household 2.53   N: Children 309

TABLE 11.18 - Ages of the Heads of the Households and Their Wives

Ages	Head %	Wife %
15-20	--	8.8
21-30	30.0	29.4
31-40	23.6	25.0
41-50	22.9	20.6
51-60	13.2	11.0
61 +	8.9	
Vagne		

Migration as a source of change of population and the family is a familiar phenomenon for Taskorpu. Some sixty years ago the main body of the population migrated from Bulgaria to Taskopru. Since the second world war some more relatives of the old migrants have also settled in the village. Hence the high ratio of those born outside of Turkey (Table 11.19).

TABLE 11.19 - Place of Birth

	The Head %	The Wife %
Taskopru	31.9	25.7
Nearby Villages	4.9	8.8
Nearby Towns	11.8	17.6
Nearby City	9.0	10.3
Other Regions	7.5	7.3
Foreign Countries	34.7	27.9
Not Clear		2.2

Husband N: 144   Wife N: 136

The newcomers are very much a part of the old population. They have integrated immediately. Houses were given or rented to them, close to their relatives and they have become integrated by marriage and work in the community. For all purposes they are true Taskopru population.

What changes the village more is the immigration from the other parts of Turkey. They are not integrated either spatially or socially. Their houses are on the outskirts of the village and as yet no marriage has taken place between them and the old population. However they made full use of the commercial institutions in the village such as coffee shops, grocery stores, busses, and wage work in and around the village. They also enter into patron-client relations with a village notable who functions as a labor broker for factories. Their participation in political activities is also significant as during the last elections the labor broker has won the elections for headmanship with their votes. Whether fully integrated or not the importance of family is the same for them as well, since they are also rural in origin.

As mentioned in the section on traditional leadership, in rural settlements, in general, and in Taskopru in particular since no other dominant social organization exists, family and intrafamily relations carry special weight. In this organization the elder male members were the decision makers in the everyday activities of the families as well as in extraordinary times such as disputes, marriages, or ceremonies of the stable village life. To live in the same house, to use the same resources, and to carry the responsibility of the future of the household members was the main source of their influence and authority. Now that 75 percent of the household are nuclear families and have separate resources for a living and another 15 percent does not have any older male member, such a dominance and relationship has become almost extinct. The importance of the elders in the community now does not go beyond a simple respect behavior. Our various approaches to check the influence of the elder males on the younger generation always gave the same result: It has disappeared.

When we asked the heads of the households who could be influential on the younger members of the community only 12.5 percent agreed that the elders of their families could exercise any influence while another 16.6 percent claimed that nobody could tell them what to do. The rest of the answers all indicated anonymous relations outside of the family, new patronage relations with the headman or "the influential rich member" of the village (Table 11.20). When the question was asked in a more specific way as to whom they would ask for advice and help when things went wrong, the answers did not change much either. Today the intrafamily relations are rather different than the extrafamily ones. Although in general the role of the elders as leaders has radically diminished, their place in settlement of disputes in the family is still important for nearly one fourth of the heads of the households. Actual aid either as money or material in something

like building their homes is also present in more than 25 percent
of the cases (Table 11.21).

TABLE 11.20 - Whose Word Carries Weight With Young People

	%
Nobody	16.6
Youth leader	16
Family elders	12.5
Teachers	2.8
Headman	25.7
Influential Village People	4.1
Headman-Teachers-Imam	12.5
Not Clear	9.7

N: 144

TABLE 11.21 - Whom They Go to For Help in Building Their Homes

	Money %	Advise %	Material %
Nobody	58.5	61.0	44.7
Skilled Workers	--	5.7	29.2
Family	19.5	13.0	6.5
Village Influentials	6.5	8.1	4.9
Friends	2.4	3.2	2.4
Anonymous organizations (Bank, Trade Union, Coop)	2.4	--	--
Not Clear	10.6	8.9	12.2

But closer examination of the tables will show that family in
general and the elders of the family in particular are remembered
much less frequently as a source of influence and leadership than
other agencies (Table 11.22 and 11.23).   The most dominant
characteristics is the extreme self-reliance of the respondents.
In all our inquiries about their problems and the agency they would
follow as leader the overwhelming majority answered that they rely
only on themselves and they will ask help from nobody, family or
otherwise.

TABLE 11.22 - Whose Word Carries Most Weight in the Village

	%
The Headman	57.6
Rich influential	23.6
Teachers	2.8
Imam	1.4
Nobody	4.9
Others	1.4
Not clear	8.3

N: 144

TABLE 11.23 - Whose Word Carries Weight Next to the
Most Influentials in the Village

	%
Muhtar	17.4
Rich influential	22.9
Teachers	13.9
Imam	4.2
Village elders	1.4
Nobody	7.6
Others	1.4
I Don't Know-Not Clear	31.2

It is quite understandable that, as the village opened up to cash cropping and industrial wage work the knowledge and experience of the elder generation became obsolete. But as an adjustment mechanism and security agency family is still the most important institution in the community. Although elder male members lost their leadership role, family as such did not change its place in the important role it plays in the life of its members. Only now it is the active age group among the kin who has more to say. Among the separate households of the same kin various mutual help patterns have also developed.

The decision and initiation for such help usually comes from the younger household heads. Many times this help is directed towards the older kin. The network of relations among the kin is still close and contacts take place in the respective houses. But ultimately as is discussed below non-kin networks are more significant and are equally information. Accordingly they take place in coffee shops (Table 11.24).

TABLE 11.24 - Whom Do They Consult for Family Problems

	%
Nobody	18.7
Wife	50.7
Family elders	21.5
Sons	6.9
Friends	2.1

N: 144

Here the position of women in the family and community comes to the foreground. As mentioned before the least organized group, at least outside of the family, is the women. Without much contact with outside, they are confined to their delicate and important job of keeping intrafamily relations among fathers, sons, daughters, daughters-in-law and grandchildren in harmony and organizing the processing of goods for consumption.

They are further responsible for the utilization and allocation of the consumption resources of the family in the house. But cash income and a smaller nuclear family have radically changed their traditional roles and relations.

Consultation with household members now means, with the nuclear structure of the family, to ask one's wife about problems. Those who never think to consult their wife are still some one fifth of the households. But they are mainly the older heads of the households. More than half mainly asks their wife's opinion. The new more competitive life, and limited members in the household, seem to bring man and wife together. However when we asked the opinion of some of the women on the behavior of their men they said that "yes, they ask our opinion, but do they as they please." For a pessimistic interpretation this comment may devalue the significance of the survey answers mentioned above. But for an optimistic view one can see that the women are aware of the relative importance of consultation. In fact, one of the women who complained about it was the very person who first went to Germany to work, then made not only her husband but his brother also come and join her. Furthermore she has explained that she made her husband and his brother's family agree to come back at the time they made a final return. She is also one of the two women who works as a saleswoman in her grocery store in the village and obviously manages it as well. So the direction of the complaints on advising clearly demonstrates the consciousness of the women to make their advice be taken seriously.

In fact gone are the days in Taskopru village when women did not count outside of the house. First of all they are not as "local" as one expect from a rural community. More than one third of them have come from outside the village. More than fifty percent of them are primary school graduates, and are working in agriculture, in factories, and as domestics. Two of them are grocery store manager-saleswomen. The women of the families who own land work their land and in their own gardens. Work for cash now takes women out of their narrow family circles and begins to integrate them into a much larger group of women in contact with men and complex organizations. Here something has to be said about the consequences of sex segregation for women in Turkey. Traditionally women have a lot to say in the house. In fact, she is the sole arbiter in her family affairs. Men's main attitude towards the home and the women folk at home is a "studied" indifference as long as it does not create problems outside.

As has been observed in other studies in Turkey and in other Middle Eastern societies, the segregated women are never passive, dependent individuals without personalities. They lead a life independent of their husbands, with work as well as social occasions to be together. The women's world has its own social structure, independent of their other roles. Women organize, conduct, and participate in a wide range of work activities, sociabilities, and ceremonies, at a distance from the world of men.

To it they bring their own leaders, skilled specialists, and loyal followers. The separate structure allows freedom of action for women, away from men.

The separated women of Turkey, and Taskopru are independent - they have freedom of movement in their own limited sphere. This gives them a substantial field for self assertion and psychological independence of men. How much this traditional independence of women from men will last cannot be predicted. At the moment this psychological independence asserts itself in development actions.

A voluntary organization among village women and the "leaders" that appeared among them is a good case in which to see this potential.

Here one should talk about the Associated Country Women of the World's activities in Taskopru as a voluntary association in action and assess its impact as a type of leadership of such organizations in small settlements, in addition to the action women can originate. The local branch of the ACWW was established in Taskopru in 1968 by R. Hanim. The wife of the larger cash cropper settled in the village in 1950. By 1968 village had become a fruit and vegetable growing community as explained above. She had become involved with the association through a seminar organized by FAO's collaboration with the ACWW and the Ministry of Village Affairs of Turkey. Her enthusiasm and initiation elicited a response from some young women. Twelve women, mostly wage workers in orchards and/or domestics in town, and two women from land owning families joined her for action. Through R. Hanim they collaborated with another women's voluntary organization in Istanbul. Their first activity was a literacy campaign. For this course a young women village teacher was appointed by the Ministry of Education. The twelve members of the association also participated. Thirty four women between the ages 14 to 74 took the course. Among those who came was the wife and the two grown up daughters of the Imam - the religious leader. An impressive ceremony had been arranged for the distribution of diplomas. But the following year when they had to sign documents for national elections many used their thumbs to press a signature again.

However all graduates became members of the association. Later the association showed films and organized festivities. When accused of making everybody communist, they bought a carpet for the mosque to prove their appreciation of old values. They further collaborated with branches of the association in developed countries. They gave scholarships for four girls to go to teacher's training schools and/or a school for midwives. They also sent two students abroad to participate in different courses. When R. Hanim moved out of the village, although the space she had provided in their farm and all the utilities acquired by the association were left totally to the organization, its activities were reduced. Perhaps it is not only that R. Hanim moved out. But some of the main activities lost their relevance. For instance

simple literacy does not answer any more to the needs of the
community. Even primary school is not sufficient. While all the
actions of the ACWW were going on, the school itself evolved from
three classes and two teachers to four teachers and five classes in
1970. Today it has six teachers (one headmaster), five classes and
full attendance of the primary school age groups. But now further
vocational education is in demand. Also for instance in 1970 for
couple of years CARE provided special type of jars and the
association held a course on home canning. A little later the
state also built and equipped a small locale for canning. The
latter has never been used, since the Turkish market has been
flooded by the products of the large commercial canning enterprises
who even compete in international markets. As for the women who
learned home canning, only those who still have the special jars do
it as a part of good housekeeping. However one has to see that
ACWW experience was important for village women since it was the
first time they had a functional relationship beyond their small
community. It was also their first experience even if still in a
women's sphere where they could use their skill of human relations
in a non-family formal organization, with a structured leadership-
follower relation. How much this experience is transferable is
certainly open to discussion.

INFORMAL NETWORKS AND PATRONAGE

The traditional interaction among the male population of rural
communities does not take place in houses. No man can visit
another one for business or companionship in his house, even if he
is ill in bed. A house is the women's domain. The place to see
and interact for men for a long time now has been the coffee shop
of the village. Before it was a guest room (oda) provided by a
wealthy influential villager to be used to the same purpose. He
was supposed to furnish the room, supply it with heat as well as
light. The village men would come sit and walk in a well defined
protocol. There is no man in the village who could refuse to go to
the coffee shop if he wants to be an integrated member of the
community. Today there are three coffee shops in the Village. In
the slack season, Sundays and holidays and at night the place is
full. During the busy hours and days there are only the very old
there or those who had asked some one to meet them there.

The time spent in coffee shop is not a continuous discussion
of "serious" affairs. The pattern is that people trickle in
according to their own schedule, go and sit next to their buddies,
or join a group playing cards or backgammon. Or they may just sit
alone. As time goes by they shift around. Usually nothing much
happens. But at one point someone starts to talk about some
subject that interests some more people, then more join in the
discussion and if it is an issue that concerns a large group it
becomes a regular meeting. However it has no chairman, rapporteur
or any such structured organization. It rewards those who talk
loud or who have made a point. If somebody keeps talking
"nonsense" either the group shuts him up, or they leave him and

turn to their games or to small group chatting. If there is one of
the "patrons" his clientele may listen to him, but as they decide
by themselves he cannot hold a monolithic court for long. Thus the
informal networks are pretty much a public interaction because of
this very culture-specific coffee shop attendance.

The largest coffee shop was at the center of the business
section in the village where a grocery store, a repair shop, and a
school are clustered. As the village is growing two more coffee
shops have opened. It is interesting that these coffee shops do
not yet have their own customers. Many go to all of them and any
talk could turn to a serious discussion in any one of them. Still
the important one seems to be the large one at the center. If one
would like to see someone away from the eyes of others it has to be
at a quiet period during the day, or one of the off center coffee
houses, or better yet, the Yalova coffee shops.

Informal networks are not structured in the village. This can
be seen in the coffee shops, where the teachers or the imam or the
patrons can talk but their influence would not be open and
conspicuous. As indicated above whatever informal patronage takes
place -- such as borrowing money, signing papers for formal
transactions, taking advice for business deals, even seeking
support when going to town to buy large items such as tractors,
refrigerators, spare parts -- is done here. No offices for the man
who act as patron have evolved. There are now several reference
groups. There seems to be a differential grouping according to
age, occupation, the way of earning one's living and patronage. An
industrial wage worker's interest is very different, from a small
orchard growers; whereas a grower does not have much in common with
those who want to know about possible new agricultural work right
at a time when crop is sold. However those who are helped by the
same patron stick together.

The coffee shop is nowadays a most important institution in
this village where organizational development is very low and
villagers' access to policy making circles is very narrow. Wage
policies, work openings, possible local customers, change in
banking policies are all not only discussed but relevant
transactions also take place here in the coffee house.

Those who need female labor for their cold storage plants come
to the village coffeeship and leave word where and when women
should apply. Men let their women know about it. After work
starts in cold storage establishments word spreads through women,
too. But the starting point is the coffee shop. The same goes for
buyers. They come and find the orchard owners and discuss the
transaction. The same is true for industrial jobs. Workers let
the openings be known at coffee shops. Most important perhaps is
the discussion of wages, conditions and prices discussed and
assessed in the coffee shop. Such a continuous face-to-face
contact and open discussion of multiple subjects leads to the
problem of leadership of unstructured variable informal networks of

relations, particularly among some wage earning groups. The other relationship still formed in the coffee shop is patron-client relations particularly between small to medium agricultural producers and larger entrepreneurs. Those who have any claim on power and influence in the village can not help but come to the coffeeship to see their clients. As the coffee shop talks are not considered consultation our inquiries in the survey concerning whom they go to for advice had such a strong emphasis on "only to myself." Also as all informal coffee shop consultation is without any differentiation, the answers have favored friends, acquaintances, and similar categories. Few have seen the difference between any "friend" and village "influentials" or "patrons." But one has to notice that they have no special space to establish contact. Thus all is informal. Contacts in the orchards or in a coffee shop in the village or in the town had to be classified as friends.

The response of the heads of the households in our survey remains vague when the question is asked in a personal way. But when the same thing is generalized as to who is influential as a leader in the village, then answers become rather clear. A great majority gave as answers the muhtar-headman. This looks like avoiding trouble by indicating the "officially" responsible person. But we do not believe this as it complies actually with the objective observations. The previous and present muhtars both are claiming not only to be the official leader but also very anxious to establish their patronage with face-to-face relations in "helps" for credit, bank transactions, job finding, or important purchases as well as to serve the village in public works. The explicit issue on which the last election was based was whether water should be brought to the village, or a meeting hall for weddings or activities should be built. But implicitly two new influential men, both patrons to different groups, both self-made, were fighting for the control of the further influence in the community, where there is a definite vacuum of power for possible advancement to national politics. The deciding vote has been of the wage workers who are interested in direct help for wage work from the labor broker.

Those whose sphere of influence is still the village are more regular in their attendance to the coffee shop. Those who have established contacts with outside do not rely for the advancement of their various enterprises on the village only, but if they expect considerable help to come from here, then they attend at least periodically. Among them is B.Bey, who obviously wishes to use village politics as a spring board for national politics. In spite of the fact that all his concern for his economic activities has outgrown the village, keeps his patron-client relations alive in the village and has run for headmanship twice, and lost during the last elections.

The place of the coffee shop for leadership and influence becomes even more conspicuous when the behavior of the largest, most modern orchard owner's behavior is observed. A.Bey as discussed in the section of portraits, has never sought influence in the village either for economic or political purposes as he was an integral part of Istanbul economic life and national politics. Thus he always remained outside of the village networks for leadership and influence, and so he never went to coffee shops to join the talks. Such a behavior makes the others stand out more. Obviously patron-client relationship at this stage of change in Taskopru definitely lead us to political life and political leadership as a factor in development.

Political leadership may have great potentials for different type of organizational development. Particularly it can bring together the small producers, or divert the national development policies to the village with strategies which will make them applicable. But today's political patronage, even in its most altruistic efforts, does not imply bold enough action to bring fundamental change to the village. Their concern is limited to infrastructure: Water, electricity, roads, primary school.

As far as local leadership is concerned the imam and teachers are of interest. The opinion of the villagers of the Imam as a leader and a man of influence of first degree importance has been mentioned only by one percent and as of second degree importance (Tables 22-23) by four percent. They are definitely not comparable to the ratios of the military and other influential patrons.

The place of religion in Taskopru in relation with development is not clear. For many a villager to be Muslim means to be a member of a community with similar codes of behavior. Religious affiliations often intermix with group loyalties, and religion is more of a community religion than an individual affair. It involves identification with a community, acceptance of its ethics and rules of conduct. In this sense religion feeds on group and community loyalties and in turn reinforces them. Another important characteristic of a community religion is its concreteness. To the villager it means a set of rules and regulations about everyday behavior rather than an abstract system of ethics. With social change religious values are generally found to weaken and lose salience as a general outlook in people's everyday lives. Religiosity as a general outlook on life also diminishes and gives way to more secular values. Yet as is the case with other traditional values, this change is not simple and uni-directional but it is rather complex. It shows much variability, reversals, and reactions which go against the general trend. Such relations occur as attempts to avoid tension and to satisfy frustrated needs such as identity, security and belongingness.

The Imam's place is also undermined parallel to all other age and authority leaderships. Just like the older members of family are not anymore remembered as good opinion leaders, the same and more is true for imam. The responses to out questions searching for the conceptualization of religious behavior have remained within the limits of such simple codes of behavior as not murdering, stealing, swearing, gambling or seducing. Only two respondents asserted that religious codes of behavior do not interest them and four people included in them the human civil rights. Obviously no translation of behavior codes to patronage, trade unionism, new rights and responsibilities towards community or other aspects of recent life has found a place in their formulation of a right way of living. Inquiries about rules of behavior had very different answers from different people. The rules center around family life, or around self centered evaluation of other people in the community. Extreme emphasis on self reliance also indicates alienation from the village, and from religion as communal identity. As for the ceremonial life, frequently imams, both of this village or from another one offer some service which definitely does not have any place in regular known religious life. An example of this was a prayer for the well being sheep by another village's imam in 1963. Such a service was never heard before and obviously is not repeated again. As village gets richer it pays more attention to mosque. The repair of the village mosque has been seriously taken into account but the responsibility for seeing that it is accomplished was assigned by the talks in the coffee shop to an old man who had no part in the orchards, or in the new ways of earning a living and no interest in the various aspects of the last changing life in the village. None of the more active members wanted to do it. Thus when the mosque was made an issue, everybody had immediately agreed to the need for repairs. But the job was delegated to a less important member of the community. Should it have brought enough prestige and influence, surely, more influential members, particularly those who seek political power would have taken it over.

Teachers of secular education used to occupy a special place in village change in Turkey; at least that was the wish of the center. The school as we mentioned above grew and became a fullsize primary school. Subjectively fifteen percent of our respondents feel that the teachers are at least at a second degree influential people in the village. They remain as possibly manipulators of the state-accepted development projects -- just like we saw in literacy campaign for women. Now they are young men who act as specialized skilled people, but with dedication to teaching. Still they are the most sophisticated members of the community on the subjects of culture, politics, and change. But their leadership, compared to patronage, has remained limited. Should there be projects of development from external resources they could participate with their skill but not leadership.

NEW COMPLEX ORGANIZATIONS

Unplanned, spontaneous changes in the community brought the usual complex organizations to Taskopru as well. Complex organizations mean at the same time differentiation and specialization so that different people in the village have differential relationship with each one of the organizations and again in the same organization. As the types of works changes, as large organizations appeared with jobs which require different skills, and contacts with different circles, the influence or help channels also changed. The work in new circumstances required new relations in new organizations. Trade unions, craft associations, such as drivers or minibuses, banks, insurance companies, social security organizations all became a part of life in the village, let alone factories, large orchards, and cold storage establishments that brought wage labor. To these, buyers of fruit of different types and white collar jobs must be added.

These circles demand anonymous relations and they do solve the problems of the people for credit, job security, and organization of work conditions. Some 14 percent of the respondents are aware that such anonymous complex organizations can solve problems. But still when it is bank credits, or even social security organizations, some help from the patrons may solve the question much faster. In such small circles patronage even in its modernized aspects is the mode of interaction. Its meaning for leadership could be positive or negative for each case in question. Patronage develops out of the interest of both parties. But once established it becomes a hinderance for further change -- as it stands in the way of the development of anonymous complex organizations and relations. Furthermore patron-client relations always extend themselves into political party organizations which means further institutionalization of the dependency!

CONCLUSIONS

We discussed development as a specific form of change, and the implications it has for leadership in a village in the Western Marmara region of Turkey. The hope was to be able to see actual micro-process of change at least in one community where we could see how development and leadership interacted. What has been seen is that local communities change their basic structure always with effective external interference. For agricultural communities, particularly important is the introduction and establishment of cash cropping. When the market economy enters not only is income increased but a whole set of new relations in terms of credit and marketing also become a part of life. Equally important is the fact that new groups such a agricultural and industrial wageworkers also merge in the old homogeneous village.

New agricultural practices, and new occupational groups enter into different relationships and look up to different persons and groups for leadership. The old traditional leadership in terms of one single influential man, patron, (Aga) with his responsibilities for the welfare of the peasants, who controls the uniform limited production of cereal, disappeared fast.

The introduction of new crops came about through a new entrepreneur from outside who employed the villagers as wage workers thereby demonstrating and teaching the techniques, the

assets and potentials of fruit growing. The leadership of the
first large fruitgrower in the villager, who came from the
metropolis, although he never intended to be a leader, became one
as his teaching was disinterested, his methods successful, and he
carried prestige. These characteristics comply with the findings
of many studies in social psychology. But A.Bey's leadership was
limited to the introduction of various forms of cash crops. The
necessary credit and marketing facilities required other types of
contacts and supports. Such new relations have brought new
dependencies to the village. A new type of patron-client
relationship has arisen between the small producers and few local
larger producers in lending money --even if with formal documents
-- and helping in various external contacts. This new type of
influence and leadership eventually extends into political
activities such as headmanship and political party affiliation.

Government extension service, although it is supposed to be a
model and act as leader, remains ineffective even in the case where
its support is specifically asked by the villagers as we say in the
case of the cattle of B. Bey. Their knowledge as well as their
bureaucracy seems to be dysfunctional. Further more, the extension
service never included one of the important needs in the life of
individuals namely, security. One of the most important aspects of
old aga patronage was its provision of security as part of a
built-in system. It stopped some thirty years ago and no agency
has taken its place yet. The delay of the establishment of
anonymous formal organizations, particularly in marketing, credit,
and health and security furthers the dependency relations and so
the influence and leadership of certain individuals as patrons.

As for the simple infrastructural development strategies of
roads, water, electricity, and literacy in general they are still
external efforts. What is significant is that when these are local
efforts it is too expensive and not used so as to become a
functional part of the life of the community. Thus in general much
social and economic resource is wasted. When the change gains
acceleration the result of such efforts remains very humble and
insufficient. There is never a successful correspondence between
the type of intrastructure brought to the community and the demand
for it. Education efforts in the near past, and the level and
demand for education today in Taskopru, illustrates the
discrepancy.

Literacy and the primary school started with painstaking
efforts in Taskopru. Even in 1969 the literacy particularly of
girls was a great problem. The efforts of the ACWW to educate four
girls at the secondary school level was almost a revolutionary
activity which caused much conflict and comment in the village,
appeared so meaningless in 1978 when girls are sent to the town
with specially arranged transportation, and private tutoring is
provided for those who wish to go to a higher learning institution.
And one has to remember that the ACWW literacy campaign for women
resulted when they used thumbprints instead of signing their names

during the elections of the following year. But today almost 70 percent of the wives, all young, are primary school graduates. A similar futile effort of both the state and the voluntary organization could be seen in canning activities. The state built a small building and installed some equipment for small scale canning in the village. The association encouraged home canning with special jars provided by CARE. Now that large commercial firms provide the whole market with all types of conserved fruit and vegetables, the state installation is never used and the women who still have some jars practice home canning as a hobby. It seems that for local development strategies and leadership, diagnosis of the speed of change triggered by impact from outside is very crucial. If outside change is fast and effective very soon local action becomes dysfunctional. It has to be geared to large, complex organizations and higher degrees of differentiation.

Another aspect of development and leadership is its distortion by culture-specific factors as we saw in the case of spending cash income. As we discussed in the new levels of consumption in the village, the new consumption patterns have reached a difficult point in a very culture-specific aspect, sex segregation. In spite of the fact that both sexes are earning larger incomes, the family budget is nowadays arranged in a very unpredicted form, with dual standards of living for men and for the rest of the household. Another culture specific result is the function of coffee shops for contacts and social networks. They are a meeting place for discussions and for the emergence of issue oriented leaders. Still although coffee shops are places of general discussion, the rising leadership and patronage uses this locale for its interaction.

All in all after the analysis of the village of Taskopru one feels that one cannot stress enough the importance of the external dynamics in change, the demands of metropolitan centers for more production and drainage of surplus from rural areas, and the concomitant profound changes they cause in the village. Before such change starts the efforts of improvement remains dysfunctional. On the other hand after they break down the old system the same activities seems less then insufficient, meaningless.

NOTES

The field work for this study was made possible by a grant from the Association of Country Women of the World, for which we wish to express our gratitude.

1. See, for instance, R. Stavenhagen, "Changing functions of the community in underdeveloped countries" in Sociologia Ruralis 4:315-331 (1964), and W.F. Wertheim, "The rising waves of emancipation" in E. de Kadt and Gavin Williams, eds., Sociology and Development, London, Tavistock, 1976.

248

2.   USAID Near East Bureau, "Strategy for Rural Development," Washington, August 15, 1978, p. 6.

3.   For leadership see J.L. Freedman, J. Carlsmith, and D.D. Sears, Social Psychology (2nd edition), Englewood Cliffs, N.J., Prentice-Hall, 1974; D. Kandiyoti, "Some social psychological dimensions of social change in a Turkish village" in British Journal of Sociology 25(1):47-62 (1974); and C. Kagitcibasi, Cultural Values and Population Action Programs, Report prepared for UNESCO, 1977.

4.   After the middle of the 19th century the loss of the Ottoman provinces in the Balkan peninsula forced hundreds of thousands of Muslims to migrate to Anatolia. They settled in various parts, including in the Eastern Marmara. The details of the settlement of these refugees are poorly known. The Taskopru settlers were from Bulgaria.

5.   See Wolf-Dieter Hutteroth, "The influence of social structure on land division and settlement in Inner Anatolia" in P. Benedict, E. Tumertekin and F. Mansur, eds., Turkey: Geographic and Social Perspectives, Leiden, Brill, 1974.

6.   This form of total patronage was not the only type found in rural Turkey. Recent social changes have brought up further varieties. As examples, see A. Dubensky, "Kinship, primordial ties and factory organization in Turkey: an anthropological view" in International Journal of Middle East Studies 7:433-451 (1976), M. Kiray, Eregli: Agir Sanayiden Once Bir Sahil Kasabasi, Ankara, State Planning Organization, 1964 (chapter four), and S. Sayari, "Political patronage in Turkey" in E. Gellner and J. Waterbury, eds., Patrons and Clients in Mediterranean Societies, London, Duckworth, 1977.

7.   Narmin Abadan, Bati Almanya'daki Turk Iscileri ve Sorunlari ("Issues Concerning Turkish Workers in West Germany"), Ankara, State Planning Organization, 1964.

8.   The great novels of Emile Zola describe such changes for France. Particularly relevant, for instance, is the series known as "Histoire Naturelle et Sociale d'une Famille sous le second Empire: les Rouqon Macquart."

9.   Mubeccel Kiray, "Social stratification, values and development" in Journal of Social Issues :87-102 (1968).

10. Serim Timur, Turkiye'de Aile Yapisi, Ankara, Hacettepe Universitesi Yayinlari, 1972.

11. ibid., p. 38.

About the Contributors

PETER BENEDICT is Mission Director, U.S. Agency for International Development, Mauritania. He previously had taught at the University of Nebraska and had been with the Ford Foundation in Egypt. His major publications are Ula (E.J. Brill, 1974) and he is editor along with E. Tumertekin and F. Mansor of Turkey: Geographic and Social Perspectives (E.J. Brill, 1974).

LOUIS J. CANTORI is Associate Professor and Chairman of the Political Science Department at the University of Maryland Baltimore County. He is also Adjunct Professor, Center for Contemporary Arab Studies, Georgetown University. His previous books include The International Politics of Regions (Prentice-Hall, 1970, co-author) and Comparative Political Systems (Holbrook Press, 1974). His most recent articles are "Religion and Politics in Egypt" in M. Curtis, ed. Religion and Politics in the Middle East (Westview, 1981) and "Egyptian Foreign Policy Since the Peace Treaty With Israel" in R. Freedman, ed. The Middle East Since the Peace Treaty (Westview, forthcoming).

PETER GUBSER is President of American Near East Refugee Aid in Washington, D.C. He has carried out field work on local politics in Lebanon and Jordan. He is the author of "The Zu ama of Zahlah," Middle East Journal 27 (1973), Politics and Change in Al-Karak, Jordan (Oxford University Press, 1973), and Jordan: Crossroads of Middle Eastern Events (Westview, 1983).

ILIYA HARIK is Professor of Political Science and Director, Center for Middle Eastern Studies, Indiana University. He is the author of The Political Mobilization of the Egyptian Peasants (Indiana University Press, 1974) as well as other books. He has contributed to such journals as World Politics, American Political Science Review and the International Journal of Middle East Affairs on Lebanon, Egypt and the Middle East in general. He is the co-editor (with R. Antoun) of Rural Politics and Social Change in the Middle East (Indiana University Press, 1972).

RAYMOND HINNEBUSCH is Associate Professor of Political Science at St. Catherine's College, Minnesota. He has also taught at the American University in Cairo. He has carried out extensive field work in Syria and written several articles on local party organization in that country in the Middle East Journal, The International Journal of Middle Eastern Studies and other journals. His most recent article is "Libya: Personalistic Leadership of a Populist Revolution" in I.W. Zartman, et al, eds. Political Elites in Arab North Africa (Longman, 1982).

NICHOLAS HOPKINS is Associate Professor of Anthropology in the American University in Cairo. He has carried out field work in Mali, Tunisia and Egypt. He is author of a book on Mali, has co-edited two books, and has written numerous articles on all three countries. His most recent article on Tunisia is "Testour au XIXe Siecle," Revue d'Histoire Maghrebine, no. 17/18, 1980. His article "Nationalism and Center-Building in North Africa" will appear in The Uncertain Paths: Cohesion and Change in 19th Century Ottoman Turkey and the Maghreb, ed. S. Mardin and I.W. Zartman. His most recent field work has been agricultural mechanization in southern Egypt.

SUAD JOSEPH is Associate Professor of Anthropology at the University of California, Davis. She is the co-editor of Muslim-Christian Conflicts (Westview, 1978). Her articles have been published in several edited volumes and such journals as American Ethnologist and Studies in Third World Societies. Her most recent article is "Working the Law: A Lebanese Working Class Case" in D. Dwyer, ed. The Politics of Law in the Middle East (forthcoming).

MUBECCEL KIRAY teaches sociology at the Istanbul Technical University in Turkey. She specializes in rural sociology. Among her publications is an article, "Social Stratification, Values and Development," Journal of Social Issues (1968) and "Social Change in Cururova: A Comparison of Four Villages" in Peter Benedict, Erol Tumertekin and Fatma Mansur, eds. Turkey: Geographic and Social Perspectives (E.J. Brill, 1974). She is the editor of Social Stratification and Development in the Mediterranean Basin (Mouton, 1973).

NIRVANA KHADR has her Ph.D. in Anthropology from Boston University and teaches anthropology at the American University in Cairo. She has carried out field work in Egypt and has been active with the United Nations in Haiti and as a consultant on development projects with other agencies in the Middle East.

BARBARA LARSON is Associate Professor of Anthropology, University of New Hampshire. She has conducted extensive field work in Tunisia and Egypt and is the author of several articles on both countries. Her most recent article is "The Status of Women in a Tunisian Village: Limits to Autonomy, Influence and Power," Signs, IX (1984). Her most recent research has been on local market systems in Egypt.

RICHARD TUTWILER has his Ph.D. in Anthropology from the State University of New York, Binghamton and presently teaches at Wilkes College, Wilkes Barre, Pennsylvania. He has carried out extensive field work in the Yemen Arab Republic and has been active in development related consulting activities with the U.S. Agency for International Development.

Index

Tunisia (continued)
  bureaucracy in, 33
  center-building in, 27-30
  class relations in, 27-28, 29
  cooperative movement in, 28,
    29, 197-202, 203, 204, 205
  economic structure, 5
  estate agriculture in, 27-28
  family in, 194-195, 209(n2)
  French occupation, 197
  Islam in, 195
  land ownership in, 194
  local politics in, 195,
    205-206
  mobilization in, 202-206
  nomads in, 29
  personal income in, 30,
    196-197
  political system, 4, 5
  program development in,
    193-194, 207-209
  technology in, 9
  values, 195-196, 207, 208-209
  women in, 196, 206-207
Turkey
  cash cropping in, 10, 225-226,
    245-246
  center-building in, 21-22
  class relations in, 22
  community development in,
    212-248
  consumption patterns, 229-232,
    247
  credit in, 227-228
  economic structure, 4
  education in, 226, 244,
    246-247
  estate agriculture in, 22
  family in, 217, 233-240
  housing in, 229-230
  informal networks in, 240-243
  institutional change in,
    244-245
  Islam in, 243-244
  labor emigration, 218
  leadership in, 216-219, 233,
    235-237, 241-244, 245, 246,
    247
  local politics in, 22
  migration in, 234-235, 248(n4)
  patronage in, 241-244, 246
  personal income in, 30,
    222-229

  social change in, 212-213,
    218-219
  values, 227, 243-244
  women, 219-220, 221-222,
    231-232, 237-240, 246-247

UAR. See United Arab Republic
UCP. See Ghanima Cooperative
    Production Unit
UNFT. See Union Nationale des
    Femmes Tunisiennes
Union Nationale des Femmes
    Tunisiennes (UNFT), 206-207
United Arab Republic (UAR), 102
Unites Cooperatives de Production
    (Tunisia), 27
Urban centers
  bureaucracy and, 50
  in Egypt, 3, 46-59, 70
  growth of, 70
  leadership in, 46-59
  rural exploitation by, 30
U.S. Agency for International
    Development (USAID), 213
USAID. See U.S. Agency for
    International Development

Vinogradov, Amal, 13

Warriner, Doreen, 11, 21
Waterbury, John, 13
Women, 31
  in Tunisia, 196, 206-207
  in Turkey, 219-220, 221-222,
    231-232, 237-240, 246-247
  in Yemen, 180, 191(n20)
World Food Program, 29

Yalman, Nur, 21
Yemen, 34, 166-192
  center-building in, 22, 24
  class relations in, 179-180,
    191(n18, n19)
  cooperative movement in, 189(n7)
  decentralization, 4-5
  economic structure, 5
  education in, 181, 192(n22)
  family in, 182
  five year plans, 184
  generation gap in, 183
  Hufash Cooperative, 175,
    189-190(n9)
  ja ish system, 170-171